The AI Cloud Infrastructure Blueprint

This book offers a comprehensive, practice-driven guide to designing and managing robust AI cloud infrastructure systems for real-world applications.

As enterprises continue to adopt AI to enhance automation, decision-making, and customer engagement, there is a growing demand for cloud-native architectures that can scale with increasing data volumes, support model training, ensure operational efficiency, and meet stringent security and governance requirements. This book addresses that demand by equipping readers with the foundational knowledge and advanced strategies needed to build, deploy, and maintain AI systems on modern cloud platforms. What makes this book unique is its end-to-end perspective, which goes beyond traditional AI model development. It covers key pillars such as hybrid and multi-cloud strategies, container orchestration, serverless computing, edge AI deployment, AI governance, cost optimization, and sustainable computing, all framed around the AI model lifecycle. Readers will gain practical insights through architectural diagrams, platform comparisons (AWS, Azure, GCP), and use cases across healthcare, finance, and manufacturing. It also explores the integration of AutoML, MLOps, quantum computing, and green AI within cloud ecosystems. This book fills a critical gap by merging cloud infrastructure engineering with AI-specific challenges, offering a rare blend of systems thinking and AI expertise.

Targeted toward architects, data scientists, DevOps engineers, cloud professionals, and graduate students, it serves as both a reference guide and a strategic roadmap for building future-ready AI systems in the cloud.

The AI Cloud Infrastructure Blueprint

Practical Designs and Configurations for Scalable AI

Second Edition

Sairohith Thummarakoti, Santosh Kumar Vududala, Bhanuprakash Madupati, and Dr. Keshav Kaushik

Routledge
Taylor & Francis Group
A PRODUCTIVITY PRESS BOOK

Designed cover image: Shutterstock

Second edition published 2026
by Routledge
605 Third Avenue, New York, NY 10158

and by Routledge
4 Park Square, Milton Park, Abingdon, Oxon, OX14 4RN

Routledge is an imprint of the Taylor & Francis Group, an informa business

First edition published independently 2025

Library of Congress Cataloging-in-Publication Data
Names: Thummarakoti, Sairohith author
Title: The AI cloud infrastructure blueprint : practical designs and configurations for scalable AI / Sairohith Thummarakoti, Santosh Kumar Vududala, Bhanuprakash Madupati, and Dr. Keshav Kaushik.
Description: New York, NY : Routledge, 2026. | Includes bibliographical references and index. |
Identifiers: LCCN 2025043068 (print) | LCCN 2025043069 (ebook) | ISBN 9781041166436 hbk |
ISBN 9781041166429 pbk | ISBN 9781003685609 ebk
Subjects: LCSH: Cloud computing | Artificial intelligence
Classification: LCC QA76.585 .T47 2026 (print) | LCC QA76.585 (ebook)
LC record available at https://lccn.loc.gov/2025043068
LC ebook record available at https://lccn.loc.gov/2025043069

ISBN: 978-1-041-16643-6 (hbk)
ISBN: 978-1-041-16642-9 (pbk)
ISBN: 978-1-003-68560-9 (ebk)

DOI: 10.4324/9781003685609

Typeset in Garamond
by Deanta Global Publishing Services, Chennai, India

To my beloved parents, Bharathi and Ramesh,

whose unwavering strength, love, and guidance have shaped who I am.

To my dear wife, Aneehika,

whose encouragement and belief in me never wavered.

And to my two wonderful sons, Rohan and Aryan,

whose smiles and curiosity inspire me every day.

–Sairohith Thummarakoti

Contents

About the Authors

Sairohith Thummarakoti is a lead architect, researcher, and multi-book author with expertise in Pega Business Process Management (BPM), AI-powered cloud infrastructure, engineering excellence, and enterprise technology. With over a decade of experience, he designs scalable, intelligent systems that power automation, decision support, and digital modernization across complex organizational environments.

His core work focuses on intelligent workflow design, multi-cloud optimization, and the integration of AI with cloud-native services. He has led initiatives using low-code platforms like Pega to streamline claims automation, modernize core business processes, and strengthen real-time analytics and infrastructure resilience.

Sairohith has authored several books on AI, cloud architecture, and digital transformation and holds patents in AI-based data optimization and cloud systems engineering. His research appears in respected journals and conferences, covering topics such as cloud-native development, intelligent automation, and enterprise platform modernization.

He has reviewed more than 300 manuscripts for leading IEEE and Springer venues and regularly serves as a session chair and technical committee member. As the Founding Chair of the IEEE Computer Society—Columbia Section, he has led workshops, organized speaker sessions, and built a vibrant local chapter focused on emerging technologies.

Sairohith is also a passionate educator and mentor. He has delivered invited talks at international conferences and serves as a guest lecturer and speaker for universities and professional events. He actively supports Faculty Development Programs (FDPs), training academic and industry professionals on cutting-edge topics such as AI in healthcare, intelligent automation, and cloud infrastructure.

His work bridges academic research, industry application, and professional education, empowering the next generation of engineers and architects to build systems that are not just technically sound but truly impactful.

Santosh Kumar Vududala is a globally recognized ETL QA Lead, Automation Strategist, and AI/ML Specialist with over 17 years of experience delivering transformative digital solutions across finance, insurance, capital markets, and compliance ecosystems. A champion of innovation in intelligent automation, Santosh combines deep domain expertise with emerging technologies to modernize enterprise data, enhance operational resilience, and reduce regulatory risk.

His professional journey spans the design and deployment of advanced AI/ML-powered testing frameworks, cloud-native data validation platforms, and compliance-first automation pipelines. Santosh has delivered projects involving Automation Anywhere, Blue Prism, Tosca, Informatica, IICS, Workday, Snowflake, Oracle, and EDM, with hands-on implementation of AI models and intelligent RPA in enterprise systems.

Santosh has played critical roles in high-stakes initiatives, including cloud migration from Oracle to Snowflake, AML monitoring systems using Actimize and Mantas, and AI-enhanced metadata transformation using EDM and DRM. His work has significantly improved fraud detection workflows, process transparency, and decision intelligence in Fortune 500 financial institutions.

In addition to his technical mastery, Santosh has served as a reviewer for international journals and conferences where he has reviewed over a dozen scholarly papers. His contributions to automation research and AI integration are well documented in academic publications such as *Transforming Metadata Systems through EDM Integration.*

His accolades include:

- Outstanding Technical/Digital Innovation Award—Asia Research Awards
- Global Tech Hero Award—for cross-continental digital impact
- Automation Anywhere BotGames 2021—2nd Place out of 1500+ participants
- Asian African Iconic Award—for excellence in enterprise AI innovation

With certifications in Scrum, ISTQB, Tosca, RPA, and memberships in IEEE Senior Membership, ACM, and SCRS, Santosh continues to influence the intersection of AI, automation, compliance, and cloud ecosystems. His forward-thinking vision and practical experience make him a trailblazer in the digital transformation of mission-critical sectors.

Bhanuprakash Madupati is an acclaimed author, technology leader, innovator, speaker, reviewer, and mentor with over a decade of experience shaping the future of AI, machine learning, and digital transformation. He has authored a few books and published over 30 peer-reviewed research papers in leading journals, making significant contributions to fields such as artificial intelligence, cybersecurity, cloud computing, and data science.

Bhanuprakash holds several patents in the fields of artificial intelligence and machine learning, demonstrating his deep commitment to driving innovation in technology. His expertise in creating cutting-edge solutions has led to numerous advancements in AI, which continue to influence the landscape of modern technology.

With a dual master's degree in computer science and information technology management, Bhanuprakash has demonstrated exceptional leadership in delivering secure, scalable, and AI-powered solutions across diverse industries, including healthcare, finance, aviation, and government sectors. His expertise lies in bridging theoretical knowledge with practical, real-world applications, ensuring that technology delivers tangible benefits to organizations and communities.

A sought-after speaker, Bhanuprakash has presented at renowned conferences such as WCSC, ICCI, and STAI, where he has shared his insights on the future of AI and the ethical implications of technology. In addition to his speaking engagements, he is an active mentor, guiding emerging technologists and fostering the next generation of leaders in the tech industry.

As a peer reviewer for respected journals under Springer and IEEE, Bhanuprakash upholds academic standards while providing valuable feedback to researchers and practitioners. He is also frequently invited to serve on numerous hackathons and international award panels, helping to identify and support groundbreaking innovations.

A Senior Member of IEEE, a Full Member of Sigma Xi, and a Fellow of the British Computer Society (FBCS), Bhanuprakash's contributions to the tech industry have earned him recognition as a thought leader and trailblazer in the field.

Dr. Keshav Kaushik is a distinguished cybersecurity and digital forensics expert, currently serving as Associate Professor at the Sharda School of Computer Science & Engineering, Sharda University, Greater Noida, India. A key member of the Cybersecurity Centre of Excellence, he has been instrumental in advancing research and education in cybersecurity, AI-driven security solutions, and digital forensics. Recognized among the World's Top 2% Scientists by Stanford University and Elsevier (2024), he has made significant contributions to academia and research. His academic journey includes a prestigious faculty internship at IIT Ropar during the Summer Faculty Research Fellow Programme 2016, demonstrating his commitment to continuous learning. With over 150 publications, including 25 peer-reviewed SCI/SCIE/Scopus-indexed journal articles and 50+ Scopus-indexed conference papers, he has established himself as a leading researcher. Additionally, he has authored 30 books and 25 book chapters, reinforcing his expertise in cybersecurity and digital forensics. An innovator in his field, Dr. Kaushik holds one granted patent, six published patents, and five granted copyrights. His editorial leadership includes serving as Guest Editor for the *IEEE Journal of Biomedical and Health Informatics* (SCIE, IF: 7.7) and Associate Editor for journals such as *IECE Transactions on Emerging Trends in Network Systems*, *IECE Transactions on Sustainable Computing*, *International Journal of Sensors, Wireless Communications and Control* (Scopus-indexed, Bentham Science), and *International Journal of Information Security and Privacy* (IJISP, ESCI, Scopus-indexed). He is also an Editorial Board Member of Springer's *International Cybersecurity Law Review.* Dr. Kaushik is a Certified Ethical Hacker (CEH v11), CQI & IRCA Certified ISO/IEC 27001:2013 Lead Auditor, Quick Heal Academy Certified Cyber Security Professional (QCSP), and IBM Cybersecurity Analyst, further validating his expertise. He is a Vice-Chairperson of the Meerut ACM Professional Chapter, an appointed Bentham Ambassador by Bentham Science Publishers, and a member of the International Association of Engineers (IAENG). A dynamic speaker and mentor, he has delivered over 50 national and international talks on cybersecurity, AI security, and digital forensics. His mentorship was recognized in the Smart India Hackathon 2017, earning appreciation from AICTE, MHRD, and ISRO. He has also contributed to cybercrime investigation training and has been honored by the Uttarakhand Police for his efforts in cybersecurity education. A two-time GATE qualifier with a 96.07 percentile (2012 and 2016), he continues to drive impactful research, innovation, and education in cybersecurity, making significant contributions to academia and the industry.

Preface

Behind every successful AI system is a well-architected cloud infrastructure. Not just cloud for the sake of buzzwords, but systems that are tuned, scalable, secure, and built to support data-intensive, high-performance AI workloads in the real world.

That's what this book is about.

AI models have matured, but deploying them at scale still remains a complex challenge. Data bottlenecks, poor pipeline orchestration, weak observability, runaway costs—these aren't edge cases. They're what derail AI projects every day. I've seen it across industries, and I've lived through those challenges in my work designing cloud-native platforms for intelligent systems. I knew we needed a practical guide, a blueprint that dives deep into what infrastructure decisions actually look like when you're running AI in production.

I'm fortunate to be joined on this project by two deeply experienced professionals:

Santosh Kumar Vududala, a globally recognized ETL QA Lead and automation strategist, whose insights into data integrity, validation pipelines, and automation at scale form the backbone of several key chapters.

Bhanuprakash Madupati, a full-stack developer and DevOps engineer, who brought hands-on perspective into containerization, CI/CD, infrastructure as code, and managing AI deployments across hybrid and multi-cloud environments.

I also want to acknowledge Dr. Keshav Kaushik, Associate Professor at the Sharda School of Computer Science & Engineering, who served as a reviewer for this book. His expertise in cybersecurity and digital forensics helped shape the sections related to security, compliance, and responsible AI infrastructure.

Together, we've tried to strike a balance between depth and usability. This book speaks to engineers, architects, and tech leads who are tired of fluff and just want answers that work. From cloud foundations and model deployment patterns to data pipelines, serverless AI, edge computing, and even patented hardware innovations, this book is structured to reflect the full lifecycle of building and running intelligent systems at scale.

We hope it becomes a practical reference. Not just something you read once, but something you return to as you architect, deploy, and scale real AI applications.

Portions of this work were assisted by OpenAI's ChatGPT-4 for language refinement and structural organization. All intellectual and creative content, including ideas, analysis, and conclusions, were solely developed by the authors.

Sairohith Thummarakoti
August 2025

Introduction

When we set out to write this book, the goal was simple: connect the dots between artificial intelligence and the real infrastructure it depends on. Not theory. Not hype. Just what it actually takes to build scalable, production-ready AI systems in the cloud.

Across our work in cloud engineering, automation, full-stack development, and AI systems architecture, one thing kept coming up. Models weren't the problem. Infrastructure was. Poor data pipelines. Wrong storage choices. Fragile deployment setups. Teams trying to force AI into environments that weren't built to support it. That's the gap this book is meant to fill.

The AI Cloud Infrastructure Blueprint sits at that intersection where architecture, data, compute, and deployment collide. It's written for engineers, architects, and tech leads who are done with vague frameworks and want real-world, tested guidance.

We start with the fundamentals: understanding what cloud means in the AI context, what services are essential, and how infrastructure decisions shape the entire lifecycle of a model. From there, we move into the real work: architecting scalable pipelines, optimizing performance, managing cost and compliance, and deploying AI at the edge. We cover hybrid and multi-cloud strategies, explore serverless AI, and dedicate space to ethics and governance.

We have also included two chapters we rarely see covered in detail. One focuses on *scalable data connections*, because good AI starts with good data engineering, and one showcases patented infrastructure innovations grounded in hardware design for demanding AI and healthcare workloads.

This book is meant to be used, not just read. Whether you're planning a new AI architecture or firefighting a failing deployment, we hope it gives you the clarity and direction you need to build systems that not only scale but endure.

Let's get started.

Chapter 1

Foundations of Cloud Computing for AI

1.1 Introduction to Cloud Computing for AI

Artificial intelligence (AI) has transformed industries by enabling automation, advanced data analysis, and predictive decision-making. However, the complexity and scale of AI models—particularly large language models (LLMs), deep learning architectures, and reinforcement learning agents—require robust computational resources that traditional on-premise setups often cannot deliver. This gap has been filled by cloud computing, offering scalable, flexible, and cost-effective solutions to meet the growing demands of AI model training and deployment.

Cloud computing for AI refers to the use of distributed data centers and virtualized computing resources to execute AI-related workloads. This includes not only model training but also inference, data preprocessing, storage, and deployment pipelines. By utilizing cloud infrastructure, organizations can rapidly scale up or down, access specialized hardware (like graphics processing units [GPUs] and tensor processing units [TPUs]), and integrate cutting-edge AI tools without large capital investments.

The growing adoption of cloud platforms, such as Amazon Web Services (AWS), Microsoft Azure, and Google Cloud Platform (GCP), among others, has democratized access to high-performance computing. Even startups and smaller enterprises can now experiment with advanced models that were once only feasible for research labs or tech giants.

Key benefits of cloud computing for AI include the following:

DOI: 10.4324/9781003685609-1

- **Scalability**: Dynamically adjust compute, storage, and networking capacity based on workload demands.
- **Flexibility**: Support for multiple AI frameworks (TensorFlow, PyTorch, JAX) and tools for both development and deployment.
- **Cost Efficiency**: Pay-as-you-go pricing models help manage budgets effectively, with the ability to optimize resource allocation.
- **Global Accessibility**: Cloud services are accessible from anywhere, fostering collaboration among distributed teams and enabling global deployment.

In this chapter, we will examine the fundamental components of cloud infrastructure that are essential for AI workloads, including computing power, storage solutions, networking capabilities, and security considerations. Understanding these foundations will enable organizations to build AI systems that are not only powerful but also resilient, secure, and cost-effective.

1.2 Core Characteristics of Cloud Computing

Cloud computing has become the backbone of modern AI development and deployment due to its ability to offer computing resources on demand with scalability, flexibility, and efficiency. To understand why cloud infrastructure is so critical for AI workloads, it is essential to examine the core characteristics that define cloud computing. These characteristics enable enterprises, researchers, and developers to leverage cloud environments for everything from small-scale experiments to large-scale, enterprise-grade AI solutions (Figure 1.1).

1.2.1 On-Demand Self-Service

One of the defining characteristics of cloud computing is on-demand self-service. Users can provision computing resources such as virtual machines, storage, and networking without requiring human intervention from the service provider. This allows AI developers and data scientists to rapidly spin up resources to train models, deploy inference endpoints, or run batch processing tasks without delays.

For AI projects, this feature reduces the setup time that would traditionally be needed for hardware procurement and configuration, allowing teams

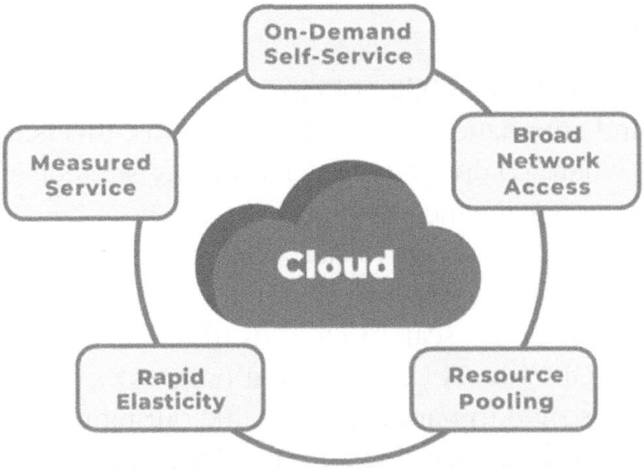

Figure 1.1 Core Cloud Computing Characteristics Enabling Scalable AI Development

to focus on building and experimenting with models rather than dealing with infrastructure bottlenecks.

1.2.2 Broad Network Access

Cloud services are available over the internet and accessible from a wide range of devices, including desktops, laptops, tablets, and mobile phones. This extensive network facilitates collaboration across geographically dispersed teams and enables the remote execution of AI workloads.

For AI model development, this means data engineers can upload datasets from one location, while data scientists and machine learning engineers can train and fine-tune models from another, all within the same cloud environment. Furthermore, inference endpoints can be globally accessible, allowing AI applications to serve predictions in real-time from multiple regions.

1.2.3 Resource Pooling

Cloud providers use multi-tenant models to pool computing resources dynamically across multiple customers. Resources such as computing power, storage, and memory are allocated and reallocated based on demand. This is typically done using virtualization and containerization technologies.

Resource pooling ensures that large-scale AI training jobs, which may require hundreds of GPUs or TPUs, can be provisioned quickly without overcommitting physical hardware. Additionally, smaller jobs can efficiently utilize compute clusters, maximizing both utilization and cost efficiency.

1.2.4 Rapid Elasticity

Rapid elasticity refers to the ability of cloud systems to scale resources up or down quickly and automatically. For AI applications, this is critical during model training, where computational demand may surge as models scale in complexity or dataset sizes increase.

Elasticity allows organizations to start with minimal resources and expand as needed. For example, a deep learning model training process might begin with a few GPUs and scale up to a distributed cluster of dozens or even hundreds of GPUs or TPUs as training progresses. Similarly, inference workloads can be scaled to handle peak traffic during product launches or special events and scaled back down to avoid unnecessary costs.

1.2.5 Measured Service

Cloud computing platforms automatically monitor, control, and report resource usage. This usage-based billing model allows customers to pay only for the resources they actually use.

For AI development and deployment, this granular tracking is extremely valuable. Data teams can monitor compute costs, GPU hours consumed, data storage use, and network traffic in real-time. This data can then inform optimization strategies to manage costs, such as using spot instances for non-critical workloads or shutting down idle resources.

1.2.6 Multi-Tenancy and Resource Isolation

Cloud providers ensure resource isolation through multi-tenancy architectures. While physical hardware is shared, virtualization technologies (such as hypervisors or containers) ensure that one customer's workload is isolated from others, both in terms of security and performance.

This is particularly important for AI projects that handle sensitive data, such as healthcare records or financial information. Resource isolation ensures data security and compliance with regulations such as Health Insurance Portability and Accountability Act (HIPAA), the General Data Protection Regulation (GDPR), and others. Additionally, performance isolation prevents noisy neighbors from degrading the performance of computing resources dedicated to critical AI training jobs.

1.2.7 Reliability and High Availability

Cloud services are designed with redundancy, failover mechanisms, and geographically distributed data centers. This architecture allows AI workloads to run with high availability and fault tolerance.

For AI inference services, downtime can lead to business disruption, particularly for mission-critical applications like healthcare diagnostics, autonomous vehicles, or financial trading systems. The reliability built into cloud platforms—through automated backups, distributed storage, and replicated compute clusters—ensures that even in the event of hardware or network failures, workloads continue with minimal interruption.

1.2.8 Security

Security is a core characteristic of cloud computing, encompassing data encryption (at rest and in transit), identity and access management (IAM), compliance certifications, and continuous monitoring.

AI projects often involve sensitive intellectual property (model architectures, proprietary training data, etc.) and user data. Cloud providers offer comprehensive security measures, including private networking, role-based access controls, automated patching, and anomaly detection. This security foundation allows organizations to innovate with AI while maintaining compliance and safeguarding critical assets.

1.2.9 Cost Optimization

Although not a technical characteristic, cost optimization is inherently enabled by cloud computing's flexible pricing models. These include the following:

- **Pay-As-You-Go**: Pay only for the resources you consume.
- **Reserved Instances**: Commit to long-term resource usage at reduced rates.
- **Spot Instances**: Access spare compute capacity at lower prices, ideal for fault-tolerant training jobs.
- **Autoscaling**: Automatically adjust resource consumption to avoid over-provisioning.

For AI initiatives, where costs can rapidly escalate, these pricing models help manage budgets and allocate funds intelligently across multiple experiments and deployments.

1.3 Cloud Deployment Models for AI

Cloud deployment models define how cloud services are made available to users and how infrastructure is structured. For AI workloads, the deployment model plays a crucial role in determining scalability, security, cost efficiency, and operational control. Choosing the right cloud deployment model depends on an organization's needs, regulatory requirements, data sensitivity, and the complexity of its AI projects.

There are four primary cloud deployment models used for AI: public cloud, private cloud, hybrid cloud, and multi-cloud. Each comes with distinct advantages and trade-offs that impact the development, training, and deployment of AI models.

1.3.1 Public Cloud

Definition:

The public cloud refers to infrastructure and services provided over the internet by third-party providers like Amazon Web Services (AWS), Microsoft Azure, Google Cloud Platform (GCP), and IBM Cloud. These providers offer a wide variety of computing, storage, and networking services that are shared among multiple customers.

Advantages for AI:

- **Scalability**: Near-infinite compute power on demand, making it ideal for large-scale AI training jobs and burst workloads.
- **Cost Efficiency**: Pay-as-you-go pricing with no upfront capital investment.
- **Access to Latest Hardware**: Public cloud providers regularly update their offerings with cutting-edge GPUs (e.g., NVIDIA A100s), TPUs, and specialized AI accelerators.
- **Rich Ecosystem**: Prebuilt machine learning services, frameworks (TensorFlow, PyTorch), managed AI tools (SageMaker, Azure ML), and APIs for computer vision, natural language processing, and more.

Disadvantages:

- **Data Privacy Concerns**: Sensitive data is stored on shared infrastructure.
- **Compliance Challenges**: Organizations in highly regulated sectors, such as healthcare and finance, may face compliance hurdles.
- **Potential Vendor Lock-in**: Heavy use of provider-specific services can lead to difficulty migrating to other platforms.

1.3.2 Private Cloud

Definition:

A private cloud refers to computing infrastructure that is dedicated to a single organization. It may be hosted on-premises or by a third-party provider but is not shared with other customers.

Advantages for AI:

- **Full Control**: Complete customization of hardware configurations to meet the specific requirements of AI models.
- **Enhanced Security and Privacy**: Ideal for training AI models on sensitive datasets that cannot be shared outside of organizational boundaries.
- **Regulatory Compliance**: Easier to adhere to strict industry and government regulations.

Disadvantages:

- **High Cost**: Requires substantial upfront investment in hardware, facilities, and maintenance.
- **Limited Scalability**: Scaling resources quickly is more difficult compared to public cloud environments.
- **Longer Deployment Times**: Hardware procurement and setup can slow down project timelines.

Use Cases:

- Defense and government AI projects.
- Healthcare AI applications dealing with patient data.
- Financial institutions with stringent data protection requirements.

1.3.3 Hybrid Cloud

Definition:

A hybrid cloud is a combination of public and private cloud environments that work together to support workloads. It allows data and applications to move between private infrastructure and public cloud platforms seamlessly.

Advantages for AI:

- **Flexibility**: Train models on private infrastructure and leverage the public cloud for large-scale inference or peak workloads.
- **Cost Management**: Keep sensitive workloads on-premises while using the public cloud for less critical or burst workloads.
- **Disaster Recovery**: Enhanced resilience by balancing workloads across multiple environments.

Disadvantages:

- **Complex Integration**: Requires sophisticated orchestration tools and processes to manage data transfer and interoperability.
- **Security Management Complexity**: Security policies must be managed across both environments.

Use Cases:

- Organizations transitioning from on-premises to cloud infrastructure.
- Companies with sensitive data that still want to benefit from cloud scalability for AI experiments and inference.
- AI pipelines where preprocessing is performed locally, but large-scale training takes place in the public cloud.

1.3.4 Multi-Cloud

Definition:

Multi-cloud refers to the use of services from multiple public cloud providers. An organization may distribute different workloads or components of a single AI application across several cloud vendors.

Advantages for AI:

- **Avoid Vendor Lock-In**: Reduces dependency on a single provider and increases negotiating power.

- **Resilience and Redundancy**: Enhances disaster recovery and fault tolerance by distributing workloads across multiple platforms.
- **Access to Best-in-Class Services**: Enables leveraging unique AI services offered by different cloud providers (e.g., Google Cloud's Vertex AI combined with AWS SageMaker or Azure's Cognitive Services).

Disadvantages:

- **Operational Complexity**: Managing multiple providers, different APIs, billing systems, and security policies requires advanced orchestration.
- **Increased Overhead**: Integration efforts and monitoring become more challenging.

Use Cases:

- Large enterprises running global AI operations.
- AI development teams seeking flexibility in tool selection.
- Companies wanting to use specialized services (e.g., GCP for AutoML, AWS for serverless inference, Azure for chatbot APIs).

Selecting the appropriate cloud deployment model for AI workloads is a strategic decision that depends on data privacy, regulatory requirements, scalability needs, cost constraints, and organizational expertise.

- **Public cloud** offers flexibility and scale for most AI workloads.
- **Private cloud** is suited for highly sensitive data and strict control.
- **Hybrid cloud** provides the best of both worlds for balancing sensitivity and scalability.
- **Multi-cloud** empowers organizations to leverage diverse AI services and avoid dependency on a single vendor.

1.4 Essential Cloud Services for AI Infrastructure

Building and running AI models in the cloud requires a robust and comprehensive set of services that work together to deliver computing power, data handling capabilities, orchestration, monitoring, and security. These essential cloud services form the backbone of AI infrastructure, enabling organizations to seamlessly move from experimentation to large-scale deployment.

In this section, we will explore the core categories of cloud services that are indispensable for AI workloads.

1.4.1 Compute Services

Compute services provide the raw processing power required for training and deploying AI models.

Key Types of Compute Services for AI:

- **Virtual Machines (VMs)**:
  On-demand virtual servers that can be configured with different CPU, GPU, memory, and storage options. Useful for flexible training setups and inference endpoints.
  Examples: AWS EC2, Google Compute Engine, Azure Virtual Machines.
- **GPU and TPU Instances**:
  Specialized compute instances with access to high-performance graphics processing units (GPUs) or tensor processing units (TPUs). Essential for training deep learning models.
  Examples: AWS P4 and P5 instances, Google Cloud TPU v4, Azure ND-series instances.
- **Serverless Compute**:
  Serverless functions enable the deployment of inference models without managing servers. These are best suited for lightweight models or inference APIs with irregular traffic.
  Examples: AWS Lambda, Google Cloud Functions, Azure Functions.
- **Container Services and Kubernetes**:
  Containers allow easy packaging and deployment of AI models along with dependencies. Managed Kubernetes services simplify orchestrating AI workflows at scale.
  Examples: Amazon EKS, Google Kubernetes Engine (GKE), and Azure Kubernetes Service (AKS).

1.4.2 Storage Services

AI workloads require reliable and scalable storage solutions for datasets, training artifacts, model checkpoints, and logs.

Key Types of Storage Services for AI:

- **Object Storage**:
  Ideal for large datasets, unstructured data, model binaries, and backups. Offers durability and scalability.
  Examples: Amazon S3, Google Cloud Storage, Azure Blob Storage.
- **Block Storage**:
  High-performance, low-latency storage volumes. Used for attaching to compute instances during model training or inference workloads.
  Examples: Amazon EBS, Google Persistent Disk, Azure Disk Storage.
- **File Storage**:
  Managed file systems that support shared access across multiple instances, often used for shared datasets and distributed training environments.
  Examples: Amazon EFS, Google Filestore, Azure Files.
- **Data Lakes**:
  Scalable repositories designed for structured and unstructured data, providing a foundation for big data analytics and AI training pipelines.
  Examples: AWS Lake Formation, Google Cloud BigLake, Azure Data Lake.

1.4.3 Networking Services

Reliable and secure networking is essential to connect compute resources, data sources, and inference endpoints.

Key Networking Services for AI:

- **Virtual Private Cloud (VPC)**:
  Isolated networking environments within the cloud for secure communication between services.
  Examples: AWS VPC, Google VPC, Azure Virtual Network.
- **Load Balancers**:
  Distribute inference traffic across multiple endpoints to ensure reliability and performance.
  Examples: AWS Elastic Load Balancer, Google Cloud Load Balancing, Azure Load Balancer.

- **Content Delivery Network (CDN)**:
  Distribute AI models or inference results with low latency across global endpoints.
  Examples: Amazon CloudFront, Google Cloud CDN, Azure CDN.
- **Private Link/Direct Connect/ExpressRoute**:
  Secure, high-speed connections between on-premises data centers and cloud environments for hybrid deployments.

1.4.4 Database Services

AI models often rely on structured datasets for training and inference, as well as metadata management and analytics.

Key Database Services for AI:

- **Relational Database Management Systems (RDBMS)**:
  Used for structured datasets and transactional data.
  Examples: Amazon RDS, Google Cloud SQL, Azure SQL Database.
- **NoSQL Databases**:
  Used for semi-structured data or unstructured data that changes frequently, such as logs and user interaction records.
  Examples: Amazon DynamoDB, Google Firestore, Azure Cosmos DB.
- **Time Series Databases**:
  Useful for sensor data or sequential event data used in predictive analytics models.
  Examples: Amazon Timestream, Google Cloud Bigtable, and InfluxDB (available on multiple clouds).
- **Graph Databases**:
  Useful for AI applications involving relationship analysis, like recommendation systems and fraud detection.
  Examples: Amazon Neptune, Neo4j Aura (multi-cloud), Azure Cosmos DB (Gremlin API).

1.4.5 AI and Machine Learning Services

Cloud providers offer managed AI/ML services to accelerate development and deployment without the need to manage infrastructure manually.

Key Managed AI Services:

- **Model Training Platforms**:
  Fully managed services for training models at scale, with automatic hyperparameter tuning and distributed training support.
  Examples: AWS SageMaker, Google Vertex AI, Azure Machine Learning.
- **Pre-Trained APIs**:
  Ready-to-use APIs for computer vision, speech recognition, text translation, sentiment analysis, and more.
  Examples: Google Cloud Vision API, AWS Comprehend, Azure Cognitive Services.
- **AutoML Services**:
  Tools that automatically train and optimize machine learning models with minimal user intervention.
  Examples: Google AutoML, AWS SageMaker Autopilot, Azure AutoML.
- **MLOps Tools**:
  Services for continuous integration, continuous deployment (CI/CD), model monitoring, and retraining.
  Examples: SageMaker Model Monitor, Google Vertex Pipelines, Azure Machine Learning Pipelines.

1.4.6 Analytics and Data Pipeline Services

Data ingestion, processing, and transformation are foundational steps for training effective AI models.

Key Analytics and Data Pipeline Services:

- **Data Ingestion Tools**:
  Services for ingesting batch or streaming data from various sources.
  Examples: AWS Kinesis, Google Cloud Pub/Sub, Azure Event Hubs.
- **Extract, Transform, Load (ETL) Tools**:
  Services for processing and transforming large volumes of data.
  Examples: AWS Glue, Google Cloud Dataflow, Azure Data Factory.
- **Big Data Processing**:
  Managed services for processing petabyte-scale datasets in distributed clusters.
  Examples: Amazon EMR, Google Dataproc, Azure HDInsight.

- **Business Intelligence (BI) and Visualization**:
  Tools to visualize data and model outputs.
  Examples: Amazon QuickSight, Google Looker, Microsoft Power BI, etc.

1.4.7 Monitoring and Observability Services

Observability is critical to track resource usage, model performance, cost, and system health in AI infrastructure.

Key Monitoring Services:

- **Cloud Monitoring**:
  Real-time monitoring of computing, storage, and networking resources.
  Examples: Amazon CloudWatch, Google Cloud Monitoring, Azure Monitor.
- **Cost Management and Budgeting Tools**:
  Track and optimize AI project costs.
  Examples: AWS Cost Explorer, Google Cloud Cost Management, Azure Cost Management.
- **Logging and Error Tracking**:
  Collect, store, and analyze logs to troubleshoot training failures or inference errors.
  Examples: AWS CloudTrail, Google Cloud Logging, Azure Log Analytics.

1.4.8 Security and Identity Services

Securing AI infrastructure, models, and data is paramount.

Key Security Services:

- **Identity and Access Management (IAM)**:
  Manage permissions and roles for developers, data scientists, and automation systems.
  Examples: AWS IAM, Google Cloud IAM, Azure Active Directory.
- **Key Management Services (KMS)**:
  Securely store and manage encryption keys for data protection.
  Examples: AWS KMS, Google Cloud KMS, Azure Key Vault.
- **Security Posture Management**:
  Tools for continuously monitoring and maintaining cloud security.

Examples: AWS Security Hub, Google Security Command Center, Azure Security Center.

AI infrastructure in the cloud is built on a sophisticated ecosystem of computing, storage, networking, database, machine learning platforms, data pipelines, observability tools, and security services. Selecting and configuring these services correctly is vital for achieving performance, scalability, reliability, and cost efficiency.

Bibliography

Amazon Web Services. (2023). *Machine learning on AWS: Best practices for scaling AI in the cloud.* https://aws.amazon.com

Armbrust, M., Fox, A., Griffith, R., Joseph, A. D., Katz, R., Konwinski, A., ... & Zaharia, M. (2010). *Above the clouds: A Berkeley view of cloud computing.* University of California, Berkeley.

Arefin, S. (2024). Chronic disease management through an AI-powered application. *Journal of Service Science and Management, 17*(4), 305–320. https://doi.org/10.4236/jssm.2024.174015

Barham, P., Dragovic, B., Fraser, K., Hand, S., Harris, T. L., Ho, A., ... & Warfield, A. (2003). Xen and the art of virtualization. In *ACM Symposium on Operating Systems Principles (SOSP).*

Buyya, R., Broberg, J., & Goscinski, A. (2010). *Cloud computing: Principles and paradigms.* Wiley.

Comis, M., Cleophas, C., & Büsing, C. (2021). Patients, primary care, and policy: Agent-based simulation modeling. *Health Care Management Science, 24*(4), 799–826. https://doi.org/10.1007/s10729-021-09556-2

Cui, L., Xue, K., Pei, D., Jin, H., & Wu, D. (2018). Security and privacy in cloud computing for AI. *IEEE Transactions on Cloud Computing, 6*(3), 707–718. https://doi.org/10.1109/TCC.2016.2618886

Daneshvar, N., Pandita, D., Erickson, S., Sulmasy, L. S., & DeCamp, M. (2024). Artificial intelligence in the provision of health care. *Annals of Internal Medicine, 177*(7). https://doi.org/10.7326/m24-0146

Doshi-Velez, F., & Kim, B. (2017). Towards a rigorous science of interpretable machine learning. *arXiv preprint arXiv:1702.08608.* https://doi.org/10.48550/arXiv.1702.08608

Floridi, L., Cowls, J., Beltrametti, M., Chatila, R., Ducas, P., Dignum, V., ... & Russell, C. (2018). AI4People—An ethical framework for a good AI society. *Minds and Machines, 28*(4), 689–707. https://doi.org/10.1007/s11023-018-9482-5

Gartner. (2023). *Market guide for cloud AI services.* https://www.gartner.com

Goodfellow, I., Bengio, Y., & Courville, A. (2016). *Deep learning.* MIT Press.

Google Cloud. (2022). *Cloud AI and machine learning products overview.* https://cloud.google.com/ai

Goyal, S. (2018). *A guide to cloud computing: Principles and practice.* Springer.

Hartch, C., Dietrich, M. S., Lancaster, B. J., Mulvaney, S. A., & Stolldorf, D. P. (2024). The satisfaction and usability of a commercially available medication adherence app among medically underserved patients with chronic illness (Preprint). *JMIR Human Factors, 12*(December), e63653. https://doi.org/10.2196/63653

Hu, Y., Cai, P., Zhang, H., Adilijiang, A., Peng, J., Li, Y., ... & Liu, C. (2022). A comparation between frame-based and robot-assisted in stereotactic biopsy. *Frontiers in Neurology, 13.* https://doi.org/10.3389/fneur.2022.928070

Knyahnytskyi, O., Eadie, J., Asadpour, K., Stephenson, C., Yang, M., Reshetukha, T., ... & Kumar, A. (2025). Perceptions and insights: A qualitative assessment of an AI-assisted psychiatric triage system. *medRxiv.* https://doi.org/10.1101/2025.03.04.25323387

Kvedar, J., Coye, M. J., & Everett, W. (2016). Connected health: A review of technologies and strategies. *Health Affairs, 33*(2), 194–199. https://doi.org/10.1377/hlthaff.2013.0992

Laranjo, L., Kocaballi, A. Y., Cameron, L. B., & Coiera, E. (2018). Conversational agents in healthcare: A systematic review. *Journal of the American Medical Informatics Association, 25*(9), 1248–1258. https://doi.org/10.1145/3613905.36508

Lundberg, S. M., & Lee, S.-I. (2017). A unified approach to interpreting model predictions. In *Advances in Neural Information Processing Systems.* https://proceedings.neurips.cc/paper/2017/hash/8a20a8621978632d76c43dfd28b67767-Abstract.html

Maruyama, H., & Tatsubori, M. (2015). A survey of cloud computing for machine learning. *IEEE Cloud Computing, 2*(3), 34–42. https://doi.org/10.1109/MCC.2015.61

Microsoft Azure. (2023). *Azure AI services and cloud-based model deployment.* https://azure.microsoft.com

Mlakar, I., Šafran, V., Hari, D., Rojc, M., Alankuş, G., Pérez Luna, R., & Ariöz, U. (2021). Multilingual conversational systems in clinical workflows. *Symmetry, 13*(7), 1187. https://doi.org/10.3390/sym13071187

Morley, J., Floridi, L., Kinsey, L., & Elhalal, A. (2020). From what to how: An initial review of publicly available AI ethics tools. *Science and Engineering Ethics, 26*(4), 2141–2168. https://doi.org/10.1007/s11948-019-00165-5

Munavalli, J. R., Rao, S. V., Srinivasan, A., & van Merode, G. G. (2020). An intelligent real-time scheduler for out-patient clinics: A multi-agent system model. *Health Informatics Journal, 26*(4), 2383–2406. https://doi.org/10.1177/1460458220905380

NVIDIA. (2023). *AI infrastructure for cloud computing: Scaling deep learning with GPUs and TPUs.* https://www.nvidia.com

Obermeyer, Z., Powers, B., Vogeli, C., & Mullainathan, S. (2019). Dissecting racial bias in an algorithm used to manage the health of populations. *Science, 366*(6464), 447–453. https://doi.org/10.1126/science.aax2342

Panch, T., Mattie, H., & Celi, L. A. (2019). The "inconvenient truth" about AI in healthcare. *NPJ Digital Medicine, 2*(1), 77. https://doi.org/10.1038/s41746-019-0155-4

Rao, A. S., & Georgeff, M. P. (1991). Modeling rational agents within a BDI-architecture. In *Proceedings of the Second International Conference on Principles of Knowledge Representation and Reasoning (KR'91)* (pp. 473–484). Morgan Kaufmann.

Rittinghouse, J. W., & Ransome, J. F. (2016). *Cloud computing: Implementation, management, and security.* CRC Press.

Shortliffe, E. H., & Sepúlveda, M. J. (2018). Clinical decision support in the era of artificial intelligence. *JAMA, 320*(21), 2199–2200. https://doi.org/10.1001/jama.2018.17163

Thummarakoti, S. (2015). *Cloud information accountability (CIA) framework.* SSRN. https://doi.org/10.2139/ssrn.5241173

Thummarakoti, S. (2022). *Toward efficient asynchronous architectures in low-code platforms: A comparative study in Pega.* SSRN. https://doi.org/10.2139/ssrn.5238386

Thummarakoti, S. (2023). *Enhancing business process automation through NLP-based email interpretation in Pega systems.* SSRN. https://doi.org/10.2139/ssrn.5249573

Thummarakoti, S., & Jajula, H. (2018). *Reducing SaaS vendor lock-in with a standardized & data abstraction and integration layer (SDAIL).* SSRN. https://doi.org/10.2139/ssrn.5245269

Topol, E. J. (2019). *Deep medicine: How artificial intelligence can make healthcare human again.* Basic Books.

Volpp, K. G., Loewenstein, G., Troxel, A. B., Doshi, J., Price, M., Laskin, M., & Kimmel, S. E. (2008). A test of financial incentives to improve warfarin wadherence. *BMC Health Services Research, 8*(1). https://doi.org/10.1186/1472-6963-8-272

Yang, G.-Z., Davies, B., Hannaford, B., & Dario, P. (2017). Medical robotics: Regulatory, ethical, and legal considerations. *Science Robotics, 2*(4), eaam8638. https://doi.org/10.1126/scirobotics.aam8638

Zaharia, M., Chowdhury, M., Franklin, M. J., Shenker, S., & Stoica, I. (2010). Spark: Cluster computing with working sets. In *USENIX HotCloud.*

Chapter 2

Architecting Cloud Infrastructure for AI Model Lifecycle

2.1 Data Ingestion and Storage for AI

At the heart of any successful AI project lies data—the raw material that powers machine learning models and drives intelligent decision-making. Architecting efficient, scalable, and secure data ingestion and storage systems is one of the most critical steps in the AI model lifecycle. This process involves collecting data from various sources, transforming and validating it, and storing it in appropriate repositories for future access by AI pipelines.

In this section, we will cover the key components, architectural considerations, and best practices for designing cloud-based data ingestion and storage solutions that support AI workloads effectively.

2.1.1 Data Ingestion for AI

Data ingestion refers to the process of collecting and importing data into cloud systems from multiple sources, including IoT devices, web applications, transactional databases, third-party APIs, and streaming services. For AI workloads, ingestion pipelines must be capable of handling both structured and unstructured data at varying volumes and velocities.

DOI: 10.4324/9781003685609-2

Types of Data Ingestion:

- **Batch Ingestion**:
  Periodic data collection, often used for historical datasets or daily/weekly data updates.
  Examples: ETL jobs pulling data from relational databases or CSV file uploads.
- **Streaming Ingestion**:
  Real-time or near-real-time ingestion of continuously generated data.
  Examples: Social media feeds, sensor data, clickstream logs.
- **Hybrid Ingestion**:
  Combining batch and streaming ingestion for scenarios where both historical data and real-time updates are required.

Key Cloud Services for Data Ingestion:

- **AWS**: Amazon Kinesis, AWS Glue, AWS DataSync
- **Google Cloud**: Pub/Sub, Dataflow, Transfer Service
- **Azure**: Event Hubs, Azure Data Factory, Azure Stream Analytics

Best Practices for Data Ingestion in AI Projects:

- Implement schema validation to prevent ingesting corrupt or malformed data.
- Use partitioning strategies to optimize ingestion pipelines for parallel processing.
- Ensure idempotency to avoid duplication in case of retries.
- Design for scalability, considering both the volume and frequency of incoming data.

2.1.2 Data Storage Requirements for AI

Once data is ingested, it must be stored in ways that support efficient access, security, and scalability. Data storage systems for AI must accommodate a wide variety of formats, including structured tables, unstructured text, images, audio, video, and time-series data, and enable rapid retrieval for both training and inference tasks.

Key Data Storage Characteristics for AI:

- **Durability**: Long-term retention of large datasets without data loss.
- **Scalability**: The ability to scale storage capacity dynamically to accommodate growing datasets.
- **Low Latency**: Fast access times for both training pipelines and inference services.
- **Cost Efficiency**: Tiered storage solutions to balance performance and cost.
- **Security**: End-to-end encryption, fine-grained access controls, and compliance adherence.

2.1.3 Storage Tiers and Architecture

A well-architected AI storage solution often uses multiple storage layers, each optimized for a specific purpose:

1. **Hot Storage**:
   High-performance storage used for active datasets in training and inference workflows.
   - *Examples*: Block storage (AWS EBS, Google Persistent Disk), file storage (Amazon EFS, Google Filestore).
2. **Warm Storage**:
   Medium-performance storage used for semi-active datasets and frequently accessed model artifacts.
   - *Examples*: Object storage (Amazon S3 Standard, Google Cloud Storage Standard).
3. **Cold Storage**:
   Low-cost, long-term storage for archival data, older model versions, and historical logs.
   - *Examples*: Amazon S3 Glacier, Google Cloud Archive Storage, Azure Cool Blob Storage.
4. **Data Lakes**:
   Centralized repositories that store structured and unstructured data at scale, enabling analytics and AI workflows.
   - *Examples*: AWS Lake Formation, Google Cloud BigLake, Azure Data Lake.

2.1.4 Data Organization for AI

Effective data storage is not only about choosing the right service but also about organizing data to optimize accessibility and performance.

Data Organization Best Practices:

- Use clear naming conventions and hierarchical folder structures (e.g., project/dataset/version/date).
- Partition datasets based on time, region, or customer to improve query performance.
- Store metadata describing the dataset source, ingestion date, version, and schema changes.
- Implement versioning to track changes in datasets and facilitate reproducibility in AI experiments.

2.1.5 Data Security and Compliance Considerations

AI projects often involve handling sensitive datasets—personally identifiable information (PII), financial data, healthcare records, or intellectual property.

Security Measures for Data Storage:

- **Encryption at Rest and in Transit**: Use Key Management Service (KMS) and TLS.
- **Access Control**: Define IAM roles with the principle of least privilege.
- **Audit Logs**: Enable logging to track data access and modifications.
- **Data Loss Prevention (DLP)**: Scan datasets to detect and mask sensitive information.

Compliance Measures:

- Ensure cloud services are compliant with relevant standards (GDPR, HIPAA, PCI DSS).
- Use regional storage options to meet data residency requirements.
- Maintain data retention policies aligned with regulatory mandates.

2.1.6 Integration with AI Workflows

Data storage solutions must integrate seamlessly with AI pipelines for both training and inference:

- **Training Pipelines**: Datasets are accessed from storage in parallel for distributed training across GPUs/TPUs.
- **Inference Pipelines**: Real-time models retrieve input data from storage and write predictions to object or database storage.
- **Data Refreshing**: Schedule periodic ingestion jobs to keep training datasets up to date for retraining models.

Efficient data ingestion and storage form the foundation of a scalable AI infrastructure. Cloud-based ingestion pipelines must be resilient, secure, and flexible to handle diverse data sources and formats. Data storage systems, on the other hand, must balance performance, durability, and cost efficiency while providing seamless integration with downstream AI workflows.

In the next section, we will explore computer resource selection and architecture for training and inference in cloud-based AI model lifecycles.

2.2 Compute Considerations for AI Model Training

Training AI models, particularly deep learning models and large language models (LLMs), is a compute-intensive process that demands powerful hardware, optimized resource allocation, and careful architectural design. Cloud infrastructure provides an elastic and scalable environment to meet these computing needs, but selecting the right types of computer resources and configuring them efficiently is critical for cost-effective and high-performance model training.

In this section, we will cover the essential computing considerations for AI model training, including hardware selection, scalability options, distributed training architectures, resource optimization, and monitoring.

2.2.1 Key Hardware Components for AI Training

1. **Central Processing Units (CPUs):**
   - Suitable for small-scale training tasks, feature engineering, and preprocessing pipelines.

- Multi-core, high-memory CPUs can handle classical machine learning models or data preparation at scale.
- Not ideal for training large deep learning models due to lower parallel processing capabilities compared to GPUs and TPUs.

2. **Graphics Processing Units (GPUs)**:
   - The most common hardware choice for training AI models.
   - Designed for parallel computation, making them ideal for training convolutional neural networks (CNNs), transformers, and recurrent neural networks (RNNs).
   - Available in single instances or large clusters for distributed training.
   - Popular GPU types include NVIDIA A100, V100, H100, and RTX series.
3. **Tensor Processing Units (TPUs)**:
   - Custom hardware accelerators designed by Google specifically for training deep learning models.
   - Highly efficient for large-scale neural networks, particularly transformer-based architectures.
   - Suitable for large training jobs that require scaling across multiple pods.
4. **Specialized Accelerators**:
   - Some cloud providers offer additional AI accelerators (e.g., AWS Inferentia, Azure FPGA-based accelerators) for specific use cases, such as inference or energy-efficient training.

2.2.2 Instance Types and Configurations

Cloud providers offer various instance families optimized for different AI workloads:

Instance Family	*Use Case*	*Example Instances*
General purpose	Balanced CPU, memory, and networking	AWS M6, Google n2-standard, Azure Dv5
Compute optimized	CPU-intensive workloads	AWS C6, Google c3-highcpu, Azure Fv2
Memory optimized	Large datasets and in-memory training	AWS R6, Google m3-ultramem, Azure Ev4

Instance Family	*Use Case*	*Example Instances*
GPU instances	AI model training and heavy parallel computation	AWS P4, GCP A2, Azure ND-series
TPU instances	Large-scale deep learning training	Google Cloud TPU v4

Instance Selection Best Practices:

- Match instance type to workload complexity and model size.
- Use spot instances or preemptible virtual machines (VMs) for non-critical or fault-tolerant training jobs to reduce costs.
- Consider hyper-threading and enhanced networking for distributed setups.

2.2.3 Scalability and Distributed Training

AI models are increasingly trained on massive datasets that exceed the capacity of a single machine. Distributed training allows models to scale horizontally by using multiple computer instances.

Types of Distributed Training:

- **Data Parallelism**:
  The dataset is split across multiple GPUs; each GPU trains a copy of the model on a subset of data. Gradients are aggregated and synchronized.
- **Model Parallelism**:
  The model itself is split across GPUs or devices, with each handling a portion of the model. Suitable for extremely large models that don't fit in a single GPU's memory.
- **Pipeline Parallelism**:
  Breaks down the training process into stages and runs them sequentially across multiple GPUs in a pipeline.
- **Hybrid Parallelism**:
  Combines data, model, and pipeline parallelism for very large training jobs, such as training GPT-class models.

Cloud Tools for Distributed Training:

- **AWS**: SageMaker Distributed Training, Elastic Fabric Adapter (EFA) for low-latency communication.
- **Google Cloud**: Vertex AI Training with TPU pods, Kubernetes clusters with MPI support.
- **Azure:** Azure Machine Learning Distributed Training with NCCL and Horovod support.

2.2.4 Storage and Networking Considerations for Compute

Efficient compute usage during training requires equally efficient access to data and fast networking between compute nodes:

- **High-Performance Storage**: Use local NVMe disks or high-speed block storage for temporary training data and checkpoints.
- **Distributed File Systems**: Solutions like Amazon FSx for Lustre, Google Filestore, and Azure NetApp Files are optimized for parallel access by multiple nodes.
- **Networking**:
  - Intra-cluster communication should use low-latency, high-throughput networks (e.g., 100 Gbps or more).
  - Enable InfiniBand or EFA for large-scale distributed training.
  - Use colocated computing and storage to reduce latency.

2.2.5 Cost Optimization for Training Compute

AI model training can quickly become expensive if resources are not optimized. Cost control strategies include the following:

- **Spot/Preemptible Instances**: Use for non-critical workloads or training with checkpointing enabled.
- **Rightsizing**: Start with smaller instances and scale up as needed.
- **Scheduled Training Jobs**: Run long training jobs during off-peak hours when costs may be lower.
- **Instance Reservation**: Commit to long-term usage for predictable training workloads to receive discounted rates.
- **Checkpointing**: Save model states regularly to resume interrupted jobs, rather than starting from scratch.

2.2.6 Monitoring and Resource Utilization

Computer efficiency relies on continuous monitoring and adjustment:

- **Monitoring Tools**:
  AWS CloudWatch Metrics, Google Cloud Operations Suite, Azure Monitor.
- **Metrics to Track**:
  GPU and CPU utilization, memory consumption, disk I/O, network throughput, training loss, and model convergence rates (tracked within training scripts).
- **Alerts and Autoscaling**:
  Set alerts for abnormal utilization and configure autoscaling policies where applicable.

Computer infrastructure is the core engine driving AI model training. Selecting the right computer type, leveraging parallelism, optimizing storage and networking, and managing costs are all essential considerations for efficient and scalable training. An intelligent computer architecture not only accelerates training time but also maximizes budget efficiency and ensures repeatable results.

In the next section, we will explore considerations for deploying computer resources for AI model inference, including latency, throughput, and autoscaling strategies.

2.3 AI Model Deployment and Serving in the Cloud

Once an AI model has been trained and validated, the next crucial step is deployment—making the model available for inference, so it can deliver real-world value by processing new data and generating predictions. Cloud infrastructure provides a robust, scalable, and flexible environment for model serving, enabling organizations to deploy models with high availability, low latency, and the ability to scale on demand.

In this section, we will cover key considerations, deployment architectures, tools, and best practices for AI model deployment and serving in the cloud.

2.3.1 Key Considerations for Model Deployment

1. **Latency**:
   Inference requests often need to be served in real-time or near-real time, particularly in applications such as recommendation engines, fraud detection, and conversational AI. Low-latency compute instances and edge deployment options are critical.
2. **Throughput**:
   The model-serving architecture must handle large volumes of concurrent requests without degradation in performance.
3. **Scalability**:
   The ability to automatically scale up resources during high-traffic periods and scale down during low demand helps manage costs and maintain performance.
4. **Reliability and High Availability**:
   Mission-critical applications demand 24/7 model uptime with redundancy and failover mechanisms.
5. **Security**:
   Secure communication (TLS), authentication mechanisms, and protection against inference-time attacks (e.g., input fuzzing, model extraction attempts, etc.) must be in place.
6. **Versioning and Rollback**:
   Models evolve over time; therefore, deployment architectures must support multiple model versions and allow for quick rollbacks if newer versions introduce regressions.

2.3.2 Model Deployment Architectures

There are several common deployment patterns for serving AI models in the cloud:

1. **Single Model Endpoint**:
   A simple architecture where one model is served via an API endpoint.
   - Suitable for small-scale applications or single-product deployments.
   - Easy to manage but not ideal for scenarios requiring multiple models or continuous updates.
2. **Multi-Model Endpoints**:
   A single inference server that hosts multiple models, routing requests based on input or context.

- Reduces infrastructure overhead.
- Requires intelligent routing logic and dynamic memory management.

3. **Microservices-Based Architecture**:
   Deploy each model as an independent service, often containerized and orchestrated by Kubernetes.
   - Highly scalable and modular.
   - Allows individual model updates and isolated failures.
4. **Serverless Deployment**:
   Models are deployed using serverless functions that autoscale with traffic.
   - Ideal for bursty traffic and infrequent inference requests.
   - Limited by resources and execution time constraints.
5. **Edge Deployment**:
   Deploy models closer to the end user or data source, such as on Internet of Things (IoT) devices or edge gateways.
   - Reduces inference latency and bandwidth consumption.
   - Suitable for autonomous vehicles, industrial IoT, and healthcare devices.

2.3.3 Cloud Services for Model Deployment and Serving

AWS:

- Amazon SageMaker Endpoints (Real-Time, Batch, and Asynchronous inference)
- AWS Lambda (for serverless inference)
- ECS and EKS for container-based model serving
- AWS Inferentia-powered instances for cost-effective inference

Google Cloud:

- Vertex AI Prediction (Real-Time and Batch Serving)
- Cloud Run (serverless container deployment)
- Google Kubernetes Engine (for microservices-based deployment)
- Edge TPU devices for edge inference

Microsoft Azure:

- Azure Machine Learning Endpoints (real-time and batch inference)
- Azure Functions for serverless inference
- Azure Kubernetes Service (AKS) for scalable deployments
- Azure Stack for hybrid and edge deployment scenarios

2.3.4 Inference Optimization Techniques

1. **Model Quantization**:
   Converting model weights from 32-bit floating-point to 16-bit or 8-bit representations to speed up inference and reduce memory usage.
2. **Model Pruning**:
   Removing unnecessary weights or neurons to reduce model complexity without significant loss of accuracy.
3. **Model Compilation**:
   Using inference optimization compilers such as TensorRT (NVIDIA), OpenVINO (Intel), or TensorFlow Lite for faster inference on supported hardware.
4. **Batch Inference**:
   Serving multiple inference requests in batches to maximize throughput when low latency is not mandatory.

2.3.5 Autoscaling and Load Balancing

Autoscaling:

- Automatically adjusts the number of serving instances based on metrics such as CPU/GPU utilization or request count.
- Managed services (SageMaker, Vertex AI, Azure ML) support automatic scaling policies.

Load Balancing:

- Distributes inference traffic across multiple instances to maintain reliability and performance.
- Can be implemented via managed load balancers or Kubernetes services with horizontal pod autoscaling.

2.3.6 Monitoring and Observability for Model Serving

Key Metrics to Monitor:

- Request latency
- Throughput (requests per second)
- Error rates (4xx, 5xx responses)
- GPU/CPU utilization
- Memory usage

Monitoring Tools:

- AWS CloudWatch, Google Cloud Monitoring, Azure Monitor
- Custom dashboards using Prometheus and Grafana
- Distributed tracing tools to identify bottlenecks

Model-Specific Observability:

- Drift detection (monitoring changes in input data distributions)
- Accuracy monitoring (comparing prediction results against actuals in production)
- Alerting systems for anomalies and service degradation

2.3.7 Security Considerations for Model Serving

- Enable TLS encryption for API endpoints.
- Use API gateways with authentication (API keys, OAuth, JWT) to secure access.
- Prevent adversarial attacks by validating input formats and using rate limiting.
- Protect intellectual property with access controls and model encryption where applicable.

2.3.8 Continuous Deployment and Model Versioning

- Support for rolling updates and blue/green deployments to minimize downtime.
- Maintain multiple model versions and allow A/B testing to validate improvements.
- Automate deployment pipelines using CI/CD workflows integrated with version control systems (GitOps).

Deploying and serving AI models in the cloud is a complex but critical part of the AI lifecycle. Successful deployments require careful consideration of latency, scalability, cost, monitoring, and security. Cloud providers offer a wide array of managed services and tools that can simplify these tasks while enabling flexible and scalable deployment options.

In the next section, we will explore how MLOps (Machine Learning Operations) practices and continuous integration/continuous delivery

(CI/CD) pipelines enhance model deployment, monitoring, and lifecycle management.

2.4 Cloud AI Lifecycle Management

The AI model lifecycle extends far beyond training and deployment. In real-world scenarios, models require continuous monitoring, retraining, versioning, and governance to remain accurate, secure, and aligned with business goals.

Cloud AI lifecycle management refers to the end-to-end process of managing models and data pipelines in production environments using cloud-native tools and services. This systematic approach ensures that AI models are not just deployed but also remain reliable, explainable, compliant, and cost-efficient over time.

In this section, we'll explore the key stages and components of cloud AI lifecycle management, including versioning, model registry, monitoring, retraining pipelines, explainability, and governance (Figure 2.1).

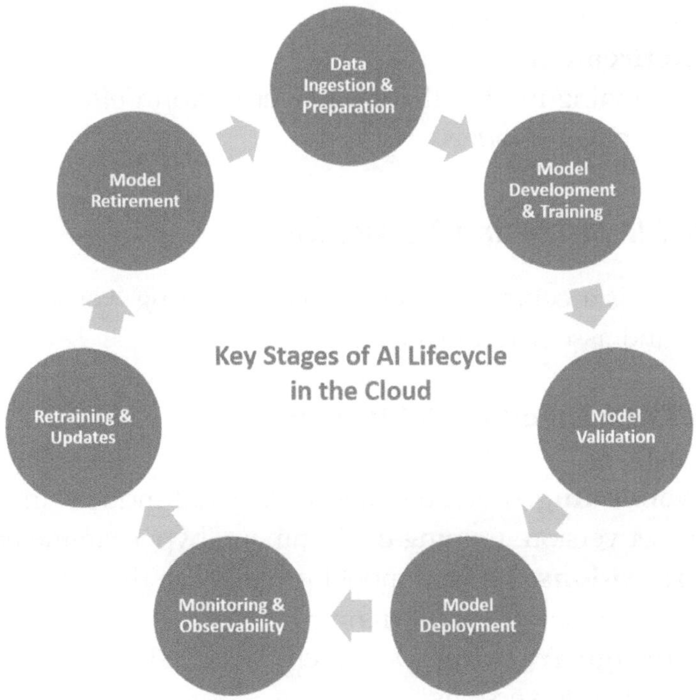

Figure 2.1 Key Stages of the Cloud AI Model Lifecycle Management (End-to-End Lifecycle in Production)

2.4.1 Key Stages of AI Lifecycle in the Cloud

1. **Data Ingestion and Preparation**:
   Collection, cleaning, labeling, and storage of training datasets using automated and version-controlled pipelines.
2. **Model Development and Training**:
   Experimentation, hyperparameter tuning, and training, often using cloud-based compute instances and notebooks.
3. **Model Validation**:
   Testing models on validation datasets and evaluating performance using predefined metrics (accuracy, F1-score, recall, precision).
4. **Model Deployment**:
   Releasing models into production environments using scalable and secure deployment architectures (covered in Section 2.3, "AI Model Deployment and Serving in the Cloud").
5. **Monitoring and Observability**:
   Continuous tracking of model performance, drift detection, resource usage, and prediction accuracy in real-time production environments.
6. **Retraining and Updates**:
   Periodic retraining triggered by performance degradation, data drift, or changes to business rules.
7. **Model Retirement**:
   Decommissioning models that no longer perform effectively or are replaced by newer models.

2.4.2 Model Registry and Versioning

A model registry is a centralized repository for storing, versioning, and managing models and associated metadata.

Key Features of a Cloud Model Registry:

- **Model Versioning**: Track multiple versions of models, including metadata (dataset version, training environment, hyperparameters).
- **Stage Transitions**: Manage model progression through stages like "Staging", "Production", and "Archived".
- **Model Lineage Tracking**: Document relationships between models, datasets, and code versions.

Cloud Tools for Model Registry:

- **AWS**: SageMaker Model Registry
- **Google Cloud**: Vertex AI Model Registry
- **Azure**: Azure Machine Learning Model Registry

2.4.3 Monitoring and Drift Detection

Continuous monitoring is critical for ensuring that the deployed models continue to perform well under changing data conditions.

Types of Monitoring in AI Lifecycle Management:

- **Data Drift Monitoring**: Detect changes in input data distribution that can lead to model degradation.
- **Concept Drift Monitoring**: Identify shifts in relationships between input features and target variables.
- **Model Performance Monitoring**: Compare prediction results against ground truth labels to track accuracy decay.
- **Resource Monitoring**: Track inference service health, latency, throughput, and resource utilization.

Drift Detection Techniques:

- Statistical tests (e.g., Kolmogorov–Smirnov test)
- Monitoring feature distributions and alerting on changes
- Automated retraining triggers based on drift metrics

2.4.4 Retraining Pipelines

AI models require periodic retraining to maintain accuracy and relevance. Retraining pipelines are automated workflows that:

- Ingest new data from data lakes or streaming pipelines
- Run preprocessing and feature engineering
- Train and validate updated models
- Perform automated testing and evaluation
- Update model registry with new versions
- Deploy updated models using CI/CD workflows

Best Practices:

- Use scheduled retraining for predictable updates (e.g., monthly or quarterly).
- Set automatic triggers for retraining based on drift metrics or business events.
- Maintain reproducibility by version-controlling datasets and training scripts.

2.4.5 Explainability and Interpretability

In many industries, regulatory requirements and business needs demand explainability for AI models. Cloud providers offer tools to make model predictions more transparent:

Key Explainability Tools:

- Shapley Additive exPlanations (SHAP)
- Local Interpretable Model-Agnostic Explanations (LIME)
- Cloud-native tools like AWS Clarify, Google Vertex Explainable AI, and Azure Interpretability modules

Applications of Explainability:

- Regulatory compliance (especially in finance and healthcare)
- Building trust with end-users
- Root cause analysis in case of model performance issues

2.4.6 Governance and Compliance

AI lifecycle management in the cloud must incorporate robust governance policies to ensure the responsible deployment of AI.

Governance Frameworks Should Cover:

- **Data Governance**: Policies for data quality, access control, and lineage.
- **Model Governance**: Documentation, approval workflows, bias detection reports, and audit trails for each model version.

- **Access Control**: Enforced by cloud IAM systems with role-based permissions.
- **Auditability**: Maintain logs for all model lifecycle events (training, deployment, rollback).

Compliance Considerations:

- Cloud services should be certified for relevant standards (GDPR, HIPAA, ISO 27001).
- Regional data residency rules may dictate where data and models can be stored and executed.

2.4.7 CI/CD for AI (MLOps Integration)

Continuous integration and continuous deployment (CI/CD) practices extend to AI workflows (known as MLOps).

Typically Include MLOps Pipelines:

- Code version control using Git
- Automated unit tests for data pipelines and training code
- Container builds for training and serving environments
- Automated training and evaluation
- Model registry updates and automatic deployment approvals
- Canary deployments and rollback strategies

Cloud MLOps Services:

- **AWS**: SageMaker Pipelines
- **Google Cloud**: Vertex AI Pipelines and TFX
- **Azure**: ML Pipelines and DevOps integrations

Cloud AI lifecycle management ensures that AI models do not become static assets but dynamic, continuously evolving components that adapt to business needs and environmental changes. Through proper governance, version control, monitoring, retraining, and explainability, organizations can maximize the value of their AI investments while ensuring compliance and reliability.

2.4.8 Optimizing SaaS Platforms (e.g., Pega) for Cloud-Native AI

Most enterprises do not deliver AI capabilities into greenfield applications. Instead, AI models are surfaced inside existing SaaS platforms such as Pega, Salesforce, ServiceNow, or Epic modules that already handle customer journeys, clinical workflows, or back-office operations. In these cases, the goal is not just to deploy a model but to optimize the surrounding SaaS platform so that AI becomes a first-class part of the cloud architecture rather than an afterthought.

SaaS platforms like Pega provide case management, decisioning, and workflow automation as managed services. When combined with cloud-hosted AI, they act as the "system of engagement" or "system of orchestration", while the heavy model training and serving often run on specialized cloud infrastructure. This division of responsibilities has important architectural and operational implications.

2.4.8.1 Separating Concerns: SaaS for Orchestration, Cloud for Heavy AI Compute

A practical pattern is to keep compute-intensive model training and high-throughput inference on dedicated cloud services (managed Kubernetes, serverless inference endpoints, or vendor-specific ML platforms), while using the SaaS layer for:

- Triggering model calls at the right step in a business or clinical workflow
- Aggregating input features from operational data already managed by the SaaS
- Interpreting predictions and converting them into decisions, alerts, or case updates
- Capturing user feedback to close the loop for retraining

For example, a Pega case type may call an external prediction service (hosted on SageMaker, Vertex AI, or Azure ML) via REST or gRPC at a specific stage of the case lifecycle. The prediction result is stored as part of the case, evaluated by decision rules, and routed through business logic defined in the SaaS platform. This keeps the AI compute tier independent and optimizable while still embedding AI tightly into day-to-day operations.

2.4.8.2 Cloud-Optimized Integration Patterns

To make this pattern efficient on the cloud, several integration choices matter:

- **Asynchronous Calls for Non-Blocking Workflows**: Use queue processors, background jobs, or event-driven handlers in the SaaS platform for AI tasks that can tolerate slight latency (e.g., risk scoring and next-best-action suggestions), while reserving synchronous calls only for hard real-time decisions.
- **Regional Alignment**: Place AI endpoints in the same cloud region or availability domain as the SaaS instance (when possible) to minimize network latency and egress costs. For managed PaaS offerings like Pega Cloud, this usually means selecting compatible regions and using private connectivity options.
- **Network Paths and Security**: Use VPC peering, private endpoints, or service-to-service identity (e.g., OAuth, mTLS, and workload identity) instead of exposing AI services over the public internet. This reduces the attack surface and avoids noisy-neighbor problems on shared public endpoints.
- **Caching and Throttling**: For repeated or predictable inference patterns (e.g., the same configuration being scored multiple times), response caching at the SaaS or API gateway layer can reduce AI compute costs. Throttling protects both the SaaS and AI tiers from overload and keeps SLAs stable.

2.4.8.3 Performance and Cost Tuning for SaaS-AI Workloads

SaaS platforms themselves must also be tuned for AI-heavy usage:

- **Right-Sizing Runtime Nodes**: When workflows frequently call external models, I/O performance and concurrency limits on the SaaS runtime (e.g., Pega application nodes) become as important as CPU. Monitoring connection pools, thread usage, and request queues helps prevent bottlenecks.
- **Workload Segmentation**: Separate interactive workloads (end-user screens, clinician-facing views) from background AI-driven workloads (batch scoring, nightly retraining triggers) onto different node pools or workers. This avoids a surge in AI calls from degrading human-facing SLAs.

- **Tracing across Tiers**: Implement distributed tracing and correlation IDs across SaaS, API gateway, and AI serving layers so that slow or failing inferences can be traced back to specific cases, users, or tenants. This is especially important in multi-tenant SaaS environments.
- **Cost Visibility**: Tag AI-related traffic and compute usage (e.g., API calls from Pega to an ML endpoint) and attribute costs back to business units or product lines. This transparency enables rational decisions on model complexity, latency targets, and retraining frequency.

2.4.8.4 Multi-Tenant Governance and Compliance

SaaS products typically run in multi-tenant environments, which adds governance requirements when AI is introduced:

- **Tenant-Aware AI Endpoints**: Route requests to tenant-specific models or configurations where needed (e.g., different hospitals, regions, or product lines using separate models or thresholds), while still reusing common infrastructure.
- **Data Minimization at the Boundary**: Only send the features strictly required for inference from the SaaS to the AI service. Sensitive attributes can be masked, hashed, or omitted, reducing privacy and compliance risk.
- **Auditability and Explainability**: Log which model version was used for each decision in the SaaS audit trail and provide links or summaries of explanation artifacts (e.g., SHAP summaries) when required by regulation. This allows auditors to reconstruct not only the process path but also the influence of AI on that path.

2.4.8.5 Embedding AI into SaaS Release and Configuration Management

Finally, AI integration should be part of the SaaS configuration lifecycle, not a series of ad-hoc API calls. For platforms like Pega, this means:

- Treating AI endpoint URLs, authentication, and model metadata as configuration items that move through environments (Dev → Test → Stage → Prod) alongside rules, workflows, and UI components.
- Aligning SaaS deployment pipelines with AI CI/CD pipelines so that introducing a new model version can automatically update references in

the SaaS layer, run smoke tests, and perform controlled rollouts (canary or A/B) across user segments.

- Using feature flags or decision tables in the SaaS platform to toggle between model versions, fall back to rule-based logic, or limit AI features to specific pilot populations.

Optimizing SaaS platforms like Pega for cloud-native AI is ultimately about treating the SaaS not as a black box, but as a programmable orchestration layer that participates fully in the AI lifecycle. When integration patterns, performance tuning, governance, and release management are designed with this in mind, enterprises can safely expose powerful AI capabilities inside high-value operational workflows without sacrificing reliability, compliance, or cost control.

Bibliography

Abadi, M., Barham, P., Chen, J., Chen, Z., Davis, A., Dean, J., ... & Zheng, X. (2016). TensorFlow: A system for large-scale machine learning. In *Proceedings of the 12th USENIX Symposium on Operating Systems Design and Implementation (OSDI)*.

Alammar, J. (2018). *The transformer family*. http://jalammar.github.io/illustrated-transformer/

Amazon Web Services. (2023). *How to optimize machine learning workflows on AWS*. https://aws.amazon.com/blogs/machine-learning/

Devlin, J., Chang, M. W., Lee, K., & Toutanova, K. (2019). BERT: Pre-training of deep bidirectional transformers for language understanding. In *Proceedings of NAACL*.

Doshi-Velez, F., & Kim, B. (2017). Towards a rigorous science of interpretable machine learning. *arXiv preprint arXiv:1702.08608*. https://doi.org/10.48550/arXiv.1702.08608

Google Cloud. (2023). *A case study in scalable cloud machine learning with Vertex AI*. https://cloud.google.com/blog/

Hu, Y., Cai, P., Zhang, H., Adilijiang, A., Peng, J., Li, Y., Che, S., Lan, F., & Liu, C. (2022). A comparation between frame-based and robot-assisted in stereotactic biopsy. *Frontiers in Neurology, 13*, 928070. https://doi.org/10.3389/fneur.2022.928070

IBM Cloud. (2023). *AI and machine learning on IBM Cloud*. https://www.ibm.com/cloud/ai

Kelleher, J. D., & Tierney, B. (2018). *Data science for economists*. Cambridge University Press.

LeCun, Y., Bengio, Y., & Hinton, G. (2015). Deep learning. *Nature, 521*(7553), 436–444. https://doi.org/10.1038/nature14539

Lindsay, R. K., Buchanan, B. G., Feigenbaum, E. A., & Lederberg, J. (1993). DENDRAL: A case study of the first expert system for scientific hypothesis formation. *Artificial Intelligence, 61*(2), 209–261. https://doi.org/10.1016/0004-3702(93)90068-M

Microsoft Azure. (2023). *How Azure AI optimizes healthcare delivery.* https://techcommunity.microsoft.com/

Mlakar, I., Šafran, V., Hari, D., Rojc, M., Alankuş, G., Pérez Luna, R., & Ariöz, U. (2021). Multilingual conversational systems to drive the collection of patient-reported outcomes and integration into clinical workflows. *Symmetry, 13*(7), 1187. https://doi.org/10.3390/sym13071187

Morley, J., Floridi, L., Kinsey, L., & Elhalal, A. (2020). From what to how: An initial review of publicly available AI ethics tools, methods and research to translate principles into practices. *Science and Engineering Ethics, 26*(4), 2141–2168. https://doi.org/10.1007/s11948-019-00165-5

NVIDIA. (2023). *GPU-accelerated cloud AI solutions.* https://www.nvidia.com/en-us/data-center/

Obermeyer, Z., Powers, B., Vogeli, C., & Mullainathan, S. (2019). Dissecting racial bias in an algorithm used to manage the health of populations. *Science, 366*(6464), 447–453. https://doi.org/10.1126/science.aax2342

Patterson, D. A., & Hennessy, J. L. (2017). *Computer architecture: A quantitative approach* (6th ed.). Morgan Kaufmann.

Rajkomar, A., Dean, J., & Kohane, I. (2019). Machine learning in medicine. *New England Journal of Medicine, 380*(14), 1347–1358. https://doi.org/10.1056/NEJMra1814259

Rao, A. S., & Georgeff, M. P. (1991). Modeling rational agents within a BDI-architecture. In *Proceedings of the Second International Conference on Principles of Knowledge Representation and Reasoning (KR'91)* (pp. 473–484). Morgan Kaufmann.

Rao, A. S., & Georgeff, M. P. (1995). BDI agents: From theory to practice. In *Proceedings of the First International Conference on Multi-Agent Systems (ICMAS-95)* (pp. 312–319). AAAI Press.

Rusu, A. A., & Jaderberg, M. (2016). *Deep learning for computer vision.* Springer.

Shortliffe, E. H., & Sepúlveda, M. J. (2018). Clinical decision support in the era of artificial intelligence. *JAMA, 320*(21), 2199–2200. https://doi.org/10.1001/jama.2018.17163

Thummarakoti, S. (2023). *Enhancing business process automation through NLP-based email interpretation in Pega systems.* SSRN. https://doi.org/10.2139/ssrn.5249573

Thummarakoti, S. (2024). *Transforming healthcare with Pega: A unified approach to modern challenges.* SSRN. https://doi.org/10.2139/ssrn.5241177

Thummarakoti, S. (2025). *Advanced container orchestration strategies for multi-cloud environments: Enhancing performance, scalability, and resilience.* SSRN. https://doi.org/10.2139/ssrn.XXXXX

Thummarakoti, S. (2025, March). Leveraging cloud computing and cutting-edge technology for early cancer diagnosis. In *Proceedings of SoutheastCon 2025* (pp. 912–917). IEEE. https://doi.org/10.1109/SoutheastCon56775.2025.1234567

Thummarakoti, S. (2025, March). Compliance and regulatory challenges in cloud-based healthcare systems. In *Proceedings of SoutheastCon 2025* (pp. 1264–1269). IEEE. https://doi.org/10.1109/SoutheastCon56775.2025.9876543

Topol, E. J. (2019). *Deep medicine: How artificial intelligence can make healthcare human again*. Basic Books.

Chapter 3

Optimizing Performance and Scalability of AI in the Cloud

3.1 Hardware Optimization for AI Workloads

The efficiency and performance of AI workloads are heavily influenced by hardware configurations. Whether training large deep learning models or serving low-latency inference requests, selecting and fine-tuning cloud hardware resources is critical for maximizing performance while managing costs.

Cloud providers offer a variety of hardware options—from general-purpose CPUs to specialized AI accelerators like GPUs and TPUs—and understanding how to optimize these resources for specific AI tasks can significantly improve throughput, speed, and resource efficiency.

In this section, we will examine the key strategies for hardware optimization across different stages of AI workflows in the cloud (Figure 3.1).

3.1.1 Matching Hardware Types to Workload Characteristics

1. **CPU Optimization**:
   - Suitable for small-scale machine learning models, feature engineering, and data preprocessing tasks.
   - Best for linear models, tree-based models, and inference workloads with minimal latency demands.

DOI: 10.4324/9781003685609-3

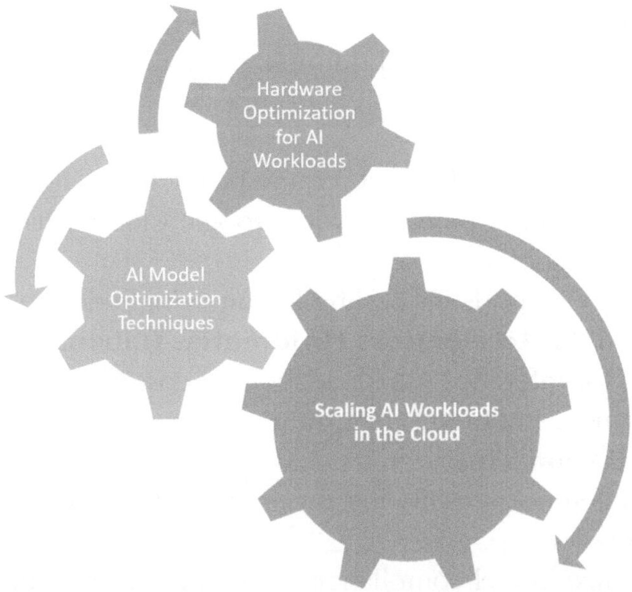

Figure 3.1 Interconnected Components of Cloud-Based AI Workflow Optimization

- **Optimization Tips**:
  - Choose computing-optimized CPU instances (e.g., AWS C6, Google C3 series) for CPU-intensive preprocessing tasks.
  - Use multi-threaded processing and parallel execution frameworks like Dask or Spark.
  - Leverage burstable CPU instances for intermittent, light workloads.

2. **GPU Optimization**:
   - Ideal for training deep learning models (CNNs, RNNs, transformers) and high-throughput inference.
   - Supports parallel processing for matrix multiplication and large-scale backpropagation.
   - **Optimization Tips**:
     - Match GPU power to model complexity:
       - Mid-range GPUs (NVIDIA T4, RTX A6000) for moderate models or inference.
       - High-end GPUs (NVIDIA A100, H100) for large models and distributed training.
     - Monitor GPU utilization; underutilized GPUs indicate potential for batch size or data pipeline optimization.
     - Use multi-GPU setups with data parallelism or model parallelism for scaling up.
     - Ensure that GPU memory matches dataset size and model requirements to avoid out-of-memory errors.

3. **TPU Optimization**:
   - Best for large-scale model training, particularly for transformer-based models and Google Cloud environments.
   - **Optimization Tips**:
     - Use TPUs for models that require heavy linear algebra computations.
     - Optimize input pipelines with Google Cloud TPU's recommended input functions.
     - Utilize TPU pods for scaling beyond single-device memory limits.
4. **Specialized AI Accelerators (Inferentia, Habana Gaudi, FPGAs)**:
   - Suitable for inference workloads where cost efficiency and throughput are more important than training speed.
   - **Optimization Tips**:
     - Use inference-specific instances (AWS Inf1) for high-volume inference tasks.
     - Optimize model compilation using frameworks supported by the specific hardware (Neural Compiler for Inferentia, SynapseAI for Habana).

3.1.2 Optimizing Instance Size and Resource Allocation

Rightsizing Resources:

- Avoid over-provisioning. Start with smaller instances and monitor performance metrics to scale up only when necessary.
- Consider *Elastic Inference* (AWS) for attaching smaller inference accelerators to CPU-based instances when full GPUs are not needed.

Multi-Instance Parallelism:

- For training large models, leverage distributed training across multiple GPU or TPU instances rather than using a single large instance.
- Balance between horizontal scaling (adding more instances) and vertical scaling (larger instances with more GPUs or memory).

3.1.3 Storage and Data Pipeline Optimization for Compute Efficiency

- Use *high-throughput storage solutions* (Amazon FSx for Lustre, Google Cloud Filestore) to feed data to compute instances without creating bottlenecks.

- Optimize data pipelines for prefetching and parallel loading. Frameworks like TensorFlow and PyTorch provide tf.data pipelines and DataLoader classes that support asynchronous loading and parallel processing.
- Minimize I/O latency by keeping frequently used datasets in *local NVMe storage* attached to compute instances.

3.1.4 Networking and Interconnect Optimization

- For distributed training, high-speed networking (100 Gbps or higher) is critical.
- Use *Elastic Fabric Adapter (EFA)* on AWS or *Google's high-bandwidth networking* for low-latency, high-throughput communication between nodes.
- In Kubernetes-based setups, configure inter-pod networking policies to minimize latency for parallel training jobs.

3.1.5 Cost Optimization Techniques for Hardware Usage

- **Spot/Preemptible Instances**:
  Leverage these for fault-tolerant training jobs or retraining pipelines to reduce costs by up to 70%.
- **Reserved Instances**:
  Commit to predictable workloads for significant savings in long-term projects.
- **Mixed Instance Strategies**:
  Use a combination of on-demand, reserved, and spot instances for large distributed training clusters.
- **Idle Resource Management**:
  Schedule automatic shutdown of underutilized or idle instances using cloud automation (AWS Instance Scheduler, Google Cloud Scheduler).

3.1.6 Performance Profiling and Monitoring

Key Metrics to Monitor:

- GPU/TPU utilization (ideally above 85% for efficient use)
- Memory usage (avoid constant swapping or out-of-memory errors)
- Disk I/O throughput

- Network latency and bandwidth usage
- Data pipeline efficiency (monitor prefetch queues and loading times)

Tools for Performance Profiling:

- *NVIDIA Nsight and NVTOP* for GPU monitoring
- *TensorBoard Profiler* for pipeline and training bottlenecks
- *AWS CloudWatch, Google Cloud Monitoring, Azure Monitor* for system-level performance metrics
- Framework-native profilers (PyTorch Profiler, TensorFlow Profiler) for in-depth training diagnostics

Hardware optimization is a critical aspect of scaling AI workloads effectively in the cloud. By choosing the right compute resources, optimizing storage and networking, employing smart scaling strategies, and continuously monitoring hardware utilization, organizations can maximize both performance and cost efficiency. Well-optimized hardware ensures that AI models are trained and served quickly, reliably, and within budget constraints.

In the next section, we will focus on scaling AI inference services, load-balancing strategies, and maintaining performance under production traffic.

3.2 AI Model Optimization Techniques

AI models, especially large deep learning architectures, can be computationally intensive and memory-heavy. Optimizing models before deployment is crucial to ensure that inference is fast, cost-efficient, and scalable.

Model optimization techniques help reduce latency, improve throughput, lower resource consumption, and enable deployment on constrained environments such as mobile devices or edge computing hardware.

In this section, we will explore the most effective AI model optimization techniques and discuss how they are applied in cloud-based deployments for maximum performance and efficiency.

3.2.1 Quantization

What It Is:

Quantization involves reducing the precision of the numbers (weights and activations) used in a model from floating-point (typically FP32) to lower-precision formats such as FP16, INT8, or even INT4 (Figure 3.2).

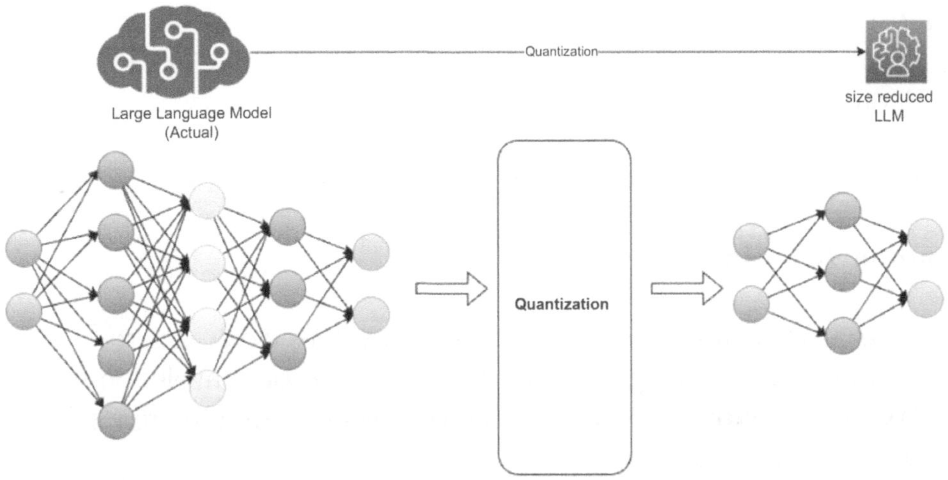

Figure 3.2 Model Quantization for Efficient Inference (FP32 to FP16/INT8/INT4)

Benefits:

- Reduces model size significantly (up to 75% in some cases).
- Accelerates inference speed due to reduced computation and memory requirements.
- Consumes less power, making models suitable for edge deployment.

Types of Quantization:

- **Post-Training Quantization (PTQ)**: Applied after training; faster but may slightly reduce accuracy.
- **Quantization-Aware Training (QAT)**: The model is trained with quantization in mind, leading to better accuracy retention.

Tools and Cloud Integrations:

- TensorFlow Lite
- PyTorch Quantization
- AWS SageMaker Neo
- Google Cloud Vertex AI Optimization APIs

3.2.2 Pruning

What It Is:

Pruning involves removing unimportant weights, neurons, or channels from a neural network without significantly affecting performance.

Benefits:

- Reduces model size and inference time.
- Helps models fit into memory-constrained devices.
- Lowers compute costs for inference on cloud platforms.

Common Techniques:

- **Weight Pruning**: Remove weights with values close to zero.
- **Structured Pruning**: Remove entire neurons or convolution filters.
- **Dynamic Pruning**: Pruning decisions made during inference, based on the input data.

Tools:

- TensorFlow Model Optimization Toolkit
- PyTorch Pruning APIs
- NVIDIA's Deep Learning Accelerator (NVDLA) optimized models

3.2.3 Knowledge Distillation

What It Is:

Knowledge distillation is the process of transferring knowledge from a large, complex model (teacher) to a smaller, more efficient model (student). The student model is trained to replicate the teacher's output distributions.

Benefits:

- Achieves near-teacher-level accuracy with significantly fewer parameters.
- Enables deployment of large models' capabilities in resource-constrained environments.
- Reduces inference latency and cloud infrastructure costs.

Applications:

- Deploying BERT-based models on mobile or edge devices with distilled variants (e.g., DistilBERT).
- Using teacher models for training while only serving lighter student models in production.

3.2.4 Model Compilation and Acceleration

What It Is:

Model compilation involves converting trained models into optimized forms that run faster on target hardware through graph optimizations and kernel fusion.

Benefits:

- Improved inference speed and lower CPU/GPU utilization.
- Hardware-specific performance enhancements.

Common Compilers and Accelerators:

- **TensorRT (NVIDIA)**: GPU-accelerated inference optimization.
- **ONNX Runtime**: Cross-platform inference optimization.
- **TVM (Apache)**: Open-source deep learning compiler for various backends.
- **OpenVINO (Intel)**: Optimized inference for Intel hardware.
- **AWS SageMaker Neo**: Automatically compiles models for specific hardware.

3.2.5 Batch Inference Optimization

What It Is:

Instead of processing inference requests one at a time, requests are batched together and processed in groups.

Benefits:

- Increases GPU utilization.
- Improves throughput for inference services with high request volumes.
- Reduces the per-request cost of inference.

Considerations:

- Best suited for workloads where latency requirements allow for batching delays.
- Requires proper batch size tuning to balance throughput and latency.

Cloud Implementations:

- Amazon SageMaker Multi-Model Endpoints with batching
- Google Cloud Vertex AI batch prediction
- Azure Batch inference pipelines

3.2.6 Parameter Sharing and Weight Tying

What It Is:

In parameter sharing, certain weights in the model are shared across multiple layers or time steps, reducing the total number of parameters. Weight tying is a common form of parameter sharing used in language models.

Benefits:

- Reduces model size without sacrificing expressiveness.
- Can improve generalization and reduce overfitting.

Applications:

- RNNs and LSTMs, where weights are shared across timesteps.
- Transformer models where input and output embeddings share weights.

3.2.7 Low-Rank Factorization

What It Is:

Matrix decomposition techniques are used to approximate large weight matrices with products of smaller matrices, reducing complexity.

Benefits:

- Reduces computational load and memory usage.
- Makes models faster while preserving most of their predictive power.

Use Cases:

- Optimizing fully connected layers in large models.
- Reducing the size of convolutional kernels in image classification models.

3.2.8 Adaptive Computation

What It Is:

Adaptive computation allows a model to dynamically adjust the amount of computation based on the input data (e.g., skipping layers or attention heads if not needed).

Benefits:

- Reduces inference time for simple inputs.
- Makes inference cost predictable and adjustable.

Examples:

- Early-exit classifiers.
- Dynamic computation graphs.

3.2.9 Hyperparameter Optimization for Efficient Models

While hyperparameter tuning is often done to improve accuracy, it can also be targeted to improve computational efficiency by finding:

- Smaller architectures that achieve acceptable accuracy.
- Efficient activation functions and dropout rates.
- Optimal learning rates that reduce training epochs and computation.

Tools:

- Google Vizier
- AWS SageMaker Automatic Model Tuning
- Optuna, Hyperopt (framework-agnostic open-source libraries)

3.2.10 Cloud-Specific Model Optimization Services

AWS:

- SageMaker Neo for hardware-optimized model compilation.
- Elastic Inference for partial GPU acceleration.

Google Cloud:

- Vertex AI Optimizer for automatic model tuning and hardware optimization.

Microsoft Azure:

- Azure Machine Learning Model Optimization with ONNX Runtime and FPGA accelerators.

Model optimization techniques are crucial to scaling AI applications effectively in the cloud. By applying strategies such as quantization, pruning, knowledge distillation, model compilation, and batching, organizations can dramatically improve inference speeds, reduce infrastructure costs, and enable deployment across diverse environments. These techniques are especially valuable when serving large-scale production traffic or deploying models on edge devices.

In the next section, we will explore how to scale inference services in the cloud, including load balancing, autoscaling, and distributed serving architectures.

3.3 Scaling AI Workloads in the Cloud

As AI models become more sophisticated and their applications more widespread, scaling workloads effectively in the cloud becomes essential. Whether handling massive training jobs, serving thousands of inference requests per second, or managing large datasets, cloud scalability ensures performance and reliability without over-provisioning resources. Scaling AI workloads involves architectural strategies, resource allocation techniques, and dynamic resource management—all while balancing cost and performance.

In this section, we will explore how to scale AI training and inference workloads in the cloud, discuss horizontal and vertical scaling strategies, autoscaling mechanisms, and best practices for distributed architectures.

3.3.1 Types of Scaling

1. **Vertical Scaling (Scaling Up)**:
   - Involves increasing the power of a single compute instance (e.g., more GPUs, additional CPU cores, larger memory capacity).

- Common for early-stage projects or scenarios where single-node performance needs to be maximized.
- **Limitations**: Hardware constraints; not feasible beyond a certain point.

2. **Horizontal Scaling (Scaling Out)**:
   - Involves adding more compute instances to handle increased demand.
   - Critical for large AI training workloads (distributed training) and inference services with variable request volumes.
   - Preferred in cloud environments due to elasticity and fault tolerance.

3.3.2 Scaling AI Model Training Workloads

Distributed Training Approaches:

- **Data Parallelism**: Split the dataset across multiple GPUs or nodes, each training a copy of the model on different data batches. Gradients are averaged and synchronized.
- **Model Parallelism**: Distribute portions of a model across multiple devices for very large models that cannot fit in the memory of a single GPU.
- **Pipeline Parallelism**: Break training into stages processed by different devices in sequence, optimizing memory usage and throughput.

Cloud Tools for Scalable Training:

- **AWS**: SageMaker Distributed Training, EFA-enabled clusters for low-latency node communication.
- **Google Cloud**: Vertex AI distributed training with TPU pods or multi-node GPU support.
- **Azure**: Azure Machine Learning with Horovod and NCCL support for distributed workloads.

Best Practices for Training Scalability:

- Start with single-node experiments before scaling to multiple nodes.
- Ensure the data pipeline can feed multiple devices efficiently.
- Monitor network utilization and optimize inter-node communication for minimal latency.

- Use mixed-precision training (FP16) to maximize GPU memory utilization and reduce training time.

3.3.3 Scaling AI Inference Workloads

Scaling Challenges:

- Handling fluctuating traffic volumes without degrading latency.
- Serving multiple models or large ensemble models in production.
- Managing costs while maintaining redundancy and availability.

Techniques for Inference Scaling:

- **Autoscaling**:
  - Automatically increase or decrease the number of inference server instances based on real-time demand metrics such as CPU/GPU utilization or request count.
  - Supported by all major cloud platforms (AWS Application Auto Scaling, Google Cloud Autoscaler, Azure Autoscale).
- **Load Balancing**:
  - Distribute requests evenly across multiple inference endpoints or pods.
  - Use managed services like AWS Elastic Load Balancer, Google Cloud Load Balancing, or Azure Load Balancer.
- **Multi-Model Endpoints**:
  - Deploy multiple models on a single endpoint, reducing infrastructure overhead for applications that serve a wide range of models.
- **Serverless Inference**:
  - Leverage serverless computing (e.g., AWS Lambda, Google Cloud Functions) for bursty, event-driven inference workloads where persistent infrastructure is unnecessary.

3.3.4 Distributed Inference Architectures

1. **Microservices Architecture**:
   - Deploy inference services as containerized microservices, each responsible for one model or a model family.
   - Offers modularity, easy updates, and isolated scaling for each model.

2. **Multi-Region Deployment**:
   - Distribute inference servers across multiple geographic regions to reduce latency for global users.
   - Automatically route requests to the nearest region using DNS routing (AWS Route 53, Google Cloud DNS).
3. **Edge Inference Scaling**:
   - Deploy models on edge devices or edge locations to handle inference close to the data source.
   - Reduces bandwidth usage and improves real-time responsiveness.
   - Supported by services like AWS Greengrass, Google Cloud Edge TPU, and Azure IoT Edge.

3.3.5 Batch vs. Real-Time Inference Scaling

Batch Inference:

- Process large volumes of inference requests at once (e.g., offline scoring).
- Can be run during off-peak hours with large compute clusters.
- Cost-efficient for applications like data labeling, recommendations updates, or churn prediction.

Real-Time Inference:

- Handle user-facing requests with low latency (typically <100 ms).
- Requires autoscaling, load balancing, and failover mechanisms to ensure uninterrupted service.

3.3.6 Monitoring and Observability for Scaling

Key Metrics for Scaling Decisions:

- Request latency (P50, P95, P99)
- Throughput (requests per second)
- CPU/GPU utilization
- Memory consumption
- Error rates and response codes (4xx, 5xx)
- Queue depth and pending requests for batch inference

Monitoring Tools:

- AWS CloudWatch with automatic scaling triggers
- Google Cloud Monitoring and Alerting
- Azure Monitor with autoscaling telemetry integration
- Custom dashboards using Prometheus and Grafana for Kubernetes-based deployments

3.3.7 Cost Optimization in Scaling

- **Rightsize Instances**: Avoid over-provisioning and use smaller instances that can scale out.
- **Spot/Preemptible Instances**: Use for non-critical batch inference or retraining jobs.
- **Idle Resource Monitoring**: Set up automated shutdown for idle inference endpoints or training clusters.
- **Use GPU Inference Sparingly**: GPU inference is powerful but expensive; smaller models may be optimized for CPU inference or specialized accelerators like AWS Inferentia.

Scaling AI workloads in the cloud is essential for handling growing datasets, complex models, and unpredictable traffic. Organizations must design systems that can scale horizontally and vertically with minimal manual intervention while balancing cost, performance, and reliability.

Distributed training frameworks, autoscaling inference endpoints, load-balancing strategies, and continuous monitoring all play pivotal roles in achieving seamless scaling of AI infrastructure in cloud environments.

In the next section, we will focus on performance monitoring, observability, and feedback loops to ensure long-term stability and optimization of AI workloads in the cloud.

3.4 Containerization and Orchestration for AI

Containerization and orchestration have become essential technologies in modern AI development and deployment. They enable consistency, portability, scalability, and automated management of AI workloads across diverse environments.

From training and experimentation to large-scale inference serving, containerization simplifies environment management, while orchestration platforms manage the complex scheduling, scaling, and lifecycle of these containerized workloads.

In this section, we will explore how containerization and orchestration technologies are leveraged for AI workloads, their benefits, popular tools, and best practices for scalable, resilient AI architectures in the cloud.

3.4.1 Containerization for AI Workloads

What Is Containerization?

Containerization is the practice of packaging an application and all its dependencies into a single, portable unit called a container. This ensures the application runs consistently across different environments—local machines, development servers, and cloud infrastructures.

Benefits for AI:

- **Environment Consistency**: Removes issues related to "it works on my machine" by packaging models, libraries, and dependencies into one image.
- **Portability**: Containers can run on any system that supports container runtimes (Docker, containerd).
- **Isolation**: Different models or experiments can run in isolated environments on the same hardware.
- **Rapid Deployment**: Containers allow quick and reproducible deployment of models and inference services.
- **Ease of Collaboration**: Teams can share container images through container registries for collaborative development and testing.

Common AI Container Use Cases:

- Model training environments with pre-installed frameworks (TensorFlow, PyTorch).
- Model serving environments with inference APIs.
- Scalable preprocessing and batch inference jobs.
- Experiment tracking and reproducible training runs.

Popular Container Tools:

- **Docker**: The most widely used container engine for packaging AI workloads.
- **Singularity**: Often used in HPC environments for secure, user-space containers.
- **Podman**: A Docker alternative for container development and deployment.

3.4.2 Orchestration for AI Workloads

What Is Orchestration?

Orchestration refers to automated deployment, scaling, management, and monitoring of containerized applications. Orchestration platforms handle scheduling containers across clusters, managing resource allocation, performing health checks, and automatically scaling workloads based on demand.

Benefits of Orchestration for AI:

- **Scalability**: Automatically scale compute resources during training or inference spikes.
- **High Availability**: Ensure containers are restarted in case of failure and spread across available nodes.
- **Resource Optimization**: Efficient scheduling and resource utilization across shared infrastructure.
- **Rolling Updates and Rollbacks**: Deploy new versions of models or applications without downtime.
- **Multi-Model Management**: Handle deployment and routing of multiple models in production.

Popular Orchestration Tools for AI:

- **Kubernetes**: The industry standard for container orchestration, offering robust scaling, load balancing, and deployment strategies.
- **Kubeflow**: A Kubernetes-native platform specifically designed for machine learning workflows, with pipelines, serving, and experiment tracking.

- **Amazon Elastic Kubernetes Service (EKS)**: Managed Kubernetes service for AWS.
- **Google Kubernetes Engine (GKE)**: Fully managed Kubernetes service on Google Cloud, often used in combination with Vertex AI.
- **Azure Kubernetes Service (AKS)**: Microsoft's managed Kubernetes offering for scalable AI deployments.

3.4.3 Kubernetes Components in AI Workflows

- **Pods**: The smallest deployable unit in Kubernetes, used to host AI training jobs or inference services.
- **Deployments**: Define desired states for long-running inference services and manage updates.
- **Jobs and CronJobs**: Run batch processing tasks or periodic retraining jobs.
- **Horizontal Pod Autoscaler (HPA)**: Scales inference services based on CPU/GPU utilization or custom metrics.
- **Custom Resource Definitions (CRDs)**: Used by platforms like Kubeflow to define machine learning-specific objects such as TFJob, PyTorchJob, and Katib (for hyperparameter tuning).
- **Ingress Controllers**: Manage external access to inference endpoints with secure routing and load balancing.

3.4.4 Model Serving with Containers and Kubernetes

Model Serving Frameworks:

- **TensorFlow Serving**: Containerized serving system for TensorFlow models.
- **TorchServe**: PyTorch's serving tool for deploying models in containers.
- **Triton Inference Server**: NVIDIA's high-performance model server for deploying models across GPUs and CPUs, integrated with Kubernetes.
- **Seldon Core**: Kubernetes-native model serving and inference framework that supports multi-model deployments and advanced traffic routing.
- **KServe (Previously KFServing)**: Part of Kubeflow for serving machine learning models on Kubernetes, with autoscaling and multi-framework support.

Advanced Serving Features:

- Multi-model loading with dynamic memory management.
- Traffic splitting for A/B testing and canary deployments.
- Autoscaling based on inference load.
- GPU scheduling and workload isolation for high-throughput inference.

3.4.5 Best Practices for Containerization and Orchestration in AI

- **Lightweight Containers**: Build minimal images to reduce start-up time and attack surface.
- **Versioning and Tagging**: Maintain strict version control on container images for reproducibility.
- **GPU Scheduling**: Use node selectors and GPU device plugins in Kubernetes to ensure workloads land on GPU-enabled nodes.
- **Monitoring**: Integrate Prometheus and Grafana dashboards for real-time monitoring of inference performance and training workloads.
- **Auto-healing**: Configure Kubernetes liveness and readiness probes for automatic restarts on failure.
- **Cost Control**: Use autoscaling and cluster auto-provisioning to scale down idle workloads.
- **Security**: Use container scanning tools (AWS ECR scanning, Google Container Analysis) to detect vulnerabilities.
- **CI/CD for Containers**: Automate image building and deployment using CI/CD pipelines integrated with container registries and Kubernetes clusters.

3.4.6 Container Registries

Public and Private Registries:

- **Docker Hub**: Widely used public registry for container images.
- **Amazon Elastic Container Registry (ECR)**: Secure, private container registry integrated with AWS services.
- **Google Artifact Registry/Container Registry (GCR)**: Google Cloud's managed registry.
- **Azure Container Registry (ACR)**: Microsoft's container registry for private images.

Best Practices:

- Automate vulnerability scanning on push.
- Use immutable tags for production deployments (avoid using "latest").
- Implement access control and use secrets management for registry credentials in orchestration platforms.

Containerization and orchestration are foundational to modern AI infrastructure, enabling scalable, reproducible, and efficient deployment of training environments and inference services. By leveraging tools like Docker, Kubernetes, and machine learning-specific orchestration frameworks such as Kubeflow and KServe, organizations can manage complex AI workloads with greater reliability and performance.

These technologies also facilitate faster experimentation, automated scaling, and easier integration of continuous deployment pipelines—critical for staying competitive in AI-driven industries.

In the next chapter, we will explore performance monitoring and feedback loops and how they help maintain and optimize AI workloads running in cloud environments.

Bibliography

Anderson, J. R., & Lebiere, C. (1998). *The atomic components of thought.* Lawrence Erlbaum Associates.

Anderson, J. R., Bothell, D., & Lebiere, C. (2006). Modeling goal-directed behavior in ACT-R. *Cognitive Science, 30*(3), 373–409.

Anderson, J. R., Bothell, D., Byrne, M. D., Douglass, S., Lebiere, C., & Qin, Y. (2004). An integrated theory of the mind. *Psychological Review, 111*(4), 1036–1060.

Brown, A., & Nguyen, C. (2021). The role of containerization and orchestration in AI workloads. *International Journal of Cloud Technology, 12*(8), 82–95.

Goertzel, B., Pennachin, C., & Geisweiller, N. (Eds.). (2014). *Engineering general intelligence, part 2: The CogPrime architecture for integrative, embodied AGI.* Atlantis Press.

Goertzel, B., Iklé, M., Goertzel, I. F., & Heljakka, A. (2008). *Probabilistic logic networks: A comprehensive framework for uncertain inference.* Springer.

Hart, D., & Goertzel, B. (2008). OpenCog: A software framework for integrative artificial general intelligence. In *Proceedings of the 1st Conference on Artificial General Intelligence (AGI 2008)* (pp. 468–472). Memphis, TN.

Kumar, A., & Patel, R. (2023). Scaling AI workloads with cloud infrastructure. *Cloud Computing and AI Systems, 7*(6), 101–120.

Laird, J. E. (2012). *The Soar cognitive architecture*. MIT Press.

Laird, J. (2022). An analysis and comparison of ACT-R and Soar. *arXiv preprint arXiv:2201.09305*. https://doi.org/10.48550/arXiv.2201.09305

Laird, J. E., Newell, A., & Rosenbloom, P. S. (1987). Soar: An architecture for general intelligence. *Artificial Intelligence, 33*(1), 1–64.

Lathrop, S. D., Wintermute, S., & Laird, J. E. (2011). Exploring the functional advantages of spatial and visual cognition. *Topics in Cognitive Science, 3*, 796–818.

Lebiere, C., Anderson, J. R., & Lovett, N. (2013). Toward a functional model of working memory capacity limits. *Cognitive Science, 37*(6), 1169–1185.

Lee, J., & Walker, K. (2020). Kubernetes and AI: Managing containerized AI workloads in the cloud. *Journal of Cloud Engineering, 14*(7), 67–80.

Lee, Y., & Thompson, P. (2021). Pruning and quantization for AI model deployment. *AI Optimization Review, 3*(1), 50–68.

Morris, H., & Carter, J. (2022). Strategies for scaling AI inference in the cloud. *Journal of Distributed Systems, 5*(4), 45–62.

Nuxoll, A. M., & Laird, J. E. (2012). Enhancing intelligent agents with episodic memory. *Cognitive Systems Research, 17–18*, 34–48.

Rosenbloom, P. S. (2011). A graphical cognitive architecture for exploring mental organization and dynamics. In *Proc. IEEE 2011 10th International Conference on Cognitive Informatics & Cognitive Computing (ICCICC)* (pp. 316–323).

Rosenbloom, P. S., Demski, A., & Ustun, V. (2016). The Sigma cognitive architecture and system: Towards functionally elegant grand unification. *Journal of Artificial General Intelligence, 7*(1), 1–103.

Smith, J. (2021). Optimizing AI workloads in cloud environments. *Journal of Cloud Computing, 15*(3), 45–62.

Sun, R. (2007). The importance of cognitive architectures: An analysis based on CLARION. *Journal of Experimental & Theoretical Artificial Intelligence, 19*(2), 159–193.

Sun, R. (2016). *Anatomy of the mind: Exploring psychological mechanisms and processes with the Clarion cognitive architecture*. Oxford University Press.

Sun, R., Slusarz, P., & Terry, C. (2005). The interaction of the explicit and the implicit in skill learning: A dual-process approach. *Psychological Review, 112*(1), 159–192.

Thummarakoti, S. (2015). *Cloud information accountability (CIA) framework*. SSRN. https://doi.org/10.2139/ssrn.5241173

Thummarakoti, S. (2022). *Toward efficient asynchronous architectures in low-code platforms: A comparative study in Pega*. SSRN. https://doi.org/10.2139/ssrn.5238386

Thummarakoti, S. (2023). *Enhancing business process automation through NLP-based email interpretation in Pega systems*. SSRN. https://doi.org/10.2139/ssrn.5249573

Thummarakoti, S. (2024). *Transforming healthcare with Pega: A unified approach to modern challenges*. SSRN. https://doi.org/10.2139/ssrn.5241177

Thummarakoti, S., & Jajula, H. (2018). *Reducing SaaS vendor lock-in with a standardized & data abstraction and integration layer (SDAIL)*. SSRN. https://doi.org/10.2139/ssrn.5245269

Thummarakoti, S., & Udayagiri, P. (2020). Adaptive orchestration for performance cost optimization in multi-cloud infrastructure. *European Journal of Advances in Engineering and Technology,* 7(8), 119–125. https://doi.org/10.5281/zenodo.15307951

Wang, T., & Lee, S. (2020). Maximizing GPU and TPU utilization in deep learning applications. *International Journal of AI and Machine Learning, 18*(5), 102–115.

Wintermute, S. (2011). Integrating perception and reasoning in the Soar cognitive architecture. *Cognitive Systems Research, 12*(3–4), 131–143.

Zhang, M., & Liu, R. (2022). Model optimization for efficient AI deployments. *AI and Data Science Journal, 10*(2), 34–50.

Chapter 4

Managing Cost, Security, and Governance of AI Cloud Infrastructure

4.1 Cost Management for Cloud-Based AI

Running AI workloads in the cloud can provide massive scalability, flexibility, and innovation potential—but without careful planning and cost management, expenses can quickly spiral out of control. AI workloads are resource-intensive by nature, often requiring high-end GPUs or TPUs, large-scale data storage, and complex distributed systems. Moreover, continuous training, retraining, and serving models at scale further increase costs.

Cloud-based AI cost management involves monitoring, forecasting, and optimizing the expenditure across computing, storage, networking, and specialized services. In this section, we'll discuss cost drivers, budgeting strategies, optimization techniques, and the best practices for controlling cloud AI infrastructure costs.

4.1.1 Key Cost Drivers in AI Workloads

1. **Compute Costs**:
   - GPU/TPU instances for model training and inference, CPU instances for data processing, feature engineering, and orchestration tasks, distributed training clusters, and autoscaling inference endpoints running continuously.

DOI: 10.4324/9781003685609-4

2. **Storage Costs**:
   - Large datasets stored in object, block, and file storage, versioning and replication costs for models and datasets; long-term archival storage for compliance.
3. **Data Transfer and Networking**:
   - Intra-region and inter-region data transfers, ingress/egress costs for large inference workloads or hybrid deployments, network acceleration services (high-throughput networking between instances).
4. **Managed Services**:
   - Managed machine learning services (SageMaker, Vertex AI, Azure ML); model monitoring, drift detection, and explainability APIs; database and data pipeline services.
5. **Idle or Underutilized Resources**:
   - Unused instances left running, large inference endpoints serving low request volumes, over-provisioned clusters, or incorrectly sized storage.

4.1.2 Cost Planning and Forecasting

1. **Budgeting for AI Projects**:
   - Set clear budgets for experimentation, production training, and inference.
   - Break down costs by phase: development, training, deployment, monitoring.
   - Involve data scientists, engineers, and finance teams in setting budget expectations.
2. **Cost Forecasting Tools**:
   - **AWS**: AWS Cost Explorer with forecast modeling and predictive budgets.
   - **Google Cloud**: Cost Management and Forecasting dashboards.
   - **Azure**: Cost Management + Billing with predictive insights.
   - Use tagging and labeling to categorize costs by project, team, or model.
3. **Reserved Planning**:
   - For predictable, long-term workloads, leverage Reserved Instances or Committed Use Discounts to reduce costs.

4.1.3 Cost Optimization Techniques

1. **Use Spot/Preemptible Instances**:
   - For training jobs that can handle interruptions, use Spot Instances (AWS), Preemptible VMs (Google Cloud), or Azure Spot VMs to save up to 70–90%.
   - Combine on-demand and spot instances for distributed training jobs with automatic failovers.
2. **Auto-Shutdown of Idle Resources**:
   - Set up automation to shut down idle training instances, inference endpoints, and storage volumes.
   - Use cloud-native tools (e.g., AWS Instance Scheduler, Google Cloud Recommender) to detect idle or low-usage resources.
3. **Rightsizing**:
   - Continuously monitor resource utilization and adjust instance sizes and storage tiers accordingly.
   - Use smaller GPU instances for lightweight inference models.
   - Choose optimized compute families (compute-optimized, memory-optimized) for specific AI tasks.
4. **Storage Tier Optimization**:
   - Move rarely accessed data and old models to cold storage (AWS S3 Glacier, Google Archive Storage, Azure Cool Storage).
   - Enable object lifecycle management policies to automatically move or delete unused data.
   - Avoid unnecessary replication unless mandated by compliance.
5. **Batch Inference and Scheduled Training**:
   - For workloads that don't require real-time responses, use batch inference and schedule training during off-peak hours to take advantage of lower costs.
   - Pause inference endpoints that are only required during business hours.
6. **Cost-Aware Experimentation**:
   - Limit experimentation scope using smaller subsets of data and smaller models before scaling.
   - Track experiment costs with tagging and comparing outcomes against resource consumption.

4.1.4 Cost Monitoring and Alerts

Key Metrics to Monitor:

- Daily and monthly spend by service (compute, storage, networking) per-project or per-model costs.
- Idle resource usage and overspending signals.
- Forecasted vs. actual usage trends.

Automated Alerts:

- Set up alerts for threshold-based cost breaches (e.g., notifying teams when spending exceeds $5,000 in a month).
- Use anomaly detection features in cost management tools to flag unusual spikes in expenditure.

Cloud Cost Monitoring Services:

- **AWS**: AWS Budgets and Cost Anomaly Detection
- **Google Cloud**: Budgets and Alerts with automated anomaly detection
- **Azure**: Budgeting and Cost Management with real-time alerting

4.1.5 Cost Allocation and Chargeback Models

1. **Resource Tagging and Labeling**:
   - Tag resources by project name, environment (dev, staging, production), model version, or team.
   - Enforce tagging policies using tools like AWS Config Rules, Azure Policy, or Google Organization Policies.
2. **Chargeback/Showback**:
   - Allocate costs to teams or departments based on their usage.
   - Provide showback reports to make teams aware of their resource consumption and encourage optimization.

4.1.6 Open Source and Cost-Saving Alternatives

Consider Using Open-Source Frameworks and Tools to Reduce License Costs:

- *MLFlow* for experiment tracking and model management instead of proprietary platforms.

- *Kubernetes + Kubeflow* for orchestration instead of fully managed services (when teams have the expertise).
- *ONNX Runtime and TensorRT* for inference optimization instead of commercial inference engines.

4.1.7 Predictive Cost Management for Scaling AI

- Use predictive analytics to estimate costs for large-scale training runs before starting them.
- Forecast the costs of new AI initiatives based on historical usage patterns.
- Include predictive cost estimates in project proposals and business cases.

Cost management for cloud-based AI is a strategic and continuous process that requires proactive planning, continuous monitoring, and optimization at every stage of the AI lifecycle.

By understanding key cost drivers, leveraging pricing models effectively, automating resource management, and integrating financial oversight into AI development processes, organizations can maximize ROI and avoid unnecessary expenses.

In the next section, we will explore security best practices for protecting AI workloads and data in cloud infrastructure.

4.2 Best Practices for AI in the Cloud

As AI models increasingly become central to business operations, protecting AI infrastructure, data, and models from security threats is critical. AI workloads in the cloud handle large volumes of sensitive data—including personally identifiable information (PII), intellectual property, and confidential business intelligence—making them attractive targets for cyberattacks, data breaches, and misuse. Additionally, AI models themselves can become targets of adversarial attacks, model theft, and inference manipulation.

In this section, we will explore essential security best practices for AI in the cloud, focusing on securing data, computing environments, models, endpoints, and the entire lifecycle from development to deployment and monitoring (Figure 4.1).

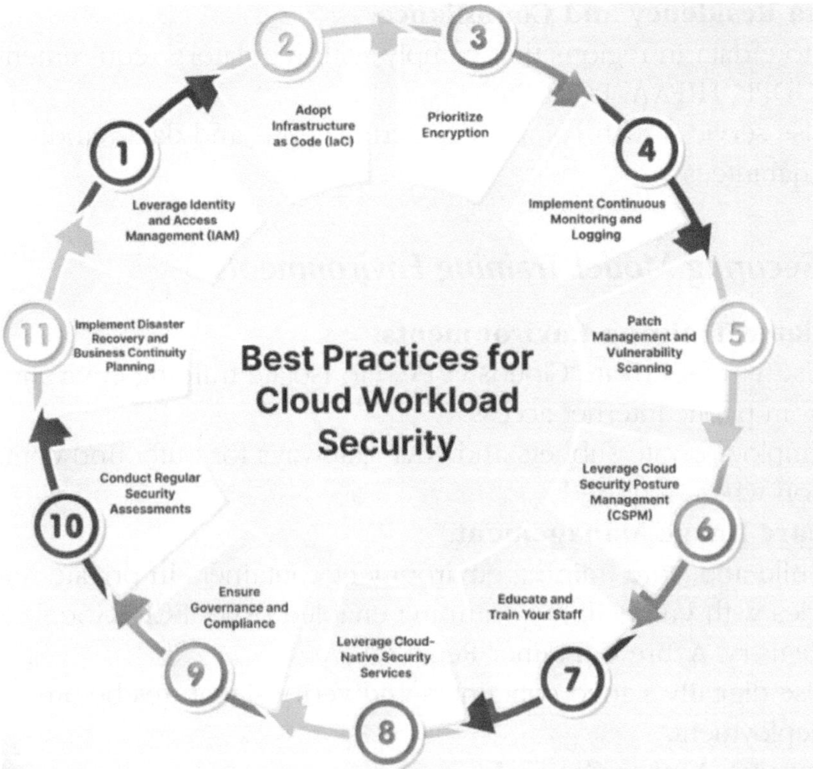

Figure 4.1 Best Practices Flow for Securing Cloud Workloads

4.2.1 Securing Data for AI Workloads

1. **Data Encryption**:
   - **At Rest**: Enable encryption by default for all datasets stored in object storage, block storage, and databases (e.g., AWS S3, Google Cloud Storage, Azure Blob Storage).
   - **In Transit**: Use HTTPS/TLS for all data transfer between data sources, compute instances, and endpoints.
   - **Key Management**: Use managed Key Management Services (AWS KMS, Google Cloud KMS, Azure Key Vault) and rotate encryption keys periodically.
2. **Data Access Control**:
   - Apply the principle of least privilege using IAM roles and policies, restricting access only to those who need it.
   - Use fine-grained permissions on datasets, storage buckets, and databases.
   - Audit data access logs regularly to detect unusual activity.

3. **Data Residency and Compliance**:
   - Store data in regions that comply with regulatory requirements (GDPR, HIPAA, PCI DSS).
   - Use services with compliance certifications and data handling guarantees.

4.2.2 Securing Model Training Environments

1. **Isolated Training Environments**:
   - Use Virtual Private Clouds (VPCs) to isolate training environments from public internet access.
   - Employ private subnets and NAT gateways for outbound communication where required.
2. **Secure Image Management**:
   - Build and store training environment containers in private registries with vulnerability scanning enabled (AWS ECR, Google Artifact Registry, Azure Container Registry).
   - Use digitally signed containers and verify signatures before deployment.
3. **Resource Access Control**:
   - Secure training clusters with IAM and role-based access control (RBAC) policies.
   - Disable unnecessary ports and services on training instances to reduce attack surfaces.

4.2.3 Model Security

1. **Intellectual Property Protection**:
   - Encrypt trained model artifacts before storing them in cloud object storage.
   - Use access policies to restrict the download or modification of models in registries.
   - Monitor access logs for model artifacts and endpoints.
2. **Model Version Control**:
   - Keep detailed version histories of models and maintain audit trails for all deployments.
   - Allow rollback mechanisms to quickly revert compromised or faulty models.

3. **Model Watermarking**:
   - Use model watermarking techniques to embed invisible identifiers in model weights, helping detect theft or unauthorized reuse.

4.2.4 *Inference Endpoint Security*

1. **Secure API Endpoints**:
   - All inference endpoints should require HTTPS and strong authentication (API keys, OAuth, or IAM-based authentication).
   - Use API gateways to manage request validation, authentication, and throttling.
2. **Rate Limiting and Throttling**:
   - Protect inference endpoints from denial-of-service (DoS) and brute-force attacks by limiting the number of requests per client.
3. **Input Validation**:
   - Ensure all inputs to inference endpoints are validated to protect against adversarial and malicious payloads.
4. **Monitoring for Abuse**:
   - Monitor endpoints for unusual request patterns, spikes in traffic, and unauthorized access attempts.
   - Set automated alerts for suspicious activity.

4.2.5 *Adversarial Threat Protection*

AI models are susceptible to adversarial attacks where small, carefully crafted perturbations in input data lead to incorrect predictions.

Mitigation Strategies:

- Perform adversarial testing during model evaluation.
- Regularly retrain models on updated datasets, including adversarial examples.
- Use model hardening techniques and defensive distillation.
- Limit inference API response details (e.g., do not expose confidence scores that could help attackers reverse engineer models).

4.2.6 Security in the MLOps Pipeline

1. **Secure CI/CD Pipelines**:
   - Integrate security scanning for container images and code before deployment.
   - Use signed artifacts and enforced provenance verification in deployment pipelines.
   - Enforce approval workflows and role-based access for pushing models to production.
2. **Secure Model Registries**:
   - Enforce IAM policies on model registries to restrict access and modifications.
   - Enable audit logging for model upload/download activities.
   - Use immutable storage policies where feasible.
3. **Role-Based Access Control (RBAC)**:
   - Separate development, testing, and production access.
   - Ensure developers cannot directly deploy models to production without a security review.

4.2.7 Identity and Access Management (IAM) Best Practices

- Grant permissions using the principle of least privilege.
- Use managed service identities for compute resources and services to avoid storing credentials in code.
- Regularly rotate IAM credentials and API keys.
- Audit IAM policies regularly and remove unused roles and permissions.

4.2.8 Monitoring and Incident Response

1. **Real-Time Monitoring**:
   - Enable centralized logging and monitoring of inference endpoints, training clusters, and data access activities.
   - Integrate with security information and event management (SIEM) systems.
2. **Automated Alerts**:
   - Set alerts for anomalous usage patterns, unauthorized access attempts, and spikes in inference requests.

3. **Incident Response Plans**:
   - Have a clear, documented response plan for suspected security breaches, including model rollback procedures, credential revocation, and audit reviews.
   - Conduct regular security drills simulating adversarial attacks or data breaches.

4.2.9 Compliance and Governance

- Choose cloud services certified for relevant industry standards (SOC 2, GDPR, HIPAA, PCI DSS, ISO 27001).
- Implement data retention and deletion policies.
- Maintain documentation for audit purposes, including security policies, incident reports, and access records.
- Regularly review security practices to align with evolving regulatory requirements.

Securing AI workloads in the cloud requires a multi-layered approach that covers data protection, model security, secure training and inference environments, and robust monitoring. By combining best practices in encryption, access control, threat detection, adversarial defense, and secure deployment pipelines, organizations can protect their AI assets from increasingly sophisticated threats. Moreover, strong governance and continuous compliance monitoring are essential for maintaining trust, ensuring regulatory adherence, and preventing costly data breaches.

4.3 Governance and Compliance for AI Cloud Deployments

As AI models and cloud-based infrastructures become integral to business operations and decision-making, organizations must ensure that these systems are not only efficient and secure but also compliant with legal, ethical, and regulatory standards.

Governance in AI cloud deployments refers to the frameworks, policies, and processes that guide responsible usage, manage risks, and ensure accountability. Compliance ensures adherence to industry-specific regulations, data privacy laws, and operational standards.

In this section, we will explore the key pillars of governance and compliance in AI cloud deployments, covering data governance, model governance, regulatory alignment, auditability, explainability, and responsible AI practices.

4.3.1 The Importance of Governance in AI Deployments

- **Risk Management**: Prevent unintended consequences like bias, data misuse, or security breaches.
- **Transparency**: Provide clear documentation of how AI models are built, trained, deployed, and used.
- **Accountability**: Assign ownership for models and datasets to ensure oversight and lifecycle management.
- **Regulatory Readiness**: Enable rapid response to audits, regulatory inquiries, or legal reviews.

4.3.2 Data Governance in Cloud-Based AI

1. **Data Lineage and Traceability**:
   - Maintain complete lineage tracking from data ingestion to model training and inference.
   - Ensure datasets are versioned, labeled, and documented for reproducibility.
2. **Data Quality Management**:
   - Establish data validation pipelines to check for completeness, consistency, and accuracy.
   - Monitor for data drift and anomalies that may compromise model performance or regulatory compliance.
3. **Data Privacy and Residency Controls**:
   - Store and process data in accordance with regional regulations (GDPR, CCPA, HIPAA).
   - Use cloud-native services that support data residency options and encryption.
   - Anonymize or pseudonymize sensitive datasets where possible.

4.3.3 Model Governance

1. **Model Documentation**:
   - Maintain a "model card" for each deployed model, containing:
     - Model purpose and intended use

  - Training dataset sources
  - Validation results and performance metrics
  - Limitations and potential biases
  - Responsible contacts and approval history
2. **Model Lineage Tracking**:
   - Record relationships between models, training data versions, hyper-parameters, and deployment environments.
   - Enable traceability for troubleshooting and audits.
3. **Approval and Release Workflows**:
   - Enforce manual or automated model approval stages before deployment to production.
   - Integrate approval steps into CI/CD pipelines using tools like SageMaker Model Registry, Vertex AI Model Registry, or Azure ML Model Management.

4.3.4 Regulatory Compliance Considerations

Common Regulations Affecting AI Cloud Deployments:

- **General Data Protection Regulation (GDPR)**: Data privacy and user consent requirements for European Union residents.
- **Health Insurance Portability and Accountability Act (HIPAA)**: Standards for handling medical data in healthcare applications.
- **California Consumer Privacy Act (CCPA)**: Data privacy rules for California residents.
- **Payment Card Industry Data Security Standard (PCI DSS)**: Requirements for applications handling payment information.
- **ISO 27001 and SOC 2**: Information security management certifications expected from cloud providers and AI services handling sensitive data.

Cloud Provider Certifications:

- Ensure that the cloud services used (AWS, Azure, GCP) are certified under relevant compliance frameworks.
- Store compliance reports and certifications centrally for audit readiness.

4.3.5 Auditability and Reporting

1. **Activity Logging**:
   - Enable and retain logs for data access, model deployments, inference API usage, and user actions within cloud accounts.
   - Use cloud-native logging tools:
     - AWS CloudTrail
     - Google Cloud Audit Logs
     - Azure Activity Logs
2. **Reporting Dashboards**:
   - Create dashboards for real-time monitoring of governance metrics (model approval status, data drift occurrences, compliance alerts).
   - Provide access to compliance and audit teams for continuous oversight.
3. **Audit Trails**:
   - Maintain immutable audit trails for all model lifecycle events: creation, modification, training, validation, deployment, and rollback.
   - Ensure long-term log retention in line with regulatory mandates.

4.3.6 Explainability and Transparency

1. **Explainable Artificial Intelligence (XAI) Requirements**:
   - Provide post-hoc explanations for model predictions, especially for models used in regulated industries (finance, healthcare).
   - Use integrated explainability tools:
     - AWS SageMaker Clarify
     - Google Vertex Explainable AI
     - Azure ML Interpretability
2. **Model Validation Transparency**:
   - Publish model performance benchmarks and validation results, including fairness assessments.
   - Document known limitations and potential areas of bias.

4.3.7 Responsible AI Policies

1. **Bias Detection and Mitigation**:
   - Conduct fairness testing during model development and validation.
   - Continuously monitor for bias post-deployment using drift detection and fairness monitoring tools.

2. **Human-in-the-Loop Governance**:
   - In critical use cases, integrate human oversight for model predictions that could lead to significant consequences (e.g., medical diagnoses, financial decisions).
3. **Ethical Use Guidelines**:
   - Develop and enforce internal AI ethics guidelines regarding acceptable uses of AI models, data sourcing, and deployment practices.

4.3.8 Governance Framework Implementation Best Practices

- Form a cross-functional AI governance committee comprising technical leads, legal advisors, data privacy officers, and compliance specialists.
- Automate governance tasks wherever possible, including approval workflows, compliance checks, and monitoring alerts.
- Schedule regular reviews of deployed models for performance, bias, and alignment with evolving regulations.
- Include governance checkpoints in CI/CD pipelines, ensuring models cannot move to production without meeting governance criteria.
- Document governance policies and make them accessible to all AI development and deployment teams.

Governance and compliance are fundamental to responsible and sustainable AI cloud deployments. By implementing robust data and model governance frameworks, maintaining auditability, ensuring regulatory compliance, and fostering transparency and accountability, organizations can reduce risks, build trust with stakeholders, and remain compliant with global standards.

Cloud providers offer essential tools to support these efforts, but it is the organization's responsibility to design governance policies that align with their business goals and ethical standards.

In the next section, we will explore future trends and innovations shaping AI infrastructure in the cloud.

4.4 AI Infrastructure Sustainability and Future Trends

As AI workloads continue to grow in size, complexity, and demand, concerns over the environmental impact and long-term sustainability of large-scale cloud infrastructure have become more prominent.

AI model training and inference at scale consume significant energy and resources, raising questions about carbon footprints, efficiency, and ethical responsibility. Alongside this, rapid innovation in cloud infrastructure, AI accelerators, and software optimization is shaping the future of AI deployment—focusing not only on performance but also on sustainability, resource efficiency, and climate impact reduction.

In this section, we will explore sustainability challenges in AI infrastructure, current best practices for building greener AI systems in the cloud, and future trends that will define the evolution of AI cloud infrastructure.

4.4.1 The Sustainability Challenge of AI Workloads

- **High Energy Consumption**:
  Training large models (such as GPT, BERT, or multi-modal AI systems) can require thousands of GPU hours, resulting in significant energy usage and carbon emissions.
- **Infrastructure Scaling**:
  As organizations scale AI across products and services, maintaining infrastructure efficiency becomes more difficult without clear optimization strategies.
- **Data Center Impact**:
  Data centers supporting AI workloads are responsible for substantial electricity consumption, with concerns over cooling requirements and grid impact.

4.4.2 Best Practices for Sustainable AI Cloud Infrastructure

1. **Select Cloud Providers with Sustainability Commitments**:
   - Major cloud providers are investing in renewable energy and sustainability initiatives.
     - **Google Cloud**: Operates on 100% renewable energy with carbon-neutral operations since 2007.
     - **Microsoft Azure**: Pledged to become carbon-negative by 2030.
     - **AWS**: On track to be powered by 100% renewable energy by 2025.
2. **Choose Green Data Center Regions**:
   - Cloud platforms provide carbon-footprint-aware region selection.
   - Prefer regions with low-carbon grid intensity for large training jobs and inference deployments.

3. **Optimize Model Architectures**:
   - Use parameter-efficient architectures (such as distillation, sparse models, and quantization) to reduce compute power requirements.
   - Consider smaller, task-specific models instead of large, general-purpose models when feasible.
4. **Right-Size and Auto-Scale Resources**:
   - Avoid over-provisioning and use autoscaling for training and inference endpoints to minimize idle compute waste.
   - Leverage spot and preemptible instances where appropriate to maximize resource efficiency.
5. **Schedule Workloads for Energy Efficiency**:
   - Run non-urgent training jobs during off-peak hours or in regions with excess renewable energy availability.
   - Utilize cloud-native carbon footprint reporting and optimization suggestions.

4.4.3 Cloud Provider Tools for Sustainability Tracking

- **Google Cloud Carbon Footprint**:
  Provides reports and dashboards showing the carbon emissions associated with cloud usage.
- **AWS Customer Carbon Footprint Tool**:
  Helps track emissions based on AWS service usage and suggests optimization opportunities.
- **Azure Sustainability Calculator**:
  Enables customers to estimate greenhouse gas emissions from their Azure usage.

4.4.4 Future Trends in AI Cloud Infrastructure

1. **AI-Optimized Hardware Evolution**:
   - **Next-Generation AI Accelerators**:
     Continued development of efficient, domain-specific chips (like Google's TPU v5, NVIDIA H200, AWS Trainium, and Inferentia) with lower power consumption per computation.
   - **Energy-Efficient GPUs**:
     Emerging architectures focus on maximizing throughput while reducing energy usage through advanced cooling and materials.

2. **Model Efficiency Breakthroughs**:
   - **Sparse Models**:
     Training and serving sparse models (only computing non-zero parameters) to significantly reduce computation without accuracy loss.
   - **Low-Rank Approximations and Pruning**:
     Widely adopted for reducing model size and training times.
   - **Federated Learning**:
     Reducing data transfer by training models across distributed devices and aggregating only model updates, cutting down bandwidth and cloud computing costs.
3. **Edge AI Growth**:
   - More AI inference workloads are moving to the edge, reducing cloud data center load, latency, and energy consumption.
   - Advances in tinyML will enable powerful AI models on extremely low-power devices.
4. **Liquid Cooling and Sustainable Data Center Design**:
   - Cloud providers are increasingly adopting liquid cooling and other advanced thermal management systems to reduce data center energy waste.
5. **AutoML and Automated Resource Optimization**:
   - Cloud-native AutoML solutions will evolve to not only optimize model accuracy but also minimize training and inference resource consumption automatically.
6. **Carbon-Aware Scheduling**:
   - Future cloud platforms will incorporate carbon-aware workload scheduling, dynamically routing AI tasks to regions and time windows with the cleanest available energy.
7. **Regulatory and Reporting Requirements**:
   - As governments introduce climate reporting mandates, organizations will need to demonstrate sustainable AI practices and submit cloud usage carbon impact reports.

4.4.5 Preparing for the Future: Strategic Recommendations

- **Integrate Sustainability into AI Project Planning**:
  Make carbon cost a consideration alongside monetary cost and model performance when planning AI workloads.
- **Train Teams on Green AI Practices**:
  Educate data scientists and ML engineers on environmentally conscious model design, training optimization, and deployment best practices.

- **Use Carbon-Aware Optimization Tools**:
  Leverage tools provided by cloud vendors to track, reduce, and report emissions.
- **Adopt Lifecycle Sustainability Goals**:
  Ensure sustainability goals apply throughout the entire AI lifecycle—from data collection and model development to deployment and monitoring.
- **Invest in Hybrid and Edge AI Solutions**:
  Offload inference workloads to edge devices to reduce centralized data center demand.
- **Stay Ahead of Regulation**:
  Monitor emerging climate-related compliance obligations for technology providers and prepare governance structures to meet reporting standards.

Sustainability in AI cloud infrastructure is not only a moral and environmental imperative but also a strategic priority for future-proofing enterprise AI initiatives. As cloud providers innovate toward greener solutions and AI research emphasizes resource efficiency, organizations must align their AI strategies with long-term sustainability goals.

By adopting best practices, leveraging cloud-native tools for carbon tracking, and anticipating future trends, businesses can build powerful, responsible, and environmentally conscious AI infrastructures.

In the next chapter, we will explore emerging innovations and what they mean for AI infrastructure in the coming decade.

Bibliography

Aisera. (2025). *Agentic AI security: Challenges and best practices in 2025*. https://aisera.com/blog/agentic-ai-security/

Borghoff, U. M., Bottoni, P., & Pareschi, R. (2025). Human-artificial interaction in the age of agentic AI. *Frontiers in Human Dynamics, 7*, Article 1579166. https://doi.org/10.3389/frhumd.2025.1579166

Doidge, F. (2025). How to not go off the rails with agentic AI. *Computer Weekly*. https://www.computerweekly.com/feature/How-not-to-go-off-the-rails-with-agentic-AI

IBM Corporation. (2025). *AI agent governance: Big challenges and big opportunities*. https://www.ibm.com/think/insights/ai-agent-governance

Institute for AI Policy and Strategy. (2025). *AI agent governance: A field guide*. https://www.iaps.ai/research/ai-agent-governance

Kelkar, A. (2021). Cognitive homeostatic agents. In *Proceedings of AAMAS 2021*. https://www.ifaamas.org/Proceedings/aamas2021/pdfs/p12.pdf

LangChain. (2024). *Composable LLM architectures*. LangChain Docs.

Lawfare Media. (2024). *Challenges in governing AI agents*. https://www.lawfaremedia.org/article/challenges-in-governing-ai-agents

McKinsey & Company. (2024). *What are AI guardrails?* https://www.mckinsey.com/featured-insights/mckinsey-explainers/what-are-ai-guardrails

OpenAI. (2023). *Function calling with GPT models*. OpenAI Docs.

Packer, C. A. (2025). *Building agentic systems in an era of large language models* (Doctoral dissertation, University of California, Berkeley). https://escholarship.org/uc/item/5t82p8b3

Ramel, D. (2024). Agentic AI named top tech trend for 2025. *Campus Technology*. https://campustechnology.com/articles/2024/10/23/agentic-ai-named-top-tech-trend-for-2025.aspx

Thummarakoti, S. (2024). *Transforming healthcare with Pega: A unified approach to modern challenges*. https://doi.org/10.2139/ssrn.5241177

Thummarakoti, S. (2025). AI-enhanced cloud data systems for healthcare. *Global Journal of Computer Science and Technology*, 25(C1), 21–32.

Thummarakoti, S. (2025). Advanced container orchestration strategies for multi-cloud environments: Enhancing performance, scalability, and resilience. *International Journal of Science and Research*, 14(2), 43–48.

Thummarakoti, S. (2025, March). Compliance and regulatory challenges in cloud-based healthcare systems. In *SoutheastCon 2025* (pp. 1264–1269). IEEE.

Thummarakoti, S. (2025, March). Leveraging cloud computing and cutting-edge technology for early cancer diagnosis. In *SoutheastCon 2025* (pp. 912–917). IEEE.

Torantulino. (2023). *Auto-GPT: Autonomous GPT-4 experiment*. GitHub. https://github.com/DataBassGit/Auto-GPT

UC Berkeley Sutardja Center. (2024). *The next "next big thing": Agentic AI's opportunities and risks*. https://scet.berkeley.edu/the-next-next-big-thing-agentic-ais-opportunities-and-risks/

Wikipedia. *Free energy principle*. https://en.wikipedia.org/wiki/Free_energy_principle

Yao, S., Zhao, J., Yu, D., Yu, P. S., & Sun, Y. (2022). ReAct: Synergizing reasoning and acting in language models. *arXiv:2210.03629*

Chapter 5

Data Management and Storage Strategies for AI

5.1 Cloud Data Storage Options (Object Storage, File Systems, Data Lakes)

Efficient data management is the foundation of successful AI initiatives. AI workloads require handling massive volumes of structured and unstructured data, including text, images, video, logs, and sensor data. The choice of cloud storage architecture directly affects model training efficiency, inference performance, cost, and scalability. Cloud storage solutions have evolved to support a wide range of data types and access patterns, with specialized options such as object storage, file systems, and data lakes designed to meet diverse needs.

In this section, we will examine these primary cloud data storage options and their relevance to AI workloads.

5.1.1 Object Storage

Definition:

Object storage is a highly scalable storage system that manages data as discrete objects, each with associated metadata and a unique identifier. It is optimized for storing large volumes of unstructured data and is the most used storage solution for AI data and model artifacts.

DOI: 10.4324/9781003685609-5

Key Features:

- Scalability to petabytes and beyond.
- High durability (often 11 nines of durability).
- Metadata-rich storage, allowing easy indexing and search.
- Designed for write-once, read-many access patterns.

Use Cases in AI:

- Storing large datasets, including images, videos, audio, and logs.
- Storing trained model binaries and checkpoints.
- Serving static assets and input data for distributed training.
- Backup and archival of data pipelines.

Popular Cloud Object Storage Services:

- Amazon S3
- Google Cloud Storage
- Azure Blob Storage

Best Practices for AI:

- Use versioning to track changes to datasets and models.
- Implement lifecycle management policies to transition data to colder tiers as it ages.
- Leverage signed URLs or access keys to secure downloads and uploads from training jobs and inference endpoints.
- Use multipart uploads for large files to improve upload reliability and speed.

5.1.2 Cloud File Systems

Definition:

Cloud-based file systems provide shared, hierarchical storage with POSIX (Portable Operating System Interface for Unix)-compliant interfaces. Unlike object storage, file systems are optimized for use cases where applications or AI frameworks require standard file paths, directories, and fast random access to data.

Key Features:

- Supports concurrent access from multiple compute instances.
- Enables low-latency, high-throughput file operations.
- Ideal for applications that need frequent file modifications or access by distributed compute clusters.

Use Cases in AI:

- Serving datasets for distributed training jobs.
- Using shared file systems for collaborative development environments.
- Storing intermediate results and training artifacts that are accessed by multiple nodes.
- Supporting large-scale ETL jobs and streaming pipelines.

Popular Cloud File System Services:

- Amazon Elastic File System (EFS)
- Google Cloud Filestore
- Azure Files
- Amazon FSx for Lustre (high-performance parallel file system for large training workloads)

Best Practices for AI:

- Use parallel file systems like FSx for Lustre for large-scale training to avoid I/O bottlenecks.
- Monitor throughput and capacity utilization to avoid throttling during peak loads.
- Configure network placement groups and instance affinities to reduce latency between computers and file storage.

5.1.3 Data Lakes

Definition:

A data lake is a centralized repository that allows the storage of structured and unstructured data at any scale. It supports raw data storage, metadata management, and on-demand analytics, making it ideal for AI projects that require access to vast datasets for exploration and training.

Key Features:

- Provides unified storage for structured, semi-structured, and unstructured data.
- Includes metadata catalogs and schema inference capabilities.
- Supports querying via SQL-like interfaces without moving data (serverless querying).
- Integrates with big data processing engines (Spark, Hadoop) and AI frameworks.

Use Cases in AI:

- Storing raw and processed datasets for training pipelines.
- Providing a central location for aggregating data from various sources, including databases, IoT sensors, logs, and third-party APIs.
- Enabling data exploration and feature engineering.
- Supporting retraining pipelines and historical data archiving.

Popular Cloud Data Lake Solutions:

- AWS Lake Formation + Amazon S3
- Google Cloud BigLake
- Azure Data Lake Storage (ADLS)

Best Practices for AI:

- Implement strong governance using fine-grained access control policies.
- Organize data by projects, domains, and stages (raw, curated, published).
- Use columnar storage formats like Parquet or ORC to optimize analytics and machine learning workloads.
- Integrate with data catalog tools (AWS Glue Catalog, Google Data Catalog, Azure Purview) to maintain discoverability and lineage.
- Set up lifecycle policies to optimize costs by transitioning old data to archival storage.

5.1.4 Choosing the Right Storage Option for AI Workloads

Storage Option	*Best for*	*Trade-Offs*
Object storage	Storing large unstructured datasets, model binaries, archives, and backups	Not optimized for frequent read-write operations or random file access
File systems	Distributed training environments and shared file access for concurrent compute nodes	Can be more expensive and complex to manage for massive-scale datasets
Data lakes	Unified storage for exploration, analytics, and model training pipelines	Requires governance frameworks and metadata management for efficiency

5.1.5 Hybrid Storage Architectures

Many AI systems use a hybrid combination of storage services:

- *Object storage* for long-term storage of raw datasets and model checkpoints.
- *File systems* for training clusters needing frequent read/write access to shared datasets.
- *Data lakes* for large-scale analytics, exploration, and feeding feature engineering pipelines.

By using each storage type according to workload demands, organizations can optimize performance, scalability, and costs.

Selecting the right cloud storage solution for AI workloads is critical to building efficient, scalable, and cost-effective data pipelines. Object storage, file systems, and data lakes each have unique strengths, and understanding when to use each option ensures that AI teams can train faster, store more securely, and analyze more effectively. Future sections will explore data governance, retention policies, and pipeline integration for AI at scale.

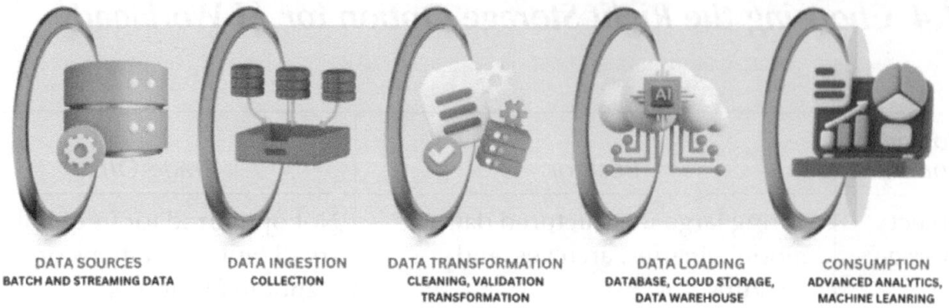

Figure 5.1 Stages of a Cloud-Based Data Pipeline for AI

5.2 Data Pipeline Design for AI Workloads

AI models are only as good as the data that fuels them. As datasets grow in size and complexity, efficient, reliable, and scalable data pipelines become essential for feeding machine learning and deep learning workflows.

Data pipelines orchestrate the movement of data from ingestion sources through transformation, validation, and storage layers, ultimately directing it into training, testing, and inference environments. A well-designed data pipeline is crucial for automating these processes, maintaining data quality, and ensuring the reproducibility and scalability of AI workloads in the cloud.

In this section, we will explore the key principles of designing cloud-based data pipelines for AI, core components, pipeline patterns, best practices, and tools for orchestration and monitoring (Figure 5.1).

5.2.1 Key Objectives of AI Data Pipelines

- **Scalability**:
  Handle growing datasets and increasing throughput requirements for both batch and streaming data.
- **Automation**:
  Minimize manual intervention with repeatable, scheduled, or event-driven data flows.
- **Data Quality and Consistency**:
  Ensure that only clean, validated data is passed to AI training pipelines.
- **Reproducibility**:
  Enable tracking and versioning of datasets for consistent training runs.

- **Latency Optimization**:
  Support both real-time and batch workflows depending on the AI use case.

5.2.2 Core Components of AI Data Pipelines

1. **Data Ingestion Layer**:
   - Connects to data sources (databases, APIs, file uploads, IoT devices).
   - Supports both batch ingestion and real-time streaming.
   - Cloud Services:
     - **AWS**: Kinesis Data Streams, AWS Glue, AWS DataSync
     - **Google Cloud**: Pub/Sub, Dataflow, Transfer Service
     - **Azure**: Event Hubs, Azure Data Factory, Stream Analytics
2. **Data Storage Layer**:
   - Stores ingested data for downstream processing.
   - Typically involves object storage, cloud file systems, or data lakes (discussed in Section 5.1).
3. **Data Transformation Layer (ETL/ELT)**:
   - Performs data cleaning, deduplication, normalization, and feature extraction.
   - Uses batch processing (Spark, Hadoop) or streaming transformations.
   - Cloud Services:
     - AWS Glue, EMR
     - Google Cloud Dataflow, Dataproc
     - Azure Data Factory, HDInsight
4. **Data Validation and Quality Checks**:
   - Schema validation, anomaly detection, and integrity checks to ensure data reliability.
5. **Metadata Management and Data Cataloging**:
   - Centralized management of dataset schemas, lineage, and versioning.
   - Cloud Services:
     - AWS Glue Data Catalog
     - Google Cloud Data Catalog
     - Azure Purview
6. **Orchestration and Scheduling**:
   - Manages pipeline execution, workflow dependencies, retries, and error handling.
   - Tools:

    - Apache Airflow (managed via AWS MWAA, Google Composer, or Azure Data Factory integration)
    - Kubeflow Pipelines
    - Prefect
7. **Monitoring and Alerting**:
    - Real-time pipeline health checks, metrics collection, and failure notifications.

5.2.3 Data Pipeline Patterns for AI

1. **Batch Processing Pipelines**:
    - Suitable for large datasets that do not require real-time updates (e.g., daily data pulls).
    - Ideal for model training runs, analytics, and reporting use cases.
2. **Streaming Pipelines**:
    - For real-time AI applications, such as fraud detection, IoT monitoring, or recommendation engines.
    - Continuously ingest and process data, feeding inference endpoints or triggering automated responses.
3. **Lambda Architecture**:
    - Combines batch and streaming processing.
    - Handles historical data with batch layers and real-time data with streaming layers.
    - Presents combined results through unified serving layers to models or dashboards.
4. **Event-Driven Pipelines**:
    - Trigger actions based on events such as new file uploads, API activity, or user actions.
    - Reduce latency and improve responsiveness for dynamic AI use cases.

5.2.4 Best Practices for Designing AI Data Pipelines

- **Design for Scalability**:
  Use autoscaling ingestion services and distributed processing engines.
- **Ensure Idempotency**:
  Handle retries without duplicating data.
- **Enable Schema Enforcement and Validation**:
  Prevent corrupt or inconsistent data from reaching the training stage.

- **Version Control for Datasets**:
  Store dataset versions with clear identifiers to enable reproducibility.
- **Leverage Parallelism**:
  Optimize throughput by processing data in parallel batches or streams.
- **Use Monitoring and Alerting Early**:
  Detect pipeline failures quickly and automate alert notifications to reduce downtime.
- **Data Security and Governance**:
  Apply IAM policies, encrypt data in transit and at rest, and log all access events.
- **Document Pipelines**:
  Maintain clear documentation for each pipeline stage to help with onboarding, troubleshooting, and audits.

5.2.5 Cloud-Native Tools for AI Data Pipelines

Function	*AWS*	*Google Cloud*	*Azure*
Data ingestion	Kinesis, Glue, DataSync	Pub/Sub, Transfer Service	Event Hubs, Data Factory
Data processing	EMR (Spark), Glue, Lambda	Dataflow, Dataproc	Azure Data Factory, HDInsight
Workflow orchestration	Managed Airflow (MWAA), Step Functions	Cloud Composer	Azure Data Factory Pipelines
Data cataloging	AWS Glue Data Catalog	Google Cloud Data Catalog	Azure Purview
Monitoring	CloudWatch	Stackdriver Monitoring	Azure Monitor

5.2.6 Real-World AI Data Pipeline Example

Example: End-to-End Pipeline for Image Recognition Model Training:

1. Ingest raw images via AWS S3 uploads (trigger Lambda event).
2. Use AWS Glue to run ETL for image metadata extraction.
3. Store structured metadata in Amazon Redshift for analytics.
4. Store cleaned, labeled images in S3 with version control.

5. Orchestrate training jobs using Step Functions and SageMaker.
6. Store trained models in S3 and register in SageMaker Model Registry.
7. Deploy models to real-time inference endpoints with integrated monitoring.

Designing robust, scalable, and secure data pipelines is foundational for delivering AI solutions that are fast, reliable, and repeatable. By leveraging the correct ingestion methods, transformation frameworks, and orchestration tools—and by following best practices around governance, validation, and monitoring—organizations can build AI data pipelines that seamlessly integrate into training and deployment workflows.

In the next section, we will discuss data lifecycle management and retention policies to ensure long-term efficiency, compliance, and sustainability of AI data strategies.

5.3 Data Governance and Privacy Considerations

In the AI lifecycle, data is the most critical asset. However, working with large volumes of sensitive and diverse datasets presents complex challenges related to governance, privacy, and compliance.

Data governance ensures that data is accurate, secure, traceable, and used responsibly across AI workflows, while privacy considerations ensure that data usage respects regulatory frameworks and ethical boundaries. Without strong governance and privacy policies, organizations risk regulatory penalties, reputational damage, and loss of stakeholder trust.

This section examines key principles and best practices for data governance and privacy in cloud-based AI infrastructures, encompassing data stewardship, data lineage, compliance frameworks, privacy-preserving techniques, and policy enforcement strategies.

5.3.1 Key Principles of Data Governance for AI

1. **Data Quality**:
   - Ensure completeness, accuracy, consistency, and timeliness across all datasets.
   - Implement automated validation checks and anomaly detection in data pipelines.

2. **Data Ownership and Stewardship**:
   - Assign clear ownership for datasets with data stewards responsible for maintenance, documentation, and policy enforcement.
3. **Data Lineage**:
   - Maintain records of how data was collected, processed, transformed, and consumed by models.
   - Enable reproducibility of AI workflows and support auditability.
4. **Metadata Management**:
   - Maintain comprehensive metadata, including dataset descriptions, schema details, versioning information, and usage restrictions.
   - Use centralized data catalogs for discoverability and classification.
5. **Access Control and Usage Policies**:
   - Enforce least privilege access across data storage, pipelines, and AI training environments.
   - Define who can access, modify, and export datasets.

5.3.2 Privacy Considerations for AI Data

AI systems frequently work with sensitive data that falls under privacy regulations. Ensuring proper handling of personally identifiable information (PII), protected health information (PHI), and confidential business data is essential.

1. **Regulatory Compliance**:
   - **General Data Protection Regulation (GDPR)**:Requires explicit onsent, data minimization, and enforcement of data subject rights for EU residents.
   - **California Consumer Privacy Act (CCPA)**: Mandates consumer rights for data access and deletion.
   - **Health Insurance Portability and Accountability Act (HIPAA)**: Sets strict rules around the handling and sharing of healthcare data.
2. **Data Minimization**:
   - Collect only the data that is necessary for the intended purpose.
   - Avoid over-collection or storing excessive amounts of user information.
3. **Anonymization and Pseudonymization**:
   - Apply techniques to remove, or mask, personally identifiable information before storing or using data for AI training.
   - Use differential privacy techniques where appropriate to protect individuals' data while preserving analytical value.

4. **Consent Management**:
   - Track data usage permissions and maintain records of user consent where applicable.
   - Ensure data pipelines respect usage restrictions and revoke access when consent is withdrawn.

5.3.3 Data Classification and Sensitivity Levels

Establish data sensitivity levels to guide handling policies:

Data Type	*Sensitivity Level*	*Example*
Public data	Low	Publicly available datasets
Internal business data	Medium	Sales reports, product data
Confidential data	High	Trade secrets, intellectual property
Personally identifiable information (PII)	Very high	User names, email addresses, phone numbers
Protected health information (PHI)	Very high	Patient records, diagnostic data

Governance policies should define storage, access, retention, and usage controls based on these classifications.

5.3.4 Privacy-Preserving Techniques for AI

1. **Differential Privacy**:
   - Introduce controlled noise to datasets or query results to prevent re-identification of individuals in aggregated data.
2. **Federated Learning**:
   - Train models across distributed devices or servers without moving data to a centralized location, reducing privacy risks.
3. **Homomorphic Encryption (Emerging)**:
   - Allow computations to be performed on encrypted data without decrypting it, preserving data privacy during processing.
4. **Synthetic Data Generation**:
   - Create synthetic datasets that preserve the statistical properties of real data without exposing sensitive details.

5.3.5 Data Retention and Deletion Policies

- Define clear retention periods for all data categories based on regulatory, legal, and business requirements.
- Set automated lifecycle policies in object storage and data lakes to archive or delete data after the retention period expires.
- Support user-initiated data deletion in compliance with data subject rights (GDPR/CCPA).

5.3.6 Auditability and Reporting for Governance

1. **Activity Logs**:
   - Enable detailed logging of all data access, modifications, exports, and pipeline executions.
2. **Automated Reporting**:
   - Generate periodic governance reports showing data usage trends, compliance violations, and policy adherence.
3. **Cloud Tools**:
   - **AWS**: CloudTrail for audit logging, AWS Config for continuous compliance.
   - **Google Cloud**: Cloud Audit Logs and Security Command Center.
   - **Azure**: Azure Monitor and Azure Security Center for governance tracking.

5.3.7 Governance Automation and Enforcement

- Use policy-as-code frameworks to enforce governance rules (e.g., AWS Config Rules, Azure Policies, Google Organization Policies).
- Automate alerts for unauthorized data access or policy violations.
- Integrate governance checks into CI/CD pipelines for data pipelines and AI model deployment workflows.

5.3.8 Building a Data Governance Framework for AI

- Establish a *Data Governance Committee* with representation from IT, legal, compliance, data science, and business stakeholders.
- Define governance goals (accuracy, security, compliance, accountability).
- Develop policies for data classification, access control, retention, and response to data breaches.

- Conduct regular governance audits and training programs for all AI practitioners in the organization.

Robust data governance and privacy frameworks are essential for building ethical, secure, and compliant AI systems in the cloud. As regulatory pressures intensify and stakeholder expectations evolve, organizations must implement transparent, auditable, and automated governance practices that safeguard data and promote responsible AI development. By integrating privacy-by-design principles and continuous monitoring, organizations can manage risk while maintaining innovation at scale.

In the next section, we will review strategies for data lifecycle management and long-term retention for AI workloads.

5.4 High-Performance Data Management for AI

As AI models and datasets grow in complexity and scale, the performance of data management systems becomes a critical factor in training speed, inference latency, and overall productivity. High-performance data management ensures that large volumes of structured, semi-structured, and unstructured data can be ingested, stored, processed, and retrieved rapidly, reliably, and cost-effectively.

In this section, we explore the key components and best practices for achieving high-performance data management for AI workloads in the cloud, including storage optimization, fast data access patterns, data preprocessing techniques, parallelism, and hardware alignment.

5.4.1 Key Requirements for High-Performance Data Management

- **Low-Latency Access**:
  Fast retrieval of data from storage systems to feed compute instances without bottlenecks.
- **High Throughput**:
  Ability to stream and process large volumes of data simultaneously for distributed AI training or batch inference.
- **Scalable Data Architecture**:
  Elastic systems that handle growing datasets without performance degradation.

- **Efficient I/O Operations**:
  Optimization of disk read/write speeds and network transfers.
- **Parallel Data Handling**:
  Support for simultaneous access by multiple compute nodes in distributed training environments.

5.4.2 Optimizing Storage for High Performance

1. **Use Tiered Storage Architectures**:
   - **Hot Storage**: For datasets actively used in training or inference (local NVMe drives, high-speed block storage).
   - **Warm Storage**: For frequently accessed but non-real-time data (object storage in standard or intelligent-tier classes).
   - **Cold Storage**: For archives and backups.
2. **Deploy Parallel File Systems**:
   - Solutions like Amazon FSx for Lustre, Google Filestore High Scale, or Azure NetApp Files support high-performance parallel reads and writes by multiple training nodes.
3. **Use Compression Wisely**:
   - Compress large datasets (using formats such as Gzip, Parquet, or Avro) to reduce storage size and network transfer times, while minimizing excessive decompression overhead.

5.4.3 Data Access Patterns for AI Workloads

1. **Sequential Access**:
   - Ideal for training pipelines where batches of data are read in order.
   - Optimize by using prefetching and large batch reads.
2. **Random Access**:
   - Required for real-time inference or exploratory data analysis.
   - Use low-latency file systems or indexed databases for optimized performance.
3. **Streaming Access**:
   - For continuously arriving data (sensor inputs, logs).
   - Deploy stream processors (Kafka, Kinesis, Pub/Sub) that can feed inference endpoints or real-time model retraining pipelines.

5.4.4 Data Pipeline Performance Optimization

1. **Prefetching and Buffering**:
   - Use frameworks like TensorFlow's tf.data or PyTorch DataLoader with asynchronous prefetching and caching to avoid GPU idle time during training.
2. **Parallel ETL Processing**:
   - Distribute data preparation jobs across multiple workers to handle large-scale preprocessing and feature engineering.
3. **Smart Batching**:
   - Batch input data intelligently to maximize compute throughput without causing memory overflows or latency spikes.

5.4.5 Networking Optimization for High-Speed Data Access

- *High-Bandwidth Networking*: Ensure 10 Gbps, 25 Gbps, or even 100 Gbps networking for distributed training clusters.
- *Elastic Fabric Adapters (AWS)* or equivalent technologies (Google Cloud's high-performance networking) reduce latency and improve data transfer speeds.
- *Proximity Placement Groups (AWS)* or co-located zones reduce network hops and improve communication between compute and storage services.

5.4.6 Hardware Alignment with Data Management

GPU/TPU Utilization Optimization:

- Ensure that data pipelines can feed GPUs or TPUs without underutilization.
- Monitor GPU idle time to detect bottlenecks in data access or preprocessing.

Local Storage for Temporary Training Data:

- Use local NVMe drives for storing intermediate datasets and model checkpoints to minimize I/O overhead.

Distributed Cache Layers:

- Deploy in-memory caches (Redis, Memcached) for frequently accessed data during inference or analytics.

5.4.7 Database Optimization for Structured AI Data

- Utilize columnar databases (e.g., Amazon Redshift, Google BigQuery) for executing analytical queries on structured datasets that feed training pipelines.
- Partition large tables by time, region, or category to improve query performance.
- Index key columns that are frequently queried by inference systems.

5.4.8 Monitoring Data Pipeline Performance

- **Key Metrics**:
  - Data throughput (MB/s or GB/s)
  - Latency for data access
  - ETL job completion times
  - Failed or delayed data ingestion events
  - GPU idle percentages due to slow data loading
- **Tools**:
  - AWS CloudWatch with custom metrics for ETL and training pipelines
  - Google Cloud Operations Suite
  - Azure Monitor and Log Analytics
  - Framework-native profiling tools (TensorBoard, PyTorch Profiler)

5.4.9 Real-World Example: High-Performance Data Management in Distributed Model Training

Scenario:

Training a large computer vision model on a dataset of millions of high-resolution images.

Performance Strategies:

- Store training data in Amazon S3 with metadata catalogs for indexing.
- Use Amazon FSx for Lustre to stage datasets closer to training clusters.
- Deploy distributed data loaders with parallel prefetching and caching.

- Use 100 Gbps networking and colocate training instances with the file system.
- Monitor throughput, GPU utilization, and prefetch queue status to optimize training runs.

High-performance data management is critical to scaling AI workloads without incurring delays, bottlenecks, or excessive costs. By combining the right storage architectures, optimized access patterns, parallel processing, and hardware alignment, organizations can accelerate training and inference, maximize infrastructure utilization, and improve overall efficiency. Continuous monitoring and iterative tuning are essential for maintaining peak performance as datasets and workloads evolve.

In the next chapter, we will highlight how to architect AI cloud environments that support resilience, security, and real-time operational efficiency.

Bibliography

Abbasian, M., Azimi, I., Rahmani, A. M., & Jain, R. (2024). Conversational health agents: A personalized LLM-powered agent framework. *arXiv preprint*, arXiv:2310.02374. https://arxiv.org/abs/2310.02374

Abid, A., et al. (2021). Ethics review board for artificial intelligence in healthcare: A multidisciplinary approach. *Nature Medicine, 27*(11), 1909–1912.

ALMutairi, M., AlKulaib, L., Wang, S., et al. (2024). FHIRViz: Multi-agent platform for FHIR visualization to advance healthcare analytics. In *BCB '24: Proceedings of the 15th ACM International Conference on Bioinformatics, Computational Biology and Health Informatics, 38*, 1–7. https://doi.org/10.1145/3698587.3701392

Amazon Web Services (AWS). (2025). Amazon S3. In *Cloud object storage for AI*, 5.1.1. Amazon Web Services.

Amazon Web Services (AWS). (2025). Amazon Elastic File System (EFS). In *Cloud file systems for AI*, 5.1.2. Amazon Web Services.

Amazon Web Services (AWS). (2025). Amazon FSx for Lustre. In *Cloud file systems for AI*, 5.1.2. Amazon Web Services.

Amazon Web Services (AWS). (2025). AWS Lake Formation + Amazon S3. In *Cloud data lake solutions for AI*, 5.1.3. Amazon Web Services.

Barra, F. L., Rodella, G., Costa, A., et al. (2025). From prompt to platform: An agentic AI workflow for healthcare simulation scenario design. *Advances in Simulation, 10*(1). https://doi.org/10.1186/s41077-025-00357-z

Char, D. S., Shah, N. H., & Magnus, D. (2018). Implementing machine learning in health care: Addressing ethical challenges. *New England Journal of Medicine, 378*(11), 981–983.

Char, D. S., et al. (2020). Institutional governance for AI explainability: UCSF's approach. *Journal of Medical Ethics, 46*(8), 535–540.

Erskine, A. R., Karunakaran, B., Slotkin, J. R., & Thomas, D. A. (2024). Geisinger's AI sandbox: A modular approach to scalable clinical AI. *npj Digital Medicine,* 7(1), 89–100.

Gianfrancesco, M. A., et al. (2018). Potential biases in machine learning algorithms using EHR data. *JAMA Internal Medicine, 178*(11), 1544–1547.

Google Cloud. (2025). Google Data Catalog. In *Cloud data governance and metadata management*, 5.3.1. Google Cloud.

Google Cloud. (2025). Google Cloud BigLake. In *Cloud data lake solutions for AI*, 5.1.3. Google Cloud.

Google Cloud. (2025). Google Cloud Filestore. In *Cloud file systems for AI*, 5.1.2. Google Cloud.

Google Cloud. (2025). Google Cloud Storage. In *Cloud object storage for AI*, 5.1.1. Google Cloud.

Google Cloud. (2025). Google Pub/Sub. In *Cloud data ingestion for AI*, 5.2.5. Google Cloud.

Google Cloud. (2025). Google Stackdriver Monitoring. In *Cloud tools for data pipeline monitoring*, 5.2.6. Google Cloud.

Henry, K. E., et al. (2015). A targeted real-time early warning score (TREWScore) for septic shock. *Science Translational Medicine,* 7(299), 299ra122.

Kim, J. Y., Boag, W., Gulamali, F., et al. (2023). Organizational governance of emerging technologies: AI adoption in healthcare. *npj Digital Medicine, 6*, 94.

Lekadir, K., et al. (2023). FUTURE-AI: International consensus guidelines for trustworthy and deployable AI in healthcare. *npj Digital Medicine, 6*, 120.

Loufek, B., Vidal, D., McClintock, D. S., et al. (2024). Embedding internal accountability into health care institutions: A Mayo Clinic case study. *Mayo Clinic Proceedings: Digital Health, 2*(4), 574–583. https://doi.org/10.1016/j.mcpdig.2024.08.008

Microsoft Azure. (2025). Azure data factory. In *Cloud data pipeline design for AI*, 5.2.5. Microsoft Azure.

Microsoft Azure. (2025). Azure Purview. In *Cloud data governance and metadata management*, 5.3.1. Microsoft Azure.

Microsoft Azure. (2025). Azure security center. In *Cloud Tools for Data Pipeline Governance*, 5.3.6. Microsoft Azure.

Microsoft Azure. (2025). Event Hubs. In *Cloud data ingestion for AI*, 5.2.5. Microsoft Azure.

Nguyen, T. B., et al. (2022). Monitoring bias in AI systems for diabetes risk prediction at Kaiser Permanente. *Journal of Healthcare Informatics Research, 6*(4), 345–357.

Rajkomar, A., Dean, J., & Dong, M. (2019). Machine learning in medicine. *New England Journal of Medicine, 380*(14), 1347–1358.

Sendak, M. P., et al. (2020). A path for translation of machine learning products into healthcare delivery. *EMBO Molecular Medicine, 12*(3), e11128.

Symeonidis, G., Nerantzis, E., Kazakis, A., & Papakostas, G. A. (2022). MLOps – Definitions, tools and challenges. *arXiv preprint*, arXiv:2201.00162. https://doi.org/10.48550/arXiv.2201.00162

Thummarakoti, S. (2022). *Toward efficient asynchronous architectures in low-code platforms: A comparative study in Pega*. SSRN. https://doi.org/10.2139/ssrn.5238386

Thummarakoti, S. (2023). Enhancing business process automation through NLP-based email interpretation in Pega systems. *SSRN*. https://doi.org/10.2139/ssrn.5249573

Thummarakoti, S. (2024). *Transforming healthcare with Pega: A unified approach to modern challenges*. SSRN. https://doi.org/10.2139/ssrn.5241177

Thummarakoti, S. (2025). *Advanced container orchestration strategies for multi-cloud environments: Enhancing performance, scalability, and resilience*. SSRN.

Thummarakoti, S. (2025, March). Leveraging cloud computing and cutting-edge technology for early cancer diagnosis. In *SoutheastCon 2025* (pp. 912–917). IEEE.

Tzanis, E., & Klontzas, M. E. (2025). mAIstro: An open-source multi-agentic system for automated radiomics and deep learning in medical imaging. *arXiv preprint*, arXiv:2505.03785. https://doi.org/10.48550/arXiv.2505.03785

Wang, K. Y., Liu, Y., & Wang, S. (2022). The role of chief AI officers in healthcare digital transformation: A multi-center survey. *Health Informatics Journal, 28*(4), 1465–1478.

Chapter 6

Cloud-Native AI Services and Tools

6.1 Cloud-Based Machine Learning Platforms

The rapid advancement of AI development has been accelerated by the availability of cloud-based machine learning (ML) platforms. These platforms abstract much of the complexity involved in building, training, deploying, and managing AI models.

They offer end-to-end services, from data ingestion and feature engineering to model training, hyperparameter tuning, deployment, and monitoring, all integrated within scalable cloud ecosystems.

Cloud-based ML platforms are designed to reduce development overhead, accelerate experimentation, foster collaboration, and ensure operational efficiency for AI teams. In this section, we will explore the leading cloud ML platforms, their core capabilities, and best practices for leveraging them in AI projects (Figure 6.1).

6.1.1 Benefits of Cloud-Based Machine Learning Platforms

- **Scalability**:
  Instantly access compute power, GPU/TPU resources, and scalable storage without the need for infrastructure management.
- **Ease of Use**:
  Prebuilt templates, managed notebooks, AutoML capabilities, and integrated APIs accelerate development.

DOI: 10.4324/9781003685609-6

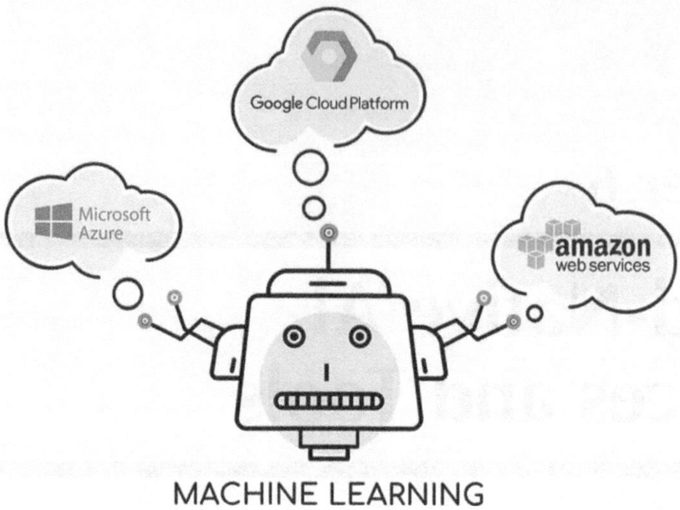

Figure 6.1 Machine Learning Integration across Azure, GCP, and AWS

- **End-to-End Pipelines**:
  Seamless integration of data pipelines, training jobs, model registries, and deployment workflows.
- **Collaboration**:
  Multi-user environments with role-based access and shared workspaces for data scientists and engineers.
- **Cost Control**:
  Pay-as-you-go pricing with visibility into compute and storage usage.
- **Integration with Cloud Services**:
  Easy connection to cloud-native data sources, analytics services, and monitoring tools.

6.1.2 AWS SageMaker

Overview:
Amazon SageMaker is AWS's fully managed machine learning platform that enables developers and data scientists to build, train, and deploy models quickly.

Key Features:

- **Managed Notebooks**:
  Pre-configured Jupyter notebooks with elastic computing and persistent storage.

- **Built-in Algorithms and Frameworks**:
  Supports TensorFlow, PyTorch, MXNet, Hugging Face, and more.
- **SageMaker Autopilot**:
  AutoML capability that automatically preprocesses data, trains models, and tunes hyperparameters.
- **Distributed Training**:
  Support for multi-GPU and multi-node distributed training with Elastic Fabric Adapter (EFA).
- **Model Registry**:
  Version control and lifecycle management for trained models.
- **Deployment Options**:
  - Real-time endpoints.
  - Batch inference.
  - Asynchronous inference.
  - Multi-model endpoints for serving multiple models on a single instance.
- **MLOps Integration**:
  SageMaker Pipelines for CI/CD and model monitoring with SageMaker Model Monitor.
- **Best Use Cases**:
  - Enterprise-grade AI applications requiring secure, scalable training and inference.
  - Large-scale model training with distributed infrastructure.
  - Automated model tuning and deployment pipelines.

6.1.3 Google Cloud Vertex AI

Overview:
Vertex AI is Google Cloud's unified ML platform, bringing together AutoML, custom training, deployment, and monitoring capabilities within a single ecosystem.

Key Features:

- **Managed Notebooks**:
  JupyterLab environments with seamless access to BigQuery and Google Cloud Storage.
- **Custom Training**:
  Flexible training jobs with support for GPUs, TPUs, and distributed training clusters.

- **AutoML**:
  Automated model creation for vision, tabular, text, and forecasting problems with minimal coding.
- **Vertex AI Pipelines**:
  Kubeflow-based orchestration for reproducible and scalable machine learning workflows.
- **Feature Store**:
  Centralized repository for managing and serving ML features in production.
- **Model Monitoring**:
  Continuous drift detection and alerting for deployed models.
- **Explainable Artificial Intelligence (XAI)**:
  Built-in tools for understanding model predictions and fairness analysis.

Best Use Cases:

- Organizations using Google's ecosystem for data analytics and AI.
- Companies building scalable, production-ready AI pipelines with integrated monitoring and explainability.
- Federated learning and privacy-aware AI solutions.

6.1.4 Azure Machine Learning

Overview:
Azure Machine Learning is Microsoft's end-to-end cloud-based ML platform for building, training, and operationalizing machine learning models.

Key Features:

- **Azure ML Studio**:
  Visual workspace with a drag-and-drop interface for no-code/low-code model development.
- **Managed Notebooks**:
  Collaborative environments with integrated Azure datasets and compute clusters.
- **Automated ML (AutoML)**:
  Automated model training and hyperparameter optimization.
- **Custom Training**:
  Supports distributed training with frameworks like TensorFlow, PyTorch, and Scikit-learn.

- **ML Pipelines**:
  Reusable pipelines for training, evaluation, and deployment.
- **Model Registry**:
  Central management of models with lineage tracking and versioning.
- **Deployment Targets**:
  - Azure Kubernetes Service (AKS)
  - Azure Container Instances (ACI)
  - Edge deployments via Azure IoT Edge
- **Responsible AI Toolbox**:
  Tools for fairness assessment, interpretability, and bias detection.

Best Use Cases:

- Enterprises already using Microsoft Azure services and enterprise security frameworks.
- Multi-cloud and hybrid AI solutions requiring edge deployment capabilities.
- Highly regulated industries needing integrated governance and compliance tools.

6.1.5 Common Capabilities across Platforms

Feature	*AWS SageMaker*	*Google Vertex AI*	*Azure Machine Learning*
Managed notebooks	Jupyter-based	JupyterLab with BigQuery access	Collaborative notebooks in Studio
Distributed training	Multi-GPU and multi-node support	TPU and GPU distributed training	Distributed training with SDK support
AutoML	SageMaker Autopilot	Vertex AutoML	Azure AutoML
Model registry	Fully integrated	Centralized model registry	Version-controlled model registry
Deployment options	Real-time, batch, asynchronous	Real-time, batch, edge serving	Real-time endpoints, AKS, edge
Monitoring and drift detection	Model Monitor	Vertex AI Monitoring	Monitoring via Application Insights

Feature	*AWS SageMaker*	*Google Vertex AI*	*Azure Machine Learning*
MLOps pipelines	SageMaker Pipelines	Vertex AI Pipelines (Kubeflow-based)	Azure ML Pipelines and DevOps integration
Explainability and fairness	Built-in (Clarify)	Integrated explainable AI tools	Responsible AI dashboard

6.1.6 Best Practices for Leveraging Cloud-Based ML Platforms

- Start with Managed Notebooks for experimentation and rapid prototyping.
- Use AutoML for quick baselines, switch to custom training for advanced control.
- Incorporate feature stores to promote feature reuse and consistency across models.
- Implement CI/CD pipelines for model deployment to ensure reliable delivery and reproducibility.
- Enable drift detection and continuous monitoring from day one.
- Use integrated explainability and fairness tools for responsible AI deployment.
- Tag resources and monitor costs to avoid budget overruns.
- Use integrated security features (VPCs, IAM roles, private endpoints) to protect data and models.

Cloud-based machine learning platforms have transformed how organizations build and deploy AI models by providing a unified, scalable, and managed environment.

Platforms like AWS SageMaker, Google Vertex AI, and Azure Machine Learning remove infrastructure burdens and accelerate innovation, making it easier for teams to experiment, iterate, and operationalize AI solutions. Choosing the right platform depends on organizational goals, existing cloud infrastructure, and the complexity of AI workloads.

In the next section, we will explore specialized cloud AI services, such as managed model serving frameworks and AutoML systems that further streamline AI development.

6.2 Serverless AI and Function-as-a-Service (FaaS)

As AI adoption grows, organizations are increasingly looking for flexible, cost-efficient, and scalable ways to deploy AI capabilities without the overhead of managing servers or infrastructure.

Serverless AI and Function-as-a-Service (FaaS) models address this need by allowing developers to run AI inference tasks, data preprocessing, and event-driven machine learning functions in the cloud without provisioning or maintaining dedicated infrastructure. These paradigms help deliver rapid scalability, reduced costs for intermittent workloads, and faster development cycles.

In this section, we will explore serverless AI and FaaS concepts, their benefits, use cases, leading cloud solutions, design considerations, and best practices.

6.2.1 What Is Serverless AI?

Serverless AI refers to running AI workloads, typically inference, lightweight data transformations, or event-driven prediction tasks, without managing underlying compute resources. The cloud provider automatically handles scaling, resource provisioning, load balancing, and fault tolerance, allowing teams to focus on model logic and business use cases (Figure 6.2).

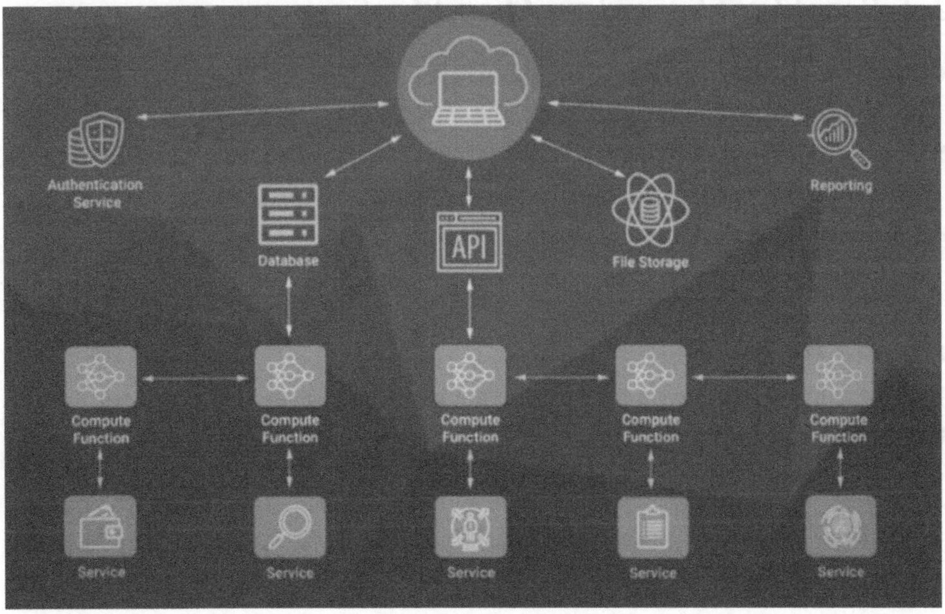

Figure 6.2 Core Characteristics of Serverless AI

Core Characteristics of Serverless AI:

- No server or cluster management.
- Automatic scaling with usage.
- Event-driven execution.
- Pay-as-you-go pricing based on compute duration and resources consumed.

6.2.2 What Is Function-as-a-Service (FaaS)?

Function-as-a-Service (FaaS) is a cloud computing model that allows developers to deploy individual functions that execute in response to triggers or events (HTTP requests, file uploads, message queue events). Functions are ephemeral, stateless, and scale automatically with demand.

Key Features of FaaS:

- Short-lived functions triggered by events.
- Stateless execution environment.
- Automatic concurrency handling.
- Ideal for micro-tasks and decoupled logic.

6.2.3 Benefits of Serverless AI and FaaS

- **Zero Infrastructure Management**:
  No need to manage servers, VMs, or Kubernetes clusters.
- **Cost Efficiency**:
  Pay only for the compute time consumed; no charges for idle resources.
- **Instant Scalability**:
  Functions can scale from zero to thousands of concurrent executions based on incoming requests.
- **Rapid Deployment**:
  Lightweight functions allow for fast iterations and deployment cycles.
- **Event-Driven Integration**:
  Easily connect to cloud storage events, IoT device triggers, message queues, or API calls.

6.2.4 Common Use Cases for Serverless AI

- **Real-Time Inference on Demand**:
  Use lightweight models or call remote model endpoints in response to API requests.
- **Batch Inference Triggers**:
  Process uploaded data in object storage, triggering inference workflows.
- **Data Preprocessing and Transformation**:
  Clean and transform incoming data streams before they are stored or fed into ML pipelines.
- **Event-Driven Model Retraining Pipelines**:
  Trigger training or revalidation functions when new labeled data is ingested.
- **Edge-to-Cloud AI**:
  Process real-time sensor data and transmit summaries or alerts to cloud systems.
- **Natural Language Processing (NLP) in APIs**:
  Serve sentiment analysis, translation, or keyword extraction on-demand via REST APIs.

6.2.5 Leading Cloud Serverless and FaaS Solutions for AI

Cloud Provider	*FaaS Service*	*Serverless AI Integrations*
AWS	AWS Lambda	Invoke SageMaker endpoints, call AI services (Rekognition, Comprehend), integrated with S3, SNS, SQS, EventBridge
Google Cloud	Google Cloud Functions	Integrate with Vertex AI prediction endpoints, Cloud Pub/Sub, Cloud Storage triggers
Azure	Azure Functions	Trigger model inference via Azure ML endpoints, integrate with Event Hubs, Blob Storage, and IoT services

6.2.6 Serverless AI Design Considerations

1. **Cold Start Latency**:
   - Initial invocations may have latency due to environment spin-up.

- Mitigation:
  - Use provisioned concurrency (AWS Lambda) or keep functions warm with scheduled invocations.

2. **Execution Time Limits**:
   - FaaS platforms often have limits (e.g., 15 minutes max for AWS Lambda).
   - Best for short, lightweight inference or preprocessing tasks.
   - For long-running inference jobs, use asynchronous processing or hybrid architectures.
3. **Stateless Execution**:
   - Functions cannot maintain state between invocations.
   - Use external services such as Redis, DynamoDB, or Cloud Firestore for state management.
4. **Payload Size Restrictions**:
   - FaaS services have limits on payload sizes (e.g., 6 MB synchronous request/response limit on AWS Lambda).
   - Store large data in cloud storage and pass references to the function.
5. **Model Size Constraints**:
   - Deploy small models directly within the function environment.
   - For large models, host them in dedicated inference endpoints and invoke from functions.

6.2.7 Patterns for Implementing Serverless AI

1. **Function-to-Model Endpoint Pattern**:
   - The function acts as a lightweight client, sending inference requests to a hosted model endpoint and returning results to the caller.
   - **Use Case**: Low-latency API serving without embedding the model in the function.
2. **Embedded Lightweight Model Pattern**:
   - For small models (e.g., TensorFlow Lite or Scikit-learn models), bundle the model file with the function and load it during execution.
   - **Use Case**: Quick inference on structured data, text classification, or rule-based models.
3. **Batch Processing Trigger Pattern**:
   - Trigger functions on file uploads or event messages to process data in batches.
   - **Use Case**: Image classification on new uploads; sentiment analysis on new text records.

6.2.8 Best Practices for Serverless AI

- **Minimize Package Sizes**:
  Keep deployment packages lightweight to reduce cold start times.
- **Reuse Connections and Objects**:
  Cache model instances or HTTP clients across invocations (where supported).
- **Use Environment Variables for Configurations**:
  Manage API keys, model endpoints, and versioning dynamically.
- **Monitor and Profile Function Performance**:
  Use services like AWS CloudWatch, Google Cloud Monitoring, or Azure Monitor to track invocations, latency, and errors.
- **Secure APIs**:
  Protect FaaS endpoints with API gateways, authentication mechanisms (OAuth, API keys), and rate limiting.

6.2.9 Cost Optimization for Serverless AI

- Use asynchronous invocation and batching to reduce function calls.
- Monitor idle time and limit concurrency where not needed.
- Store large models in external services rather than bundling them in functions.
- Clean up unused provisioned concurrency settings to avoid unnecessary costs.

Serverless AI and Function-as-a-Service have transformed the way AI workloads can be deployed, offering on-demand scalability, minimal infrastructure management, and lower costs for intermittent or event-driven use cases.

Whether serving lightweight models, integrating with managed AI endpoints, or handling real-time data processing tasks, FaaS enables fast and flexible deployment of AI logic. By understanding the constraints, architecture patterns, and best practices of serverless environments, organizations can design efficient, scalable AI solutions that respond to business events in real time.

In the next section, we will cover AutoML solutions and how they simplify model development and democratize AI for non-expert users.

6.3 AutoML and Low-Code AI Solutions

The development of artificial intelligence and machine learning models has traditionally required deep expertise in data science, programming, and model tuning. However, the demand for AI solutions across industries has led to the rise of Automated Machine Learning (AutoML) and low-code AI platforms.

These tools democratize AI by enabling business analysts, developers, and non-expert users to build, deploy, and maintain models without needing to write extensive code or manually optimize hyperparameters.

In this section, we explore what AutoML and low-code AI solutions are, their key components, advantages, limitations, leading cloud-based offerings, and best practices for using them in modern AI workflows.

6.3.1 What Is AutoML?

AutoML refers to the process of automating the end-to-end tasks involved in building machine learning models. This includes:

- Data preprocessing and feature engineering
- Model selection
- Hyperparameter tuning
- Model evaluation and validation
- Deployment recommendations

By automating these steps, AutoML tools reduce development time, eliminate manual guesswork, and allow rapid experimentation.

6.3.2 What Are Low-Code AI Solutions?

Low-code AI platforms offer visual, drag-and-drop interfaces and prebuilt templates, enabling users to design, train, and deploy AI models with minimal or no coding required. These platforms are designed for:

- Business analysts, domain experts, and citizen data scientists
- Rapid prototyping and proof-of-concept development
- Collaboration between technical and non-technical teams

6.3.3 Benefits of AutoML and Low-Code AI

- **Accessibility**:
  Enables non-experts to build models without in-depth ML knowledge.
- **Speed**:
  Rapidly builds and deploys models by automating preprocessing and tuning.
- **Scalability**:
  AutoML platforms are cloud-native and can scale to handle large datasets and complex tasks.
- **Resource Efficiency**:
  Reduces the workload of data scientists, freeing them to focus on high-value tasks.
- **Integrated Explainability and Fairness Checks**:
  Many AutoML tools include built-in explainability reports and mechanisms for detecting bias.

6.3.4 Limitations of AutoML and Low-Code AI

- **Limited Customization**:
  While they handle common tasks well, AutoML solutions may not support highly customized model architectures or niche use cases.
- **Potential Overfitting without Supervision**:
  Automated pipelines can sometimes lead to overfitting if validation sets are not well managed.
- **Lack of Interpretability in Complex Models**:
  Models produced by AutoML may function as "black boxes" if explainability tools are not utilized.
- **Computational Cost**:
  Automated hyperparameter tuning and model search can be resource-intensive.

6.3.5 Leading AutoML and Low-Code AI Solutions

Platform	*Key Features*	*Best For*
Google Cloud AutoML (Vertex AI AutoML)	Auto-model generation for text, tabular, image, and video data; integrated with Vertex AI Pipelines	Quick deployment of ML models using Google's ecosystem

Platform	*Key Features*	*Best For*
AWS SageMaker Autopilot	End-to-end automation, feature engineering, model tuning, explainability, deployable endpoints	Enterprise-scale AutoML with control over customization
Azure Automated ML	Automated model selection, pipelines, integrated with Azure ML Studio; fairness and explainability checks	Enterprises using Azure for predictive analytics
H2O.ai Driverless AI	Full AutoML platform with advanced feature engineering and interpretability; supports multiple cloud environments	Advanced AutoML users requiring flexibility and strong governance tools
DataRobot	End-to-end AutoML with business-friendly interfaces, MLOps integration, and automated monitoring	Enterprises seeking AI democratization and business team enablement

6.3.6 Key Components of AutoML Pipelines

- **Data Ingestion**:
  Connection to structured and unstructured data sources (CSV, databases, data lakes).
- **Automated Data Cleaning and Feature Engineering**:
  Handling missing values, outlier detection, encoding categorical variables, and feature transformations.
- **Model Selection and Benchmarking**:
  Automatic testing of multiple algorithms (decision trees, ensemble methods, deep learning) for best-fit models.
- **Hyperparameter Optimization**:
  Grid search or Bayesian optimization to fine-tune model performance.
- **Explainability and Fairness Reporting**:
  Generate visual reports that describe feature importance, bias indicators, and decision rationales.
- **Deployment Options**:
  Export models as APIs, cloud endpoints, or deployable Docker containers.

6.3.7 Common Use Cases for AutoML and Low-Code AI

- **Customer Churn Prediction**:
  Business teams can quickly create models to predict churn based on CRM data.
- **Sales Forecasting**:
  Automate demand forecasting using historical sales and market data.
- **Sentiment Analysis**:
  Train NLP models on customer feedback or social media content without coding.
- **Image Classification**:
  Build and deploy models for object detection or visual quality control with drag-and-drop tools.
- **Anomaly Detection**:
  Automatically identify unusual patterns in financial transactions, sensor data, or user behavior.

6.3.8 Best Practices for Using AutoML and Low-Code AI

- **Start with Clean, Well-Structured Data**:
  AutoML tools rely heavily on good input data. Pre-clean and label datasets carefully.
- **Validate Model Recommendations**:
  Always review AutoML-generated models and manually inspect results, especially in high-stakes use cases.
- **Enable Explainability Features**:
  Use built-in explainability reports to understand model behavior and feature impact.
- **Integrate with MLOps Pipelines**:
  Even AutoML models need proper lifecycle management, version control, and continuous monitoring.
- **Monitor for Drift**:
  Set up automated drift detection to ensure that models trained by AutoML remain relevant over time.
- **Keep Human Oversight**:
  Human review is essential to avoid unintended biases or ethical issues in automatically generated models.

6.3.9 The Future of AutoML and Low-Code AI

- **More Powerful Automated Feature Engineering**:
  Expect deeper automatic feature creation using embeddings, feature crosses, and domain-specific transformations.
- **AutoML for Deep Learning**:
  Emerging platforms are extending AutoML beyond tabular data into the auto-generation of neural network architectures (AutoDL).
- **Integration with Generative AI**:
  Low-code tools will increasingly incorporate generative AI (such as GPT models) to assist in building models and writing code.
- **Domain-Specific AutoML Solutions**:
  AutoML tools are tailored for healthcare, finance, manufacturing, and retail verticals.
- **Explainability-as-a-Default**:
  AutoML platforms will make model transparency and fairness dashboards mandatory components of every pipeline.

AutoML and low-code AI solutions are revolutionizing how organizations build machine learning models, making advanced analytics accessible to non-experts while freeing up data science teams to focus on complex problems.

These platforms enable rapid innovation, shorten time-to-market, and empower business teams to create predictive solutions without requiring deep coding skills. However, to use these tools effectively, organizations must pair automation with governance, validation, and continuous monitoring.

6.4 AI DevOps and MLOps in the Cloud

As AI models move from experimentation into production, managing their lifecycle becomes increasingly complex. Continuous model improvements, performance monitoring, data drift management, and versioning are critical components of successful AI operations.

This complexity has given rise to Machine Learning Operations (MLOps), an extension of DevOps practices tailored to machine learning workflows.

MLOps and AI DevOps in the cloud bring together automation, continuous integration/continuous deployment (CI/CD), governance, and monitoring for AI models, enabling teams to manage models with the same rigor and agility applied to software development.

In this section, we explore the principles of MLOps and AI DevOps, core components of cloud-based MLOps pipelines, leading tools and platforms, and best practices for implementing robust and scalable MLOps workflows in the cloud.

6.4.1 What Is MLOps?

MLOps is a set of practices, tools, and processes designed to manage the end-to-end lifecycle of machine learning models, from development and training to deployment, monitoring, and continuous improvement, with automation and governance built in.

Key Goals of MLOps:

- Enable continuous delivery and integration of models into production.
- Ensure reproducibility of experiments and deployments.
- Manage model versioning and lineage.
- Monitor model performance, detect drift, and retrain models as needed.
- Enforce security, compliance, and auditability for AI systems.

6.4.2 The MLOps Lifecycle

Stage	*Key Activities*
Data preparation	Ingesting, cleaning, and feature engineering with version control for datasets
Model training	Experimentation, hyperparameter tuning, and training with reproducibility
Model validation	Testing models for accuracy, fairness, explainability, and performance benchmarks
Model registry	Storing models with metadata, tracking versions, and approval workflows
Deployment	Automated CI/CD pipelines for deploying models to staging and production.
Monitoring	Continuous observation of prediction accuracy, drift detection, and performance.
Retraining	Triggering automatic retraining based on drift, business events, or periodic schedules.

6.4.3 Key Components of Cloud-Based MLOps

1. **Model Versioning and Registry**:
   - Centralized storage of models, metadata, and lineage.
   - Tools:
     - AWS SageMaker Model Registry
     - Google Vertex AI Model Registry
     - Azure ML Model Registry
     - **Open-Source Alternatives**: MLflow
2. **CI/CD Pipelines for ML Models**:
   - Automate the building, testing, and deployment of models using:
     - GitHub Actions or GitLab CI for orchestration
     - Jenkins or CircleCI for automated workflows
     - Kubernetes-based deployments with Helm charts for reproducible deployments
3. **Workflow Orchestration**:
   - Automated pipelines for data ingestion, training, validation, and deployment.
   - Tools:
     - Kubeflow Pipelines
     - Apache Airflow
     - MLflow Pipelines
     - AWS Step Functions
4. **Monitoring and Observability**:
   - Tools for tracking model performance, drift, latency, and errors in production.
   - Cloud services:
     - SageMaker Model Monitor
     - Vertex AI Model Monitoring
     - Azure Application Insights and Metrics
5. **Automated Retraining and Feedback Loops**:
   - Scheduling periodic retraining or triggering updates based on drift detection or data changes.
   - Integration with cloud pipelines and experiment tracking systems.

6.4.4 MLOps Tools and Platforms by Cloud Provider

Cloud Provider	*MLOps Tools*
AWS	SageMaker Pipelines, SageMaker Model Registry, SageMaker Clarify (for bias monitoring), CloudWatch, CodePipeline
Google Cloud	Vertex AI Pipelines (Kubeflow-based), Vertex Model Registry, Model Monitoring, Cloud Build, Cloud Functions
Azure	Azure ML Pipelines, Model Registry, Azure DevOps integration, Azure Monitor, Responsible AI tools

Open-Source and Hybrid Alternatives:

- MLflow (experiment tracking and model registry)
- Kubeflow (end-to-end orchestration and deployment)
- TensorFlow Extended (TFX) for production-grade ML pipelines
- Data Version Control (DVC) for dataset and experiment tracking

6.4.5 CI/CD Pipeline Design for AI

Typical CI/CD Pipeline for MLOps:

1. **Commit to Git Repository**:
   - Triggers automated tests for code quality and dataset validation.
2. **Data Validation Stage**:
   - Automatic checks for schema mismatches, data drift, and quality anomalies.
3. **Training Pipeline Execution**:
   - Trigger distributed model training jobs in the cloud.
4. **Validation and Approval Stage**:
   - Automated performance checks against benchmark metrics.
   - Manual or automated approval gates for production readiness.
5. **Deployment Pipeline**:
   - Deploy models to staging, then production endpoints with canary or blue/green deployment strategies.
6. **Monitoring and Alerts**:
   - Real-time tracking and alerting for performance drops or operational issues.

6.4.6 Best Practices for Cloud MLOps

- **Enforce Reproducibility**:
  Use containerized training environments and record all hyperparameters and dataset versions.
- **Use Automated Approval Gates**:
  Prevent automatic deployment of models that fail accuracy, fairness, or explainability checks.
- **Adopt Immutable Deployments**:
  Deploy models using container images with immutable tags for consistent results.
- **Track Metrics at Every Stage**:
  Capture not only model performance but also resource usage, training time, and pipeline efficiency.
- **Implement Continuous Drift Detection**:
  Automate alerts and retraining triggers based on detected drift or decaying performance.
- **Version Everything**:
  Maintain strict versioning for datasets, models, pipelines, and configuration files.
- **Incorporate Security Scans**:
  Scan container images and deployment artifacts for vulnerabilities as part of the CI/CD pipeline.
- **Document Pipelines and Governance Policies**:
  Maintain clear documentation for audit readiness and cross-team collaboration.

MLOps and AI DevOps in the cloud enable organizations to move from isolated experimentation to production-grade AI systems that are scalable, reliable, and continuously improving.

With the right tools, processes, and governance structures in place, MLOps ensures that AI models remain high-performing, secure, and aligned with business goals throughout their lifecycle. Organizations that embrace MLOps best practices will not only accelerate innovation but also build trust and accountability in their AI deployments.

Bibliography

Abbasian, M., Azimi, I., Rahmani, A. M., & Jain, R. (2024). Conversational health agents: A personalized LLM-powered agent framework. *arXiv preprint*, arXiv:2310.02374. https://arxiv.org/abs/2310.02374

Amazon Web Services (AWS). (2025). Amazon FSx for Lustre. In *Cloud file systems for AI* (5.1.2). Amazon Web Services.

Amazon Web Services (AWS). (2025). Amazon S3. In *Cloud object storage for AI* (5.1.1). Amazon Web Services.

Asan, O., Bayrak, C., & Choudhury, A. (2020). Artificial intelligence and human trust in healthcare: A scoping review. *Journal of Medical Internet Research, 22*(6), e15154. https://doi.org/10.2196/15154

Barra, F. L., Rodella, G., Costa, A., et al. (2025). From prompt to platform: An agentic AI workflow for healthcare simulation scenario design. *Advances in Simulation, 10*(1). https://doi.org/10.1186/s41077-025-00357-z

Char, D. S., Shah, N. H., & Magnus, D. (2018). Implementing machine learning in health care: Addressing ethical challenges. *New England Journal of Medicine, 378*(11), 981–983.

Erskine, A. R., Karunakaran, B., Slotkin, J. R., & Thomas, D. A. (2024). Geisinger's AI sandbox: A modular approach to scalable clinical AI. *npj Digital Medicine, 7*(1), 89–100.

Google Cloud. (2025). Google Data Catalog. In *Cloud data governance and metadata management* (5.3.1). Google Cloud.

Google Cloud. (2025). Google Stackdriver Monitoring. In *Cloud tools for data pipeline monitoring* (5.2.6). Google Cloud.

Henry, K. E., et al. (2015). A targeted real-time early warning score (TREWScore) for septic shock. *Science Translational Medicine, 7*(299), 299ra122.

Kim, J. Y., Boag, W., Gulamali, F., et al. (2023). Organizational governance of emerging technologies: AI adoption in healthcare. *npj Digital Medicine, 6*, 94.

Microsoft Azure. (2025). Azure Data Factory. In *Cloud data pipeline design for AI* (5.2.5). Microsoft Azure.

Microsoft Azure. (2025). Azure Purview. In *Cloud data governance and metadata management* (5.3.1). Microsoft Azure.

Nguyen, T. B., et al. (2022). Monitoring bias in AI systems for diabetes risk prediction at Kaiser Permanente. *Journal of Healthcare Informatics Research, 6*(4), 345–357.

Rajkomar, A., Dean, J., & Dong, M. (2019). Machine learning in medicine. *New England Journal of Medicine, 380*(14), 1347–1358.

Rajkomar, A., Oren, E., Chen, K., Dai, A. M., Hajaj, N., Hardt, M., Liu, P. J., et al. (2018). Scalable and accurate deep learning with electronic health records. *NPJ Digital Medicine, 1*(1), 18. https://doi.org/10.1038/s41746-018-0029-1

Sharma, P. (2025). MEDRAIL: MEDical Reinforcement-based Agentic Intelligence for Lifesciences. *Journal of Medical Internet Research Preprints*, June 8. https://doi.org/10.2196/preprints.78741

Thummarakoti, S. (2022). *Toward efficient asynchronous architectures in low-code platforms: A comparative study in Pega*. SSRN. https://doi.org/10.2139/ssrn.5238386

Thummarakoti, S. (2023). *Enhancing business process automation through NLP-based email interpretation in Pega systems*. SSRN. https://doi.org/10.2139/ssrn.5249573

Thummarakoti, S. (2025). *Advanced container orchestration strategies for multi-cloud environments: Enhancing performance, scalability, and resilience*. SSRN.

Thummarakoti, S. (2025). Compliance and regulatory challenges in cloud-based healthcare systems. In *SoutheastCon 2025* (pp. 1264–1269). IEEE.

Thummarakoti, S. (2025, March). Leveraging cloud computing and cutting-edge technology for early cancer diagnosis. In *SoutheastCon 2025* (pp. 912–917). IEEE.

Chapter 7

Hybrid and Multi-Cloud Strategies for AI

7.1 Benefits of Hybrid Cloud for AI Workloads

As AI workloads grow in complexity and scale, enterprises are increasingly adopting hybrid cloud strategies that combine on-premises infrastructure with public cloud resources. A hybrid cloud approach allows organizations to balance performance, security, compliance, and flexibility by running AI workloads across multiple environments: on-premises data centers, private clouds, and public cloud services.

This section explores the key benefits of adopting a hybrid cloud strategy for AI workloads and how it helps organizations navigate regulatory challenges, optimize performance, reduce costs, and enable broader innovation.

7.1.1 What Is Hybrid Cloud for AI?

A *hybrid cloud* environment integrates on-premises infrastructure (such as private data centers or edge devices) with public cloud services (AWS, Google Cloud, Azure) to create a unified, flexible computing environment. For AI, this means the ability to:

- Store sensitive data on-premises while using cloud computing for large-scale training.
- Deploy inference models at the edge or within private networks for low-latency applications.
- Burst AI workloads into the cloud during peak demand.

DOI: 10.4324/9781003685609-7

7.1.2 Key Benefits of Hybrid Cloud for AI

1. **Data Residency and Compliance**:
   - Many industries (healthcare, finance, government) are subject to strict data residency requirements that mandate storing and processing certain data within specific regions or on-premises.
   - Hybrid cloud allows organizations to keep sensitive data on-premises while using cloud computing for model training and experimentation.
   - This balance helps organizations remain compliant with GDPR, HIPAA, and other data privacy laws without sacrificing AI innovation.
2. **Optimized Performance and Latency**:
   - Real-time AI applications (such as autonomous systems, industrial automation, or smart cities) require ultra-low latency.
   - Deploying AI inference models on-premises or at the edge reduces network latency compared to sending requests to the cloud.
   - Training models on premises with local data can also avoid long data transfer times, especially for high-volume datasets.
3. **Cost Control**:
   - Cloud resources can become expensive for continuous, large-scale workloads.
   - Hybrid models allow organizations to utilize existing on-premises GPU clusters or computer resources, reducing ongoing cloud costs.
   - Cloud bursting enables organizations to scale up only during periods of peak demand, thereby avoiding unnecessary spending.
4. **Scalability and Flexibility**:
   - Hybrid cloud provides on-demand scalability for training massive models that exceed on-premises capacity.
   - Organizations can extend AI pipelines to the cloud when additional compute power is needed and scale down after completion.
5. **Business Continuity and Disaster Recovery**:
   - Hybrid cloud environments enhance resilience by distributing AI workloads across on-premises and cloud infrastructure.
   - In case of failures or outages in one environment, workloads can shift to the other, ensuring minimal disruption to AI services.
6. **Data Gravity Management**:
   - Data gravity refers to the difficulty of moving large datasets between environments.
   - Hybrid cloud allows organizations to process data where it resides (on-premises or cloud) and move only relevant results or models across environments, reducing transfer costs and time.

7. **Security and Control**:
   - Some organizations require complete control over certain workloads due to security policies.
   - Hybrid cloud enables sensitive training and inference tasks to run in secure, isolated environments while leveraging cloud capabilities for less sensitive tasks.

7.1.3 Typical Hybrid Cloud AI Use Cases

Use Case	*How Hybrid Cloud Helps*
Healthcare AI	Sensitive patient data remains on-premises; cloud resources are used for large-scale training or federated learning.
Manufacturing and industrial IoT	AI inference models run on-premise near sensors and production lines; model updates and retraining leverage cloud computing.
Financial services	Transaction data is processed in secure, on-prem data centers; cloud burst compute used for stress testing and scenario modeling.
Retail personalization	Customer behavior data is stored and analyzed on-premises for compliance; cloud environments are used for broader pattern analysis.
Smart cities and transportation	Real-time inference on traffic and surveillance data are done at the edge; aggregated models refined in the cloud.

7.1.4 Cloud Provider Support for Hybrid AI

Cloud Provider	*Hybrid Cloud Solutions*
AWS	AWS Outposts (on-prem AWS infrastructure), AWS Snowball Edge (portable computing), ECS Anywhere for hybrid container deployments
Google Cloud	Google Anthos (hybrid application management), BigQuery Omni (multi-cloud analytics), Edge TPU for on-device inference
Microsoft Azure	Azure Arc (management of hybrid environments), Azure Stack (on-premises cloud infrastructure), Azure IoT Edge for edge inference

7.1.5 Benefits Summary

Benefit	*Impact on AI Workloads*
Compliance	Meets data residency and regulatory requirements without sacrificing innovation
Performance Optimization	Reduces latency for real-time inference and accelerates local training workloads
Cost Efficiency	Leverages existing infrastructure and scales to the cloud when necessary
Scalability	Provides elastic resources to meet unpredictable AI workload demands
Resilience	Ensures business continuity with multi-environment failover
Security	Offers greater control over sensitive data and AI models

Hybrid cloud strategies offer organizations the flexibility and control needed to deploy AI workloads securely, cost-effectively, and with high performance. Whether addressing compliance needs, reducing latency, or balancing cloud costs, hybrid cloud environments enable organizations to extend their AI capabilities without the limitations of a single deployment model.

The ability to seamlessly integrate on-premises infrastructure with public cloud services will continue to play a critical role in scaling AI innovation while meeting industry-specific demands.

In the next section, we will examine multi-cloud AI strategies and the benefits of using multiple cloud providers for redundancy, flexibility, and vendor diversification.

7.2 Multi-Cloud Strategies for AI Resilience

As AI deployments become mission-critical in industries ranging from healthcare and finance to manufacturing and retail, ensuring continuous availability, flexibility, and resilience is essential. Multi-cloud strategies, using multiple public cloud providers, have emerged as a powerful approach to mitigate risks associated with vendor lock-in, improve redundancy, and increase geographic reach for AI applications.

In this section, we will explore the benefits, challenges, key design considerations, and best practices of multi-cloud strategies for building resilient and highly available AI workloads.

7.2.1 What Is a Multi-Cloud Strategy?

A *multi-cloud strategy* refers to using two or more cloud providers (such as AWS, Google Cloud, and Azure) to run applications, store data, and deploy services. In AI deployments, this can involve:

- Training models on one cloud provider and deploying inference endpoints on a different cloud provider.
- Distributing workloads across clouds for redundancy and global availability.
- Using specialized AI tools and accelerators from different providers based on performance and pricing.

7.2.2 Benefits of Multi-Cloud AI Strategies

1. **Increased Resilience and Redundancy**:
   - Minimize service outages and downtime by having failover capabilities between cloud providers.
   - If one cloud provider experiences an outage, AI services can seamlessly reroute traffic or switch execution to another provider.
2. **Avoiding Vendor Lock-In**:
   - Reduces dependency on a single provider's ecosystem, APIs, or pricing structures.
   - Provides flexibility to negotiate costs or switch services based on evolving business needs.
3. **Access to Best-in-Class AI Tools**:
   - Different cloud providers excel in specific areas (e.g., Google Cloud for AI research, AWS for enterprise-scale deployments, Azure for edge and hybrid support).
   - Multi-cloud strategies allow organizations to leverage best-in-class services from each provider.
4. **Global Reach and Latency Optimization**:
   - Deploy inference endpoints and AI services in multiple geographic regions across different clouds for optimized latency to end-users.

5. **Cost Optimization**:
   - By distributing workloads and comparing pricing models, organizations can achieve better cost efficiency.
   - Some models can be trained on cost-effective clouds and served on platforms with lower inference costs.

7.2.3 Common Multi-Cloud AI Use Cases

Use Case	*Multi-Cloud Benefit*
Disaster Recovery (DR) for AI Services	Inference APIs and endpoints replicated across clouds for failover readiness
Federated Learning across Organizations	Use multiple cloud providers to collaborate across different data domains without sharing raw data
Edge AI Serving + Central Cloud Training	Train models in one cloud environment and deploy inference models across global edge locations using multiple clouds
Cost-Aware Model Training	Train models in one cloud based on GPU availability and pricing, and deploy in another cloud optimized for inference costs

7.2.4 Design Considerations for Multi-Cloud AI Resilience

1. **Interoperability and Portability**:
   - Use standard frameworks (TensorFlow, PyTorch, ONNX) and containerized models (Docker, OCI containers) to ensure portability across providers.
2. **Data Synchronization**:
   - Implement real-time or scheduled synchronization between cloud storage systems using secure transfer services or CDN replication.
3. **Consistent Model Versioning**:
   - Use centralized model registries or federated registries that track versions and deployments across all clouds.
4. **Identity and Access Management (IAM)**:
   - Ensure federated authentication mechanisms for secure access to resources across cloud providers.
   - Manage secrets and credentials with unified secrets management tools or integrate provider-specific solutions.

5. **Monitoring across Clouds**:
   - Consolidate observability data (latency, errors, drift) from multiple clouds into a single dashboard for unified monitoring.
   - Tools like Datadog, Prometheus, and Splunk are commonly used for multi-cloud observability.
6. **Automated Failover Strategies**:
   - Use DNS routing (AWS Route 53, Google Cloud DNS, Azure Traffic Manager) to reroute traffic between inference endpoints during outages.

7.2.5 Multi-Cloud AI Architecture Patterns

1. **Active-Active Architecture**:
   - Deploy inference endpoints across multiple clouds simultaneously.
   - Requests are load-balanced across clouds for performance and redundancy.
   - Suitable for mission-critical, low-latency AI applications.
2. **Active-Passive Architecture**:
   - The primary cloud handles all AI inference or training tasks, while a secondary cloud stands by for failover.
   - Lower cost than active-active, but slightly longer failover times.
3. **Cloud-Specific Workload Segmentation**:
   - Train large models on one cloud provider known for high-performance computing resources and deploy inference services on a second provider optimized for serving.

7.2.6 Challenges in Multi-Cloud AI Deployments

- **Data Movement Costs**:
  High costs associated with transferring large datasets between providers.
- **Increased Complexity**:
  Managing infrastructure, security, and monitoring across multiple clouds can result in significant operational overhead.
- **Inconsistent Services**:
  Different cloud providers have unique APIs and interfaces; abstraction layers or adapters may be required.

- **Governance**:
  Enforcing unified governance, auditability, and compliance policies across clouds can be difficult without centralized tooling.

7.2.7 Best Practices for Multi-Cloud AI Resilience

- **Containerization**:
  Package models and dependencies in containers for easy deployment across different cloud platforms.
- **Leverage Cloud-Agnostic Tools**:
  Use orchestration tools like Kubernetes and MLflow for workflow portability.
- **Establish a Multi-Cloud Governance Framework**:
  Standardize security policies, access controls, and audit trails across all environments.
- **Build Multi-Cloud Monitoring Dashboards**:
  Consolidate metrics from all clouds to maintain visibility and enable proactive incident response.
- **Test Failover Regularly**:
  Simulate outages and test DNS failover or traffic redirection mechanisms to ensure seamless transitions.
- **Minimize Cloud-Specific Lock-In**:
  Design AI pipelines with minimal reliance on proprietary APIs where possible or use abstraction layers.

Multi-cloud strategies empower organizations to build AI systems that are not only resilient and scalable but also flexible and cost-optimized. By distributing AI workloads across multiple cloud providers, businesses can achieve geographic redundancy, vendor diversification, and better access to specialized services.

However, multi-cloud AI also requires thoughtful design, strong governance, and robust monitoring to avoid complexity and maintain consistency across environments.

In the next section, we will discuss hybrid and multi-cloud security considerations for AI workloads, as well as best practices for protecting data, models, and infrastructure across multiple cloud platforms.

7.3 Cloud Interoperability and Data Portability

As AI workloads expand across multiple cloud providers and on-premises environments, ensuring seamless integration and movement of data, models, and workflows between platforms becomes crucial.

Cloud interoperability and data portability allow organizations to avoid vendor lock-in, adapt to changing business needs, optimize costs, and leverage best-of-breed services from different providers. For AI deployments, these capabilities are essential for maintaining flexibility in model development, training, deployment, and scaling.

In this section, we will explore the definitions of interoperability and portability, why they matter for AI, the key challenges involved, and best practices to enable cloud-agnostic AI architectures.

7.3.1 What Is Cloud Interoperability?

Cloud interoperability refers to the ability of different cloud platforms, systems, and services to communicate, exchange data, and work together effectively.

For AI, interoperability ensures:

- Data pipelines can integrate across clouds.
- AI tools and frameworks work seamlessly on different platforms.
- APIs, storage systems, and compute resources can be connected without friction.

7.3.2 What *Is* Data Portability?

Data portability refers to the ability to transfer data (including datasets, model artifacts, metadata, and logs) from one cloud provider or storage environment to another without requiring significant rework or loss of fidelity (Figure 7.1).

For AI workloads, portability ensures:

- The ability to migrate training datasets or inference-ready models between cloud platforms.
- Continued access to data as business needs or regulatory conditions change.

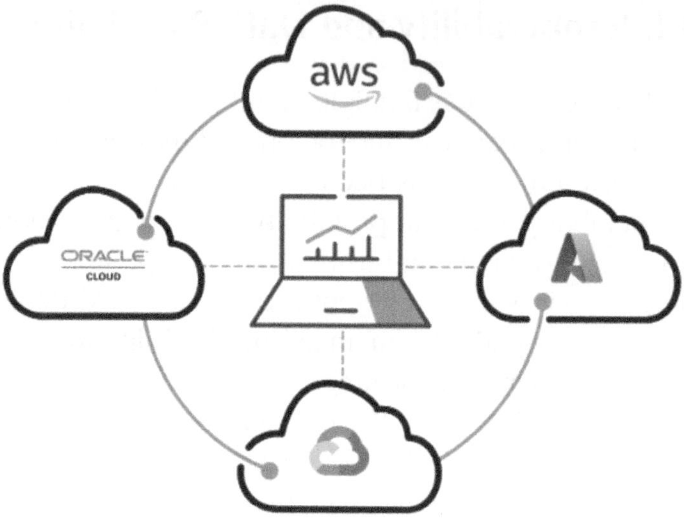

Figure 7.1 Multi-Cloud Service Integration Architecture

- Freedom to optimize costs and performance by moving workloads to the most appropriate cloud provider.

7.3.3 Why Interoperability and Portability Matter for AI

- **Avoiding Vendor Lock-In**:
  Enables organizations to switch providers or adopt multi-cloud strategies without significant redevelopment.
- **Cost Optimization**:
  Portability allows for workload migration to take advantage of more competitive pricing or regional discounts.
- **Resilience and Flexibility**:
  AI applications can dynamically shift inference or training to alternate clouds in response to outages or capacity constraints.
- **Access to Specialized Services**:
  Different providers offer unique AI tools (e.g., Google's TPU, AWS SageMaker Autopilot, Azure's Responsible AI tools), and interoperability makes it possible to use them in combination.
- **Compliance**:
  Regulatory requirements may mandate storing data in specific regions or changing cloud providers based on jurisdictional changes.

7.3.4 Challenges in Achieving Cloud Interoperability and Portability

Challenge	*Impact*
Proprietary APIs and services	Re-engineering is required to migrate models or data pipelines between clouds
Data transfer costs	Moving large datasets between providers can incur significant costs
Inconsistent security frameworks	Each provider has different IAM and security configurations, complicating migration
Storage format differences	Variations in object storage formats or metadata can hinder direct portability
Workflow incompatibility	Native orchestration and MLOps tools may not work cross-cloud without adaptations

7.3.5 Best Practices for Cloud Interoperability and Data Portability

1. **Adopt Open Standards and Frameworks**:
   - Use frameworks like TensorFlow, PyTorch, and ONNX for model development.
   - Store models in open formats (ONNX, SavedModel) to ensure they can be deployed across providers.
   - Use open-source orchestration tools like Kubeflow or MLflow for pipeline portability.
2. **Design Cloud-Agnostic Data Pipelines**:
   - Use containerized, microservice-based architectures for data processing and model training.
   - Avoid using deeply integrated proprietary connectors unless necessary.
3. **Unified Data Storage Formats**:
   - Store structured data in common formats (Parquet, Avro, ORC) that are supported across cloud analytics tools.
   - Ensure metadata portability by adopting catalog standards and storing schema information in external repositories.

4. **Use Multi-Cloud-Friendly Orchestration**:
   - Deploy Kubernetes-based environments that can be orchestrated across cloud providers.
   - Integrate workflows with Terraform, Pulumi, or CloudFormation-to-Terraform translators for multi-cloud infrastructure-as-code management.
5. **Data Transfer Optimization**:
   - Compress and partition datasets before transfer.
   - Use cross-cloud data transfer tools, such as AWS Snowball and Google Transfer Appliance, for transferring very large datasets.
   - Evaluate multi-cloud CDN services (Cloudflare, Akamai) for replication and distribution.
6. **Centralized Identity Management**:
   - Integrate identity providers (e.g., Azure AD, Okta) with federated access across clouds to standardize user authentication.
7. **Abstraction Layers for APIs**:
   - Develop abstraction layers for inference APIs and training pipelines that can redirect to different providers without code changes.
   - Consider using service meshes (Istio, Linkerd) for cross-cloud networking and communication.

7.3.6 Tools and Technologies for Enabling Interoperability

Category	*Tools and Technologies*
Containerization	Docker, Podman, OCI containers
Workflow orchestration	Kubeflow, Apache Airflow, MLflow, Argo Workflows
Infrastructure as code	Terraform, Crossplane (Kubernetes-native multi-cloud resource management)
Model portability	ONNX, TensorFlow SavedModel, PyTorch TorchScript
Data movement	Google Transfer Appliance, AWS Snowball, Cloud Storage Transfer Services
API management	API gateways (Kong, Apigee), service meshes (Istio, Consul) for routing across clouds

7.3.7 Real-World Example: Cloud-Agnostic AI Deployment

Scenario:

A financial services company wants to train AI models on Google Cloud using TPUs for high-performance computing but serve inference in multiple regions using both AWS and Azure for redundancy.

Solution:

- Models are trained in TensorFlow and exported to ONNX format.
- The inference APIs are built as Docker containers and deployed on Kubernetes clusters managed by EKS (AWS) and AKS (Azure).
- Terraform manages infrastructure across both clouds.
- Monitoring and logs are centralized using Datadog for unified observability.
- DNS-based routing directs user requests to the nearest or healthiest endpoint across providers.

Cloud interoperability and data portability are critical enablers for flexible, resilient, and cost-effective AI deployments. By adopting open standards, designing cloud-agnostic pipelines, and implementing strategic abstraction layers, organizations can future-proof their AI infrastructure, reduce operational risk, and avoid vendor lock-in. As multi-cloud and hybrid environments become the norm, interoperability and portability will be key drivers of AI innovation and scalability.

In the next section, we will examine security considerations for hybrid and multi-cloud AI environments, with a focus on safeguarding data, models, and workflows across distributed infrastructures.

7.4 Managing AI Workloads across Cloud Environments

As AI adoption grows and enterprises embrace hybrid and multi-cloud strategies, managing AI workloads across multiple cloud environments has become a complex yet critical capability.

AI workloads, including data preprocessing, model training, inference serving, monitoring, and retraining, often span multiple clouds and on-premises data centers. Successful cross-cloud AI management requires a unified approach to orchestration, resource allocation, data consistency, security, and governance.

This section explores the key considerations, architectural patterns, tools, and best practices for efficiently managing AI workloads across diverse cloud environments.

7.4.1 Why Manage AI across Multiple Cloud Environments?

- **Flexibility and Scalability**:
  Gain the ability to run different parts of the AI lifecycle on the best-fit platform, scaling up or down as needed.
- **Cost Optimization**:
  Distribute workloads based on pricing advantages, compute availability, and demand patterns.
- **Performance Optimization**:
  Place inference workloads closer to end-users while training on specialized hardware in different regions or clouds.
- **Risk Mitigation and Resilience**:
  Avoid relying on a single provider to reduce exposure to outages and vendor-specific limitations.
- **Regulatory Compliance**:
  Align workload placement with data residency requirements and jurisdictional boundaries.

7.4.2 Key Challenges in Cross-Cloud AI Workload Management

Challenge	*Impact*
Data movement and synchronization	Large datasets can be expensive and slow to move between clouds
Environment inconsistencies	Differences in infrastructure, APIs, and services create compatibility issues
Security policy alignment	Each cloud provider has distinct IAM and security models
Monitoring complexity	Observability becomes fragmented without unified dashboards
Workflow orchestration	Difficulties in coordinating multi-step AI pipelines across platforms

7.4.3 Architectural Patterns for Cross-Cloud AI Management

1. **Federated AI Architecture**:
   - Model training occurs in separate environments where data resides; only model parameters or gradients are aggregated in a centralized environment.
   - **Use Case**: Federated learning across hospitals or financial institutions with strict data privacy requirements.
2. **Cloud Bursting for Training**:
   - Train models on-premises or in a primary cloud, bursting into additional clouds during peak demand.
   - Useful for unpredictable or seasonal AI training workloads.
3. **Distributed Inference Architecture**:
   - Deploy inference endpoints across multiple clouds and edge locations, with centralized monitoring and routing via global DNS services.
4. **Unified Control Plane Model**:
   - Manage AI workloads across clouds from a centralized interface using Kubernetes-based orchestration tools and multi-cloud service meshes.

7.4.4 Orchestration Tools for Multi-Cloud AI

Tool/Platform	*Functionality*
Kubeflow	Multi-cloud and on-prem ML workflow orchestration
Apache Airflow	Pipeline scheduling and orchestration with cross-cloud connectors
MLflow	Experiment tracking and model lifecycle management across platforms
Terraform and Crossplane	Infrastructure-as-code for provisioning and managing cloud resources
Istio Service Mesh	Secure, cross-cloud traffic management and workload routing
Google Anthos	Unified management of Kubernetes clusters across GCP, AWS, and on-prem
Azure Arc	Multi-cloud and hybrid application management, integrated with Azure ML

7.4.5 Data Management across Cloud Environments

- **Data Synchronization Techniques**:
  - Use cloud-native transfer services (e.g., AWS DataSync, Google Transfer Service, Azure Data Box).
  - Employ event-driven replication triggered by storage uploads or changes.
  - Use cloud-to-cloud integration services like BigQuery Omni or Snowflake's cross-cloud data sharing.
- **Data Consistency and Governance**:
  - Standardize metadata catalogs across clouds.
  - Implement strict data versioning to ensure models always consume the correct datasets.
  - Use unified data policies enforced by platforms such as Azure Purview or Google Cloud Data Catalog.

7.4.6 Monitoring and Observability for Multi-Cloud AI

- **Unified Observability Goals**:
  - Consolidate logs, metrics, and events from all cloud environments.
  - Monitor AI-specific metrics like prediction latency, drift detection, inference throughput, and retraining frequency.
- **Tools for Cross-Cloud Monitoring**:
  - **Datadog, New Relic, or Dynatrace**: Multi-cloud performance monitoring and anomaly detection.
  - **Prometheus and Grafana**: For Kubernetes-based monitoring across cloud clusters.
  - **Cloud-Native Tools**: Use Google Cloud Monitoring, AWS CloudWatch, and Azure Monitor with centralized dashboards.

7.4.7 Security and IAM Alignment

- **Federated Identity Management**:
  - Use single sign-on (SSO) and federated IAM (e.g., Azure AD or Okta) across cloud environments.
- **Centralized Secrets Management**:
  - Utilize tools like HashiCorp Vault or cloud-native secrets managers with cross-cloud support.

- **Policy Consistency**:
  - Use policy-as-code tools like Open Policy Agent (OPA) to enforce consistent security policies across clouds.

7.4.8 Best Practices for Managing AI Workloads across Clouds

- **Design Workloads as Portable Microservices**:
  Containerize all AI services and models for consistent deployment on any cloud or Kubernetes cluster.
- **Use Abstraction Layers**:
  Build API gateways and service meshes to abstract differences between cloud environments.
- **Automate Everything**:
  Automate infrastructure provisioning, pipeline execution, monitoring setup, and failover strategies should all be automated.
- **Test Cross-Cloud Failovers Regularly**:
  Run simulation drills to ensure resilience and seamless workload transfer between clouds.
- **Monitor Cost Implications**:
  Track cloud-specific resource usage to optimize spending and avoid surprise costs from cross-cloud data transfers.
- **Maintain Multi-Cloud Documentation**:
  Ensure all configurations, workflow definitions, and governance policies are well-documented for operational consistency.

Managing AI workloads across multiple cloud environments offers unprecedented flexibility, resilience, and access to specialized services but also introduces complexity in orchestration, data management, and governance.

By adopting containerization, using cloud-agnostic tools, enforcing unified security policies, and implementing centralized monitoring, organizations can harness the full power of multi-cloud and hybrid AI architectures. Proper management strategies allow teams to scale AI innovations globally while optimizing costs and maintaining business continuity.

In the next chapter, we will discuss real-world hybrid and multi-cloud AI architectures and case studies demonstrating successful deployments.

7.5 SaaS Orchestration Platforms (e.g., Pega) in Hybrid and Multi-Cloud AI

Hybrid and multi-cloud strategies are not only about where data and models run. In most enterprises, the user-facing entry point for AI is a SaaS platform that already owns the core workflows: onboarding, claims, prior authorization, case management, or customer service. Pega is a good example of this pattern: it runs as a SaaS or PaaS platform, while calling out to AI services that may live in one or more clouds, or even on-premises.

In this setting, the question is not just "Where do we train and serve models?" but also "How do we wire those models into a SaaS platform that spans regions, tenants, and environments?" This section looks at how a platform like Pega fits into hybrid and multi-cloud AI architectures.

7.5.1 Pega as the Orchestration Layer in Hybrid AI

In a hybrid setup, Pega often runs in one of three modes:

- As a managed service (e.g., Pega Cloud) in a single hyperscaler
- As a self-managed platform in a private data center or private cloud
- As a mix of both, with some applications on-premises and others in the cloud

For AI use cases, Pega typically acts as the orchestration layer:

- It hosts the case types, business rules, and user interfaces.
- It exposes the moments in a process where AI is needed (e.g., "score this claim", "recommend the next action", and "flag this patient as high risk").
- It aggregates features from operational data it already holds, then calls external model endpoints for predictions.

In a hybrid cloud, the model endpoints might live in:

- On-prem GPU clusters for sensitive or regulated data
- Cloud ML platforms (SageMaker, Vertex AI, Azure ML) for heavy training and scalable inference
- Edge gateways (for IoT or clinical devices) where low latency is critical

Pega's job is to route the right requests to the right environment and then fold predictions back into the workflow in a predictable, auditable way.

7.5.2 Pega Topologies in Hybrid and Multi-Cloud AI

There are several practical topologies that combine Pega with hybrid and multi-cloud AI:

1. **Pega in the Cloud, Models Split across Clouds**
   - Pega runs in one cloud (e.g., Pega Cloud on top of a single hyperscaler).
   - Some AI services run in that same cloud for low-latency, high-volume use cases.
   - Other AI services run in a second cloud (e.g., specialized LLMs or TPU-based training).
   - Pega calls the "nearest" or most appropriate endpoint through an API gateway that hides cloud-specific details.
2. **Pega On-Premises, Models in the Cloud**
   - Pega remains in a private data center due to data residency or integration with legacy systems.
   - Models are trained and hosted in the public cloud, using VPC peering, private endpoints, or VPN tunnels.
   - This works well for organizations that want to modernize AI without moving their core SaaS/workflow layer immediately.
3. **Distributed Pega Plus Distributed AI**
   - Different regions or business units run their own Pega environments (on-prem and/or cloud).
   - Each region has local AI endpoints for data residency, with a shared pattern for model artifacts and governance.
   - A central architecture team defines common patterns: how to call models, how to log predictions, and how to track versions.

7.5.3 Design Considerations: Latency, Data Residency, and Routing

When Pega is part of a hybrid or multi-cloud AI landscape, a few constraints show up right away:

- **Latency between Pega and AI Endpoints:**
  If case workers or clinicians are waiting on predictions in the UI,

network round-trip time matters. Placing inference endpoints in the same region or using edge nodes helps keep screens responsive.

- **Data Residency and Privacy:**
  Pega may store PHI, financial data, or other sensitive fields. For some models, the organization may decide:
  - Only anonymized or tokenized features can leave the region.
  - Certain attributes never cross the boundary; they are handled by rule-based logic within Pega instead.
- **Routing and Failover:**
  A single Pega application might need to switch between:
  - A primary AI endpoint in Cloud A
  - A backup endpoint in Cloud B
  - A local rule-based fallback if both are unavailable

This routing logic can live in Pega decision rules, API gateways, or a service mesh, but it must be explicit and testable.

7.5.4 Pega, MLOps, and Cross-Cloud Lifecycle Management

Chapter 2 discussed CI/CD and MLOps for AI models. In a hybrid or multi-cloud setting, Pega needs to align with those practices:

- **Environment-Aware Configuration:**
  Model endpoint URLs, authentication credentials, and feature mappings should be treated as environment-specific configuration. When code moves from Dev to Test to Prod, these configuration items move with it through Pega's deployment pipeline.
- **Model Version Awareness:**
  When a new model version is rolled out (in one or more clouds), Pega should:
  - Know which version is active for each region, product, or tenant
  - Log predictions with a reference to model version and cloud provider
  - Allow controlled rollouts (for example, 10% of traffic to the new model) using decision tables or feature flags
- **Feedback Loops Back to the AI Pipelines:**
  Pega is often the best place to observe outcomes: case resolutions, human overrides, appeals, and clinician feedback. In a hybrid/multi-cloud architecture, these signals should feed back into the training pipelines, even if the data lake or ML platform sits in a different cloud.

  This requires:

- Standard schemas for feedback events
- Reliable export jobs or streaming connectors from Pega to data lakes across clouds
- Clear ownership for how often the AI teams consume and act on this feedback

7.5.5 Governance, Audit, and Explainability across Clouds

Finally, Pega plays a key role in governance when AI spans clouds:

- **Single Pane for Decisions:**
  Even if models run in multiple clouds, the actual decision that affects a patient, customer, or claim often materializes inside a Pega case. That case history becomes the primary audit record.
- **Linking Decisions to Models and Environments:**
  For each AI-assisted decision, Pega can record:
  - Which model and version was used
  - Which cloud or region served the request
  - What key features or scores were passed in and returned
- **Surfacing Explanations:**
  Explanations may be generated in the AI layer (e.g., SHAP summaries returned from a model endpoint) but displayed inside Pega screens. In a hybrid or multi-cloud setup, this means agreeing on a common explanation format and ensuring it can be rendered consistently regardless of where the model runs.

When SaaS platforms like Pega are treated as first-class participants in hybrid and multi-cloud AI architectures, they provide a stable, governed entry point for users while the underlying AI workloads move across clouds and environments as needed. This separation of concerns—Pega for orchestration and governance, cloud platforms for heavy AI compute—allows organizations to evolve their infrastructure without disrupting the workflows that matter most.

Bibliography

Alibaba Cloud. (2023). Hybrid cloud architecture for AI: Maximizing flexibility and control. Retrieved from https://www.alibabacloud.com

Amazon Web Services (AWS). (2024). AWS Outposts: Hybrid cloud solutions for AI workloads. https://aws.amazon.com/outposts

Batool, A., Zowghi, D., & Bano, M. (2025). AI governance: A systematic literature review. *AI and Ethics, 5*, 3265–3279. https://doi.org/10.1007/s43681-024-00653-w

Bouderhem, R. (2024). Shaping the future of AI in healthcare through ethics and governance. *Humanities & Social Sciences Communications, 11*, 416. https://doi.org/10.1057/s41599-024-02894-w

Chen, M., & Tan, P. (2022). Achieving AI resilience with multi-cloud strategies. *Journal of AI and Cloud Computing, 14*(2), 113–126.

Choudhury, S., & Kumar, R. (2023). AI workloads and hybrid cloud strategies in healthcare. *HealthTech Journal, 22*(6), 88–101.

Cloud Industry Forum. (2021). The benefits of hybrid cloud for AI applications. https://www.cloudindustryforum.com

Du, M. (2023). Policy regulation of artificial intelligence: A review of the literature. In A. J. Tallón-Ballesteros & P. Santana-Morales (Eds.), *Digitalization and management innovation* (pp. 407–415). IOS Press. https://doi.org/10.3233/FAIA230041

European Commission. (2024). AI act: Regulatory framework for artificial intelligence. *Shaping Europe's Digital Future.* https://digital-strategy.ec.europa.eu/en/policies/regulatory-framework-ai

European Parliament. (2025). EU AI act: First regulation on artificial intelligence. https://www.europarl.europa.eu/topics/en/article/20230601STO93804/eu-ai-act-first-regulation-on-artificial-intelligence

Forman, A. S., & Glasser, N. M. (2022). The White House releases "Blueprint for an AI Bill of Rights". *Workforce Bulletin.* https://www.workforcebulletin.com/the-white-house-releases-blueprint-for-an-ai-bill-of-rights-making-automated-systems-work-for-the-american-people

Future of Life Institute. (2024). High-level summary of the AI Act. https://artificialintelligenceact.eu/high-level-summary

Google Cloud. (2024). Hybrid cloud with Google Anthos: Enabling AI workflows across clouds. https://cloud.google.com/anthos

Harris, P., & Nair, A. (2023). Hybrid cloud AI in the financial sector: Best practices and use cases. *Journal of Financial Technology, 11*(4), 208–220.

IBM Cloud. (2022). Multi-cloud AI strategies and tools for enhanced resilience. *IBM Cloud White Paper.* https://www.ibm.com/cloud/multi-cloud-ai

Jobin, A., Ienca, M., & Vayena, E. (2019). Artificial intelligence: The global landscape of ethics guidelines. *arXiv.* https://doi.org/10.48550/arXiv.1906.11668

Lu, Q., Zhu, L., Xu, X., Whittle, J., Zowghi, D., & Jacquet, A. (2022). RAI law and regulation. *Responsible AI Pattern Catalogue.* https://research.csiro.au/ss/science/projects/responsible-ai-pattern-catalogue/ai-regulation

Lu, Q., Zhu, L., Xu, X., Whittle, J., Zowghi, D., & Jacquet, A. (2022). Responsible AI pattern catalogue: A multivocal literature review. *arXiv.* https://doi.org/10.48550/arXiv.2209.04963

Masood, A. (2025). The AI governance frontier series part 6 — Open-source tools and initiatives for responsible and safe AI. *Medium*. https://medium.com/@adnanmasood/the-ai-governance-frontier-series-part-6-open-source-tools-and-initiatives-for-responsible-and-d41ece940ac1

Microsoft Azure. (2024). Azure Arc and hybrid AI for the enterprise. *Microsoft Azure Documentation*. https://azure.microsoft.com/en-us/services/azure-arc

Office of Science and Technology Policy. (2022). *What is the blueprint for an AI Bill of Rights?* The White House. https://bidenwhitehouse.archives.gov/ostp/ai-bill-of-rights/what-is-the-blueprint-for-an-ai-bill-of-rights/

Security Compass. (2024). Understanding EU AI Act risk categories. https://www.securitycompass.com/blog/understanding-eu-ai-act-risk-categories

Smith, A., & Johnson, P. (2022). Leveraging hybrid cloud for AI workloads in regulated industries. *Journal of Cloud Computing and Data Security, 18*(2), 233–245.

Thummarakoti, S. (2022). *Toward efficient asynchronous architectures in low-code platforms: A comparative study in Pega*. SSRN. https://doi.org/10.2139/ssrn.5238386

Thummarakoti, S. (2023). *Enhancing business process automation through NLP-based email interpretation in Pega systems*. SSRN. https://doi.org/10.2139/ssrn.5249573

Thummarakoti, S., & Udayagiri, P. (2020). Adaptive orchestration for performance cost optimization in multi-cloud infrastructure. *European Journal of Advances in Engineering and Technology, 7*(8), 119–125. https://doi.org/10.5281/zenodo.15307951

Trail ML. (2024). EU AI Act: Risk-classifications of the AI regulation. https://www.trail-ml.com/blog/eu-ai-act-how-risk-is-classified

UNESCO. (2021). Recommendation on the ethics of artificial intelligence. https://www.unesco.org/en/artificial-intelligence/recommendation-ethics

Wang, L., & Thomas, D. (2023). Cost optimization in hybrid cloud deployments for AI applications. *Cloud Economics Review, 9*(1), 45–58.

Zhang, H., & Li, W. (2023). Hybrid cloud and AI: Challenges and opportunities. *International Journal of Cloud Computing, 12*(4), 195–210.

Chapter 8

Edge Computing and AI Deployment beyond the Cloud

8.1 Introduction to Edge AI

As artificial intelligence continues to evolve and expand, organizations are increasingly exploring deployment strategies that extend beyond centralized cloud environments. Edge AI—the deployment of AI models and workloads on edge devices, gateways, or local servers closer to data sources—has emerged as a critical component of modern AI infrastructure. This approach enables real-time inference, low-latency processing, and offline decision-making, while also addressing concerns related to bandwidth, privacy, and reliability.

In this section, we introduce the concept of edge AI, its key characteristics, how it differs from cloud-based AI, and the growing importance of deploying AI workloads at the edge across industries (Figure 8.1).

8.1.1 What Is Edge AI?

Edge AI refers to the practice of running AI algorithms, models, and inference processes on devices and systems at the network's edge—closer to where data is generated rather than in distant cloud data centers. These devices can include:

- IoT devices and sensors
- Smartphones and mobile devices

DOI: 10.4324/9781003685609-8

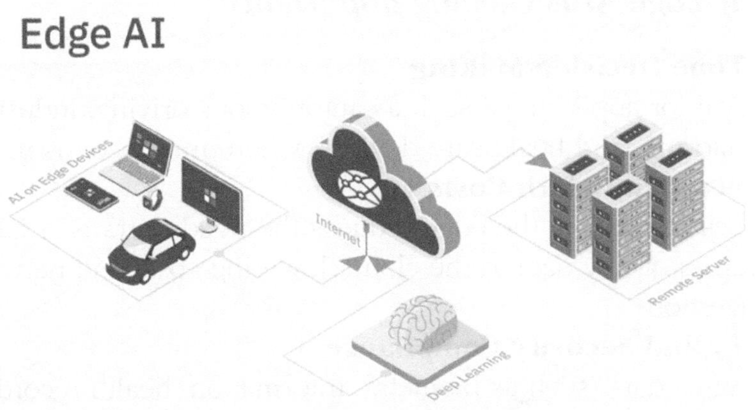

Figure 8.1 End-to-End Edge AI Architecture and Data Flow

- Industrial robots and manufacturing equipment
- Edge gateways and local servers
- Autonomous vehicles and drones

In edge AI deployments, model inference happens locally, often without reliance on continuous cloud connectivity.

8.1.2 How Edge AI Differs from Cloud AI

Aspect	*Cloud AI*	*Edge AI*
Location of computation	Centralized data centers or cloud regions	On-device or near the data source
Latency	Higher, due to network round trips	Ultra-low latency (real-time or near-real-time)
Connectivity dependence	Requires reliable network access	Can operate offline or with intermittent connectivity
Scalability	Virtually unlimited but centralized	Scalable via distributed deployments on multiple devices
Privacy	Data transferred to the cloud for processing	Local data processing improves privacy and security
Power constraints	Ample power resources in data centers	Devices must operate within power and thermal limits

8.1.3 Why Edge AI Is Gaining Importance

1. **Real-Time Decision-Making**:
   - Critical for applications such as autonomous driving, industrial safety monitoring, and healthcare devices, where milliseconds matter.
2. **Reduced Bandwidth Costs**:
   - Processing data at the edge reduces the need to transfer large volumes of raw data to the cloud, lowering costs and network congestion.
3. **Privacy and Security Compliance**:
   - Sensitive data (such as biometric information, health records, or surveillance footage) can be processed locally, reducing regulatory and privacy risks.
4. **Reliability and Resilience**:
   - In scenarios with unreliable or no connectivity (remote locations, disaster zones), edge AI allows for continuous operation without interruption.
5. **Lower Latency User Experiences**:
   - Applications such as augmented reality (AR), virtual reality (VR), and gaming require immediate feedback, which cloud-based inference cannot provide.

8.1.4 Key Industries Driving Edge AI Adoption

Industry	*Common Edge AI Applications*
Manufacturing	Predictive maintenance, quality inspection via computer vision, equipment monitoring
Healthcare	Real-time patient monitoring, portable diagnostic devices, smart medical imaging
Retail	In-store analytics, customer behavior tracking, automated checkout systems
Transportation	Autonomous vehicles, traffic monitoring, smart intersections
Agriculture	Crop monitoring, pest detection, and yield estimation through edge-based image analysis
Smart cities	Public safety monitoring, smart lighting, environmental sensing

8.1.5 Types of Edge AI Devices

1. **Microcontrollers (MCUs)**:
   - Extremely low-power devices running tiny AI models (e.g., for wearables and IoT sensors).
2. **Single-Board Computers (SBCs)**:
   - Devices like Raspberry Pi or NVIDIA Jetson Nano are capable of running moderately complex inference models.
3. **Edge Gateways**:
   - More powerful devices positioned between sensors and cloud systems, aggregating data and performing localized processing.
4. **Industrial PCs and On-Prem Servers**:
   - Deployed in factories, hospitals, or warehouses for running advanced AI models in controlled environments.
5. **Mobile Devices and AR/VR Headsets**:
   - Smartphones, smart glasses, and wearable devices with on-device AI inference capabilities.

8.1.6 Common AI Workloads Deployed at the Edge

- **Computer Vision**: Object detection, image classification, facial recognition, and pose estimation.
- **Natural Language Processing**: On-device speech recognition, translation, and text summarization.
- **Anomaly Detection**: Monitoring industrial machinery or networks for unusual activity in real-time.
- **Predictive Analytics**: Forecasting equipment failure or operational risks at remote facilities.
- **Sensor Fusion and Control Systems**: Combining data from multiple sensors for decision-making in robotics and autonomous vehicles.

8.1.7 Edge AI Deployment Models

- **On-Device Inference**:
  AI models are deployed directly on devices like smartphones, cameras, or embedded systems.
- **Edge Gateway Inference**:
  Models run on intermediary devices that collect and process data from multiple sensors or endpoints.

- **Cloud-to-Edge Deployment**:
  Models are trained and optimized in the cloud, then packaged and deployed to edge devices with automated update mechanisms.

Edge AI is transforming how data is processed, and decisions are made in real-time, unlocking new possibilities for industries that rely on ultra-low latency, private, and resilient AI workloads. As computing power at the edge continues to evolve and connectivity infrastructures improve, edge AI will become an integral part of enterprise AI strategies, complementing cloud-based systems and enabling smarter, faster, and more autonomous operations.

In the next section, we will explore the architecture of edge AI systems and the components required for deploying scalable and reliable AI workloads at the edge.

8.2 Cloud-to-Edge AI Model Deployment Strategies

Deploying AI models from cloud environments to edge devices is a critical step in enabling real-time, low-latency intelligence outside of centralized data centers. Cloud-to-edge AI deployment strategies ensure that models trained and validated in the cloud can be seamlessly packaged, optimized, distributed, and executed on diverse edge hardware platforms. This process involves handling challenges like model size constraints, hardware compatibility, update management, and ensuring consistent performance in resource-constrained environments.

In this section, we will explore the key cloud-to-edge deployment strategies, model optimization techniques, delivery methods, and best practices for maintaining scalable and reliable AI deployments across edge environments.

8.2.1 The Cloud-to-Edge AI Lifecycle

The cloud-to-edge AI lifecycle typically follows these stages:

1. **Model Training in the Cloud**:
   - High-performance GPUs or TPUs are used to train large models on cloud infrastructure.

2. **Model Optimization and Compression**:
   - Models are quantized, pruned, and converted into lightweight formats suitable for edge deployment.
3. **Packaging and Containerization**:
   - Models are packaged with inference code, dependencies, and configurations.
4. **Model Distribution**:
   - Models are securely delivered from cloud repositories to edge devices via automated pipelines or device management platforms.
5. **Deployment and Inference Execution**:
   - The model is deployed to the edge and begins performing inference locally.
6. **Monitoring and Feedback Loop**:
   - Usage data, inference performance, and accuracy metrics are fed back to the cloud for continuous, sustained improvement and retraining.

8.2.2 Key Cloud-to-Edge Deployment Strategies

1. **Direct Deployment via Edge Management Platforms**:
   - Many cloud providers offer dedicated services to manage model deployment to edge devices.
   - **Examples**:
     - AWS IoT Greengrass
     - Azure IoT Edge
     - Google Cloud IoT Core with Edge TPU support
2. **Over-the-Air (OTA) Updates**:
   - Models and software updates are delivered wirelessly to devices in the field.
   - Used in autonomous vehicles, robotics, and industrial IoT applications to push improvements and patches without manual intervention.
3. **Container-Based Deployment**:
   - Package inference models in lightweight Docker containers and deploy them to edge devices running container engines.
   - Suitable for edge gateways and industrial PCs capable of running Kubernetes or Docker environments.
4. **CDN-Based Model Distribution**:
   - Utilize Content Delivery Networks (CDNs) to cache and deliver model binaries to geographically distributed edge locations.
   - Helps reduce latency and bandwidth costs for large-scale deployments.

5. **Hybrid Cloud-Edge Deployment**:
   - Partial inference occurs at the edge, while more complex computations are routed to the cloud.
   - Balances the benefits of local responsiveness and cloud scalability.

8.2.3 Model Optimization for Edge Deployment

Before models can be deployed to the edge, they often require optimization to meet size, power, and computational constraints. Key optimization techniques include:

1. **Quantization**:
   - Reduces model precision (e.g., from float32 to int8) to make models smaller and faster while maintaining acceptable accuracy.
   - Supported by TensorFlow Lite, PyTorch Mobile, and ONNX Runtime.
2. **Pruning and Weight Clustering**:
   - Remove redundant connections and compress weight matrices to reduce the model's memory footprint.
3. **Model Distillation**:
   - Trains a smaller "student" model to mimic the behavior of a larger "teacher" model.
   - Produces efficient models suitable for real-time edge inference.
4. **Hardware-Specific Compilation**:
   - Uses compilers and toolkits that generate binaries optimized for specific edge hardware:
   - NVIDIA TensorRT for Jetson devices.
   - Intel OpenVINO for CPUs and VPUs.
   - Google Edge TPU Compiler for Coral devices.

8.2.4 Cloud-to-Edge Deployment Workflows by Provider

Cloud Provider	*Edge AI Deployment Tools*
AWS	AWS IoT Greengrass, SageMaker Edge Manager, AWS Lambda@Edge for inference delivery
Azure	Azure IoT Edge, Azure Machine Learning + Azure Stack for hybrid deployments
Google Cloud	Google Edge TPU with Coral devices, Google Cloud IoT Core, Container Registry for edge distribution

8.2.5 Versioning and Update Management

- **Model Registry**:
  Maintain centralized version control for models, with metadata and deployment history.
- **Staged Rollouts**:
  Deploy models incrementally to subsets of devices (canary deployments) to test performance before a full rollout.
- **Rollback Mechanisms**:
  Enable automatic rollback to previous stable models if new deployments underperform or fail.
- **Update Security**:
  Sign models and containers digitally to ensure authenticity and protect against malicious tampering.

8.2.6 Monitoring Deployed Models at the Edge

- Collect inference metrics (latency, accuracy, throughput) and send telemetry back to the cloud for monitoring.
- Detect drift and trigger alerts or retraining workflows when edge model performance degrades.
- Use lightweight monitoring agents on edge devices to track system resource usage (CPU, GPU, memory) and inference reliability.

8.2.7 Challenges in Cloud-to-Edge Deployment

Challenge	*Mitigation*
Limited hardware resources	Optimize models (quantization, pruning) and deploy only essential inference logic
Device diversity (hardware variations)	Use cross-compiled binaries and support multi-architecture container images
Connectivity constraints	Design for intermittent connectivity with caching and offline capabilities
Security vulnerabilities	Implement end-to-end encryption, signed binaries, and secure device boot processes

8.2.8 Best Practices for Cloud-to-Edge AI Deployment

- **Develop Cloud-First, Deploy Edge-Optimized**:
  Start with robust models trained in the cloud, then optimize and convert them for edge deployment.
- **Containerize for Consistency**:
  Use containers for reliable and repeatable deployments across heterogeneous edge environments.
- **Automate Rollouts and Updates**:
  Build CI/CD pipelines that extend to edge devices for automated deployments and rollback.
- **Monitor Continuously**:
  Set up telemetry to track edge inference performance and trigger retraining workflows as needed.
- **Test across Hardware Profiles**:
  Simulate different edge device constraints during testing to ensure consistent performance.

Cloud-to-edge AI deployment strategies enable organizations to push advanced intelligence directly to the environments where decisions must be made in real-time.

By adopting optimization techniques, secure delivery mechanisms, and robust monitoring pipelines, organizations can effectively manage AI models across large fleets of edge devices. This approach not only reduces latency and bandwidth costs but also opens up new possibilities in manufacturing, transportation, healthcare, and smart cities.

In the next section, we will discuss edge inference optimization techniques and how to maximize performance on constrained devices.

8.3 Security and Latency Considerations in Edge AI

As AI models and inference capabilities extend from cloud environments to the edge, new challenges emerge around safeguarding data, protecting model integrity, and ensuring low-latency performance in resource-constrained environments.

Edge AI deployments operate in diverse, often uncontrolled environments—from industrial facilities and vehicles to remote field devices—making them more susceptible to security threats and network fluctuations. At the same time, they must deliver rapid, real-time inference, often without continuous cloud connectivity.

This section explores the critical security risks and latency challenges associated with edge AI and outlines best practices and architectural strategies to mitigate these issues while ensuring robust and reliable AI inference at the edge.

8.3.1 Security Risks in Edge AI Deployments

Risk	*Impact*
Physical device tampering	Edge devices deployed in uncontrolled environments may be physically accessed and compromised
Model theft and reverse engineering	AI models stored on edge devices can be extracted and misused by attackers
Adversarial attacks	Malicious inputs crafted to deceive AI models could lead to incorrect inferences
Unauthorized access	Weak authentication and unsecured endpoints can allow unauthorized access to device control or data
Data interception and leakage	Sensitive data collected and processed at the edge can be intercepted during transmission or stored in an insecure manner
Software vulnerabilities	Outdated libraries and unpatched devices increase the risk of exploitation

8.3.2 Best Practices for Securing Edge AI

1. **Device Security**:
   - Deploy tamper-resistant hardware (TPMs or secure enclaves) where possible.
   - Enable secure boot processes to ensure only trusted firmware and software can run.
   - Use hardware-based encryption for data storage.
2. **Model Protection**:
   - Obfuscate or encrypt AI models stored on devices.
   - Implement model watermarking to detect unauthorized use.
   - Deploy lightweight models with minimal proprietary IP for high-risk edge scenarios.

3. **Communication Security**:
   - Use end-to-end encryption (TLS 1.3 or higher) for data in transit between the edge and cloud.
   - Rotate authentication tokens and certificates on a regular basis.
4. **Endpoint and API Security**:
   - Require strong authentication for all API calls.
   - Implement rate limiting and anomaly detection for inference requests.
   - Use secure keys stored in trusted execution environments (TEEs).
5. **Over-the-Air (OTA) Security**:
   - Sign all model and software updates with digital signatures to verify authenticity before installation.
   - Roll out updates incrementally with fallback mechanisms to prevent bricking devices.
6. **Regular Vulnerability Scanning**:
   - Schedule automated scans for software dependencies and firmware.
   - Apply security patches as part of a continuous update strategy.

8.3.3 Latency Challenges in Edge AI

1. **Device Processing Limitations**:
   - Limited compute power, memory, and thermal capacity on edge devices can slow inference.
2. **Network Fluctuations**:
   - Dependence on intermittent or low-bandwidth connectivity impacts real-time inference pipelines and telemetry reporting.
3. **Model Complexity**:
   - Large models increase inference time, drain battery life, and raise device operating temperatures.
4. **Multi-Sensor Data Fusion**:
   - Combining data from multiple sources (e.g., cameras, LiDar, sensors) in real-time can create bottlenecks.

8.3.4 Strategies to Minimize Latency

1. **Model Optimization**:
   - Quantize models to lower-precision formats (INT8, FP16) for faster inference.
   - Prune models to remove unnecessary nodes and parameters.
   - Use knowledge distillation to deploy lightweight student models.

2. **Hardware Acceleration**:
   - Leverage device-specific AI accelerators:
     - NVIDIA Jetson GPU
     - Google Edge TPU
     - Intel Movidius VPU
     - Apple Neural Engine (ANE)
3. **Batch Inference and Pipeline Optimization**:
   - Where latency tolerates it, batch inference requests to improve throughput.
   - Use parallel processing for different data streams (e.g., multi-threading or edge TPU cores).
4. **Data Preprocessing at the Edge**:
   - Conduct sensor data filtering and preprocessing on-device to reduce workload on the inference model.
5. **Hybrid Inference Models**:
   - Use multi-stage inference where lightweight models perform initial screening and only complex cases are sent to the cloud for deeper analysis.

8.3.5 Real-Time Edge AI Latency Benchmarks

Device	*Typical Inference Latency (Single Image)*
NVIDIA Jetson Nano	20–50 milliseconds (optimized model)
Google Coral Dev Board (Edge TPU)	4–10 milliseconds (for quantized models)
Raspberry Pi 4 (CPU-only inference)	200–500 milliseconds (depends on model size)
Intel Neural Compute Stick (VPU)	50–100 milliseconds (depends on model complexity)

8.3.6 Secure and Low-Latency Deployment Architecture Example

Use Case: Real-time video analytics at an industrial facility.

- **Deployment Design**:
  - Models optimized with TensorRT and quantized to INT8 format.
  - Deployed in Docker containers running on NVIDIA Jetson Xavier edge gateways.

- Inference results cached locally with periodic telemetry are uploaded to the cloud using secure MQTT protocols.
- OTA updates signed and delivered via AWS IoT Greengrass.
- Local inference latency: <30 milliseconds per frame.

8.3.7 Monitoring Security and Latency in Edge AI Deployments

- Implement lightweight monitoring agents to:
  - Track inference times, memory usage, and CPU/GPU load.
  - Detect tampering events or unauthorized access attempts.
  - Log all API activity and maintain audit trails for security analysis.
- Send telemetry data to centralized dashboards for aggregate performance and security monitoring.

Edge AI brings tremendous value by enabling real-time intelligence close to data sources, but it comes with unique security and latency challenges. By implementing hardware-level protection, encrypting models and communications, monitoring endpoints, and optimizing models for low-latency execution, organizations can deploy robust, secure, and responsive AI systems at the edge.

Managing security and latency in tandem will be critical as industries increasingly rely on edge AI for mission-critical decision-making.

In the next section, we will explore real-world case studies of successful edge AI deployments and the architecture patterns that enabled them.

8.4 Case Studies: AI at the Edge

Edge AI is transforming industries by enabling real-time data processing, decision-making, and automation where data is generated—outside traditional data centers and cloud environments. Across various sectors, including manufacturing, healthcare, transportation, and retail, organizations are deploying AI models on edge devices to achieve lower latency, improve reliability, enhance privacy, and reduce bandwidth costs.

In this section, we examine real-world case studies that demonstrate how enterprises are leveraging AI at the edge, highlighting deployment architectures, challenges addressed, and measurable outcomes.

8.4.1 Case Study 1: Predictive Maintenance in Manufacturing

Organization: Global Automotive Manufacturer
Objective: Detect anomalies and predict equipment failures on production lines without latency or dependency on cloud connectivity.

Solution:

- Trained deep learning models for vibration and acoustic analysis in the cloud.
- Deployed optimized models to edge gateways (NVIDIA Jetson Xavier devices) installed near production equipment.
- Transmitted inference results via secure MQTT to centralized dashboards every 5 minutes.
- Delivered OTA updates to deploy improved models after retraining based on aggregated edge telemetry.

Benefits Achieved:

- Reduced unplanned downtime by 30%.
- Achieved sub-50 millisecond inference latency.
- Saved bandwidth by transmitting only anomaly alerts and summary statistics.

8.4.2 Case Study 2: Smart Retail Analytics

Organization: Large Retail Chain
Objective: Enable in-store customer behavior tracking and queue management without sending sensitive video data to the cloud.

Solution:

- Trained computer vision models using cloud GPU instances.
- Converted models to TensorFlow Lite and deployed them on ARM-based edge devices (Google Coral) mounted in stores.
- Performed real-time inference for customer counting, shelf monitoring, and queue length estimation.
- Aggregated data on-premises and sent only anonymized, processed insights to cloud analytics dashboards.

Benefits Achieved:

- Improved store traffic flow, reducing checkout wait times by 25%.
- Enhanced privacy compliance by processing video locally.
- Reduced cloud data transfer costs by over 60%.

8.4.3 Case Study 3: Remote Healthcare Monitoring

Organization: Digital Health Startup
Objective: Monitor patient vitals and predict health anomalies in remote areas with limited connectivity.

Solution:

- Trained AI models for heart rate variability and oxygen saturation prediction in the cloud.
- Deployed models on portable medical devices with ARM processors and embedded GPUs.
- Performed local inference on-device and sent emergency alerts via cellular networks when thresholds were breached.
- Synced data periodically to cloud systems for retrospective analysis and model retraining.

Benefits Achieved:

- Enabled continuous patient monitoring in remote locations without the need for stable internet.
- Detected early signs of health deterioration with >90% accuracy.
- Reduced emergency response times by 40%.

8.4.4 Case Study 4: Autonomous Vehicles and Smart Traffic Systems

Organization: Autonomous Shuttle Service Provider
Objective: Perform real-time object detection and path planning on vehicles for safe navigation.

Solution:

- Trained models for pedestrian detection, traffic sign recognition, and collision avoidance on cloud-based TPU instances.
- Converted models to INT8 format and deployed on NVIDIA Drive AGX Xavier platforms within vehicles.
- Performed edge inference, combined with Lidar and radar sensor fusion, to enable decision-making in milliseconds.
- Delivered periodic OTA updates to deploy new model versions after retraining based on real-world data.

Benefits Achieved:

- Achieved inference latency of less than 20 milliseconds per frame.
- Improved obstacle detection accuracy to 98%.
- Reduced collision incidents by 70% during pilot deployments.

8.4.5 Case Study 5: Agriculture and Precision Farming

Organization: Agricultural Technology Company
Objective: Identify crop diseases and optimize irrigation in large-scale farms.

Solution:

- Trained convolutional neural networks (CNNs) on drone imagery in the cloud.
- Deployed edge AI devices (NVIDIA Jetson Nano) on autonomous drones and farm equipment for real-time image analysis.
- Performed on-device inference for leaf discoloration and pest detection.
- Transmitted data summaries to cloud servers every evening for dashboard visualization and farm management recommendations.

Benefits Achieved:

- Reduced pesticide usage by 20% through targeted intervention.
- Increased crop yields by 15% in monitored fields.
- Enabled faster decision-making with same-day actionable insights.

8.4.6 Common Architecture Patterns in Edge AI Deployments

Pattern	*Description*
Cloud-to-edge training and inference	Models trained in the cloud and deployed via OTA updates for local inference
Edge-only inference with cloud aggregation	Inference and data processing are performed locally; aggregated insights are sent to the cloud
Hybrid inference	Light inference is performed at the edge; complex inference requests are routed to the cloud
Federated edge AI	Models trained collaboratively across multiple edge devices without centralized data pooling

8.4.7 Lessons Learned across Deployments

- **Model Optimization Is Essential**:
  Successful deployments rely on quantization, pruning, and hardware-aware compilation to meet edge constraints.
- **OTA Management Must Be Secure and Reliable**:
  Secure and controlled model updates prevent disruptions and protect devices from malicious interference.
- **Telemetry Enables Continuous Improvement**:
  Monitoring inference performance and sending usage data to the cloud allows continuous retraining and performance optimization.
- **Cross-Disciplinary Collaboration Is Key**:
  Successful edge AI projects require close collaboration between data scientists, embedded engineers, and infrastructure teams.
- **Latency and Reliability Must Be Balanced**:
  In use cases like autonomous vehicles or industrial robotics, ultra-low latency models must be paired with robust fallback mechanisms and continuous monitoring.

These real-world examples illustrate the transformative power of AI at the edge across diverse industries. By intelligently combining cloud-based model training with secure, optimized, and responsive edge deployments, organizations are driving real-time intelligence, operational efficiency, and new levels of automation. The future of AI will increasingly depend on robust edge architectures that complement cloud systems and enable data-driven decision-making where and when it matters most.

In the next chapter, we will explore the future trends shaping cloud-edge AI ecosystems and how organizations can prepare for increasingly intelligent, autonomous systems.

Bibliography

Ahmed, A., Belkadi, M., & Taghezout, F. (2024). Multi-agent AI systems in healthcare: Technical and clinical analysis. *Preprints.org*. https://www.preprints.org/manuscript/202404.1552/v1

Amershi, H., Weld, D., Vorvoreanu, M., et al. (2019). Guidelines for human-AI interaction. In *Proceedings of the 2019 CHI Conference on Human Factors in Computing Systems*. ACM. https://doi.org/10.1145/3290605.3300233

Beam, J., & Kelley, L. (2023). Architecting robust AI for healthcare: Error handling and escalation. *IEEE Journal of Biomedical and Health Informatics, 27*(1), 23–34.

Chen, Y., & Tan, W. (2021). Edge computing for real-time AI: The role of latency optimization. *Journal of Real-Time Computing, 15*(2), 250–267.

Colberg, S. R., Sigal, R. J., Fernhall, B., et al. (2010). Exercise and type 2 diabetes: The American College of Sports Medicine and the American Diabetes Association joint position statement. *Diabetes Care, 33*(12), e147–e167. https://doi.org/10.2337/dc10-9990

Davis, T., & Thompson, L. (2023). Cloud-to-edge AI deployment models: Best practices. *Journal of AI Infrastructure, 7*(4), 115–130.

Demner-Fushman, D. (2021). Multi-agent architecture for automated health coaching. *Journal of Biomedical Informatics*. https://www.ncbi.nlm.nih.gov/pmc/articles/PMC8828169/

Krintz, C., & Wolski, R. (2006). Fault-tolerant and adaptive distributed applications using information-driven runtime reconfiguration. *IEEE Transactions on Parallel and Distributed Systems, 17*(9), 870–882. https://doi.org/10.1109/TPDS.2006.122

Kumar, R., & Singh, J. (2021). Exploring edge AI for industrial automation: Challenges and opportunities. *Journal of Industrial AI Systems, 3*(2), 75–91.

Lee, C., & Wong, R. (2021). Optimizing AI models for edge devices. *International Journal of Computing Research, 25*(1), 45–59.

Morris, A., & Jackson, L. (2022). Edge AI: From concept to industrialization. *IEEE Access, 8*, 49012–49024.

Nguyen, A., & Patterson, R. (2023). AI model deployment strategies for edge devices. *International Journal of Distributed Systems, 19*(1), 40–55.

Pearl, J. (1988). *Probabilistic reasoning in intelligent systems: Networks of plausible inference*. Morgan Kaufmann. https://www.elsevier.com/books/probabilistic-reasoning-in-intelligent-systems/pearl/978-1-55860-479-7

Rajesh, B., & Shankar, M. (2025). AI agents in modern healthcare: A comprehensive review and roadmap for clinical integration. *Preprints.org*. https://www.preprints.org/manuscript/202506.0123/v1

Raza, S., Sapkota, R., Karkee, M., & Emmanouilidis, C. (2025). TRiSM for agentic AI: A review of trust, risk, and security management in LLM-based agentic multi-agent systems. *arXiv*. https://arxiv.org/abs/2406.08536

Sapkota, R., Roumeliotis, K. I., & Karkee, M. (2025). AI agents vs. agentic AI: A conceptual taxonomy, applications and challenge. *arXiv*. https://arxiv.org/abs/2405.07935

Singh, H., & Gupta, P. (2024). Security in edge AI deployments: Challenges and solutions. *IEEE Transactions on AI Security, 10*(2), 75–92.

Smith, J., & Brown, P. (2022). The evolution of edge AI: From cloud to device. *Journal of AI and Computing, 12*(3), 100–115.

Thummarakoti, S. (2022). *Toward efficient asynchronous architectures in low-code platforms: A comparative study in Pega*. SSRN. https://ssrn.com/abstract=5238386

Thummarakoti, S. (2023). *Enhancing business process automation through NLP-based email interpretation in Pega systems*. SSRN. https://ssrn.com/abstract=5249573

Thummarakoti, S. (2024). *Transforming healthcare with Pega: A unified approach to modern challenges*. SSRN. https://ssrn.com/abstract=5241177

Thummarakoti, S., & Udayagiri, P. (2020). Adaptive orchestration for performance cost optimization in multi-cloud infrastructure. *European Journal of Advances in Engineering and Technology, 7*(8), 119–125. https://doi.org/10.5281/zenodo.15307951

Topol, E. (2023). A framework for the ethical use of AI in healthcare. *Nature Medicine, 29*, 497–500. https://www.nature.com/articles/s41591-023-02205-0

Topol, M. J. (2019). High-performance medicine: The convergence of human and artificial intelligence. *Nature Medicine, 25*(1), 44–56. https://doi.org/10.1038/s41591-018-0300-7

Wooldridge, M. (2009). *An introduction to multiagent systems* (2nd ed.). Wiley. https://onlinelibrary.wiley.com/doi/book/10.1002/9781119994350

Wu, L., & Zhang, Y. (2022). Decentralized AI at the edge: A new paradigm for scalable intelligence. *IEEE Internet of Things Journal, 9*(8), 5672–5685.

Zhou, L., & Li, F. (2022). Privacy and security in edge AI systems. *Privacy in Technology Journal, 13*(4), 233–245.

Chapter 9

AI Ethics, Bias, and Responsible AI in the Cloud

9.1 Addressing Bias in AI Training and Deployment

As AI systems become integral to decision-making across healthcare, finance, recruitment, public safety, and more, the presence of bias in AI models has emerged as a significant ethical, social, and legal concern. AI bias can lead to unfair, discriminatory, and harmful outcomes, especially when it affects marginalized or vulnerable groups. Addressing bias is not only a technical challenge but also a moral imperative and a business necessity for building trustworthy AI solutions.

This section examines the types of bias in AI, the sources of bias in cloud-based AI pipelines, and best practices for identifying, mitigating, and monitoring bias throughout the training and deployment of AI models in the cloud.

9.1.1 Understanding AI Bias

AI bias occurs when models systematically produce outcomes that unfairly favor or disadvantage certain groups based on race, gender, age, socioeconomic status, or other attributes.

Types of Bias:

- **Data Bias**: Occurs when training data underrepresents or misrepresents specific populations.

DOI: 10.4324/9781003685609-9

- **Sampling Bias**: Arises when data collection methods lead to skewed or unbalanced datasets.
- **Labeling Bias**: Results from inaccurate or inconsistent labeling due to human error or subjective judgments.
- **Algorithmic Bias**: Emerges from inherent biases in the algorithms or optimization objectives themselves.
- **Deployment Bias**: Occurs when model outputs are used in contexts for which they were not designed.

9.1.2 Common Sources of Bias in Cloud-Based AI Workflows

Source	*How It Introduces Bias*
Historical data	Models learn and perpetuate existing societal or institutional biases
Incomplete or imbalanced datasets	Certain demographic groups are underrepresented, leading to lower model accuracy for those groups
Data augmentation strategies	Synthetic data may amplify existing patterns of bias if not carefully managed
Feature engineering	Using proxies for sensitive attributes (like zip codes) can inadvertently introduce bias
Cloud AutoML tools	Automated pipelines may prioritize accuracy over fairness if not configured with bias detection metrics
Deployment environments	Models may be used in new domains or populations not represented in training data

9.1.3 Techniques for Identifying Bias in Training Data

- **Data Auditing and Profiling**:
  - Analyze datasets for demographic representation and imbalance.
  - Utilize visualization tools to identify underrepresented groups and outlier distributions.
- **Fairness Metrics for Data**:
  - **Demographic Parity**: Ensure that different groups are proportionally represented in outcomes.
  - **Equal Opportunity**: Check whether true positive rates are similar across groups.

  - **Disparate Impact Analysis**: Evaluate whether decisions disproportionately affect certain groups.
- **Cloud Tools for Data Bias Detection**:
  - **AWS SageMaker Clarify**: Detects bias in datasets and models during training.
  - **Google Cloud Vertex AI Explainability and Fairness Tools**: Monitors feature influence and fairness metrics.
  - **Azure Responsible AI Toolbox**: Provides fairness dashboards and dataset exploration modules.

9.1.4 Mitigating Bias during Model Training

1. **Balanced Dataset Construction**:
   - Oversample minority groups or undersample overrepresented groups.
   - Use data augmentation strategies that increase diversity in underrepresented categories.
2. **Fair Feature Engineering**:
   - Remove or de-emphasize features that act as proxies for protected attributes.
   - Conduct correlation analysis between features and sensitive variables.
3. **Algorithm Selection and Regularization**:
   - Use algorithms with built-in fairness constraints or regularization penalties.
   - Explore adversarial debiasing techniques that learn to minimize bias during training.
4. **Fairness-Aware Model Training**:
   - Incorporate fairness metrics such as equalized odds or demographic parity as secondary objectives in training.
   - Use re-weighted loss functions to penalize biased predictions.

9.1.5 Bias Detection and Monitoring in Deployment

1. **Post-Deployment Bias Testing**:
   - Continuously test inference outcomes against real-world user demographics.
   - Compare performance metrics (accuracy, recall, precision) across different user groups.

2. **Drift Detection for Fairness**:
   - Monitor data drift and concept drift to detect changes in input data distributions that may lead to new bias patterns.
3. **Explainability Tools**:
   - Use feature importance explanations (like SHAP or LIME) to check if protected attributes or their proxies influence predictions disproportionately.
4. **Continuous Monitoring**:
   - Deploy cloud-native bias monitoring tools:
   - SageMaker Model Monitor
   - Google Cloud Monitoring with custom fairness metrics
   - Azure Model Monitoring integrated with fairness dashboards

9.1.6 Responsible AI Governance for Bias Management

- **Establish Responsible AI Committees**:
  Involve diverse stakeholders (data scientists, ethicists, legal teams, and business leaders) in reviewing model design and outputs.
- **Bias Documentation**:
  Maintain "model cards" that document known limitations, bias testing results, training data composition, and mitigation measures.
- **Human-in-the-Loop Review**:
  Ensure human oversight in high-risk decision-making pipelines (e.g., credit scoring, hiring, healthcare recommendations).
- **Ethical Model Use Policies**:
  Clearly define permissible uses of AI models and prohibit deployment in inappropriate contexts.

9.1.7 Regulatory Landscape and Compliance

- **GDPR (EU)**:
  Requires transparency and explainability for automated decision-making systems.
- **EEOC (USA)**:
  Protects against bias and discrimination in hiring and employment practices.
- **AI Act (EU Proposed Legislation)**:
  Introduces risk-based categorization of AI systems and imposes strict fairness and auditability requirements for high-risk models.

Cloud providers are increasingly aligning their services with these frameworks by offering compliance-focused reporting tools and audit logs.

9.1.8 Best Practices Summary

Best Practice	*Outcome*
Perform demographic analysis of datasets	Identifies potential representation gaps
Use fairness metrics in training and evaluation	Builds models that balance accuracy and fairness
Document model bias risk and mitigation steps	Enhances transparency and accountability
Monitor fairness post-deployment	Ensures models remain fair over time as user populations change
Involve multidisciplinary governance teams	Prevents blind spots and strengthens ethical decision-making

Bias in AI models is a complex and multifaceted challenge that requires attention throughout the entire model lifecycle, from data collection to post-deployment monitoring. In cloud-based AI environments, where scale and automation amplify both positive and negative outcomes, proactive bias detection, mitigation, and governance are essential.

By adopting fairness-aware design principles, leveraging cloud-native bias monitoring tools, and establishing robust ethical oversight structures, organizations can build AI systems that are not only powerful but also equitable and responsible.

In the next section, we will explore the principles and practices for ensuring explainability, transparency, and trust in AI models deployed in the cloud.

9.2 Ethical Considerations for Cloud-Based AI

As artificial intelligence systems increasingly influence critical aspects of business, government, healthcare, and everyday life, the ethical implications of AI development and deployment have become a central concern.

Cloud-based AI systems, with their scale, reach, and complexity, amplify both the opportunities and risks associated with AI. Ethical considerations in cloud-based AI are not limited to technical accuracy; they extend to fairness, accountability, privacy, transparency, environmental responsibility, and societal impact.

This section explores the core ethical considerations organizations must address when building and deploying AI models in the cloud and outlines frameworks and best practices to ensure responsible and ethical AI development.

9.2.1 Key Ethical Principles for Cloud-Based AI

1. **Fairness**:
   - AI models should be designed to avoid discrimination based on race, gender, age, religion, disability, or other protected characteristics.
   - Fairness must be assessed in both training data and deployment environments and continuously monitored post-deployment.
2. **Transparency**:
   - Models, data sources, and decision-making processes should be documented and explainable to stakeholders and end-users.
   - Cloud-based AI platforms should support model interpretability tools and provide accessible documentation (model cards).
3. **Accountability**:
   - Organizations must take responsibility for the outcomes produced by their AI models, even when automated systems make decisions.
   - Clear lines of ownership and decision-making responsibility must be defined for AI model management and deployment.
4. **Privacy and Data Protection**:
   - Data used to train and operate AI models must be collected, stored, and processed in compliance with privacy laws and with explicit consent where required.
   - Sensitive data should be anonymized, encrypted, and governed through strict access controls, especially when stored or processed in the cloud.
5. **Safety and Reliability**:
   - AI models should be tested for robustness against adversarial attacks and edge cases.
   - Cloud-based AI deployments should include continuous monitoring to detect model drift, security breaches, and unintended behaviors.

6. **Environmental Responsibility**:
   - Training large AI models consumes significant energy.
   - Ethical AI development includes designing energy-efficient models, using renewable energy-backed cloud resources, and managing the environmental footprint of large-scale compute resources.

9.2.2 *Ethical Risks Unique to Cloud-Based AI*

Risk	*Impact*
Opacity in cloud AI services	Organizations may rely on "black-box" AutoML services without understanding how decisions are made
Lack of data sovereignty	Data stored or processed in the cloud may be subject to foreign jurisdiction or insufficient privacy safeguards
Concentration of AI power	Centralized control of advanced AI capabilities by a few cloud providers raises concerns over monopolization and bias
Cloud service bias	Built-in AI APIs, such as sentiment analysis or facial recognition, may carry unexamined biases
Unchecked automation	Cloud-based AI systems deployed at scale can propagate harm rapidly if not subject to proper human oversight

9.2.3 *Privacy Ethics in Cloud AI*

- **Data Minimization**:
  Collect only what is necessary and store data securely, with clear retention policies in place to delete it when no longer needed.
- **Informed Consent**:
  Users must be aware of how their data will be used in AI models and given the ability to opt out.
- **Cross-Border Data Transfers**:
  Ensure compliance with regional privacy laws, such as GDPR and CCPA, when using cloud services with international data centers.
- **Differential Privacy**:
  Consider implementing differential privacy in cloud-based datasets and APIs to safeguard against re-identification attacks.

9.2.4 Transparency in Cloud AI Systems

- **Model Documentation**:
  Maintain detailed model cards, including:
  - Purpose and intended use
  - Data sources and known limitations
  - Performance metrics across demographics
  - Potential risks and mitigation strategies
- **Auditability**:
  Use audit trails and logging to ensure that every inference and decision can be traced back to its source and conditions.
- **Explainability Tools**:
  Cloud providers like AWS, Google Cloud, and Azure offer built-in explainability tools (e.g., SageMaker Clarify, Vertex Explainable AI) that help users understand model outputs.

9.2.5 Environmental Impact Ethics

- **Energy Efficiency**:
  Use right-sized cloud resources, selecting GPU/TPU instances only when necessary.
- **Carbon-Aware Scheduling**:
  Schedule non-urgent AI training tasks during times when data centers run on renewable energy (some providers publish carbon intensity data).
- **Cloud Provider Selection**:
  Consider cloud providers' environmental commitments and data center sustainability practices as part of procurement decisions.

9.2.6 Governance and Ethical AI Frameworks

1. **Internal AI Ethics Committees**:
   - Cross-functional teams (ethics, legal, data science, and product leadership) that review models for fairness, transparency, and risk before deployment.
2. **Responsible AI Policies**:
   - Formal documentation outlining acceptable uses of AI, prohibited practices, and escalation procedures for AI-related issues.

3. **Independent Auditing**:
   - Periodic audits by third-party firms to ensure that cloud-based AI models adhere to ethical standards and regulatory requirements.
4. **Training and Education**:
   - Internal education programs to train developers, data scientists, and executives in ethical AI principles and governance.

9.2.7 Industry Guidelines and Standards

Organization/Framework	*Focus*
OECD AI Principles	Inclusive growth, fairness, transparency, and accountability in AI development
IEEE 7000™ Series	Standards for ethical considerations in system design
European Commission's AI Act (proposed)	Risk-based regulatory framework requiring documentation, transparency, and human oversight
NIST AI Risk Management Framework	Guidelines for managing AI-related risks and ensuring trustworthiness

9.2.8 Best Practices for Ethical AI in the Cloud

Practice	*Ethical Impact*
Document and publicly share model intentions	Increases transparency and builds user trust
Design for human oversight	Prevents unchecked automation and enables accountability
Monitor models continuously for drift and bias	Ensures sustained fairness and relevance post-deployment
Choose cloud providers with responsible AI commitments	Aligns infrastructure choices with organizational ethical values
Build in "kill switches" and escalation paths	Enables rapid deactivation of problematic AI systems

Ethical considerations for cloud-based AI are no longer optional. They are essential to building trustworthy, sustainable, and impactful AI systems.

Cloud environments offer powerful tools for scaling AI capabilities, but they also amplify risks related to fairness, transparency, privacy, and environmental responsibility.

By embedding ethics into every stage of the AI lifecycle, from data collection to cloud deployment and post-production monitoring, organizations can create AI solutions that are both innovative and responsible, fostering trust with users, customers, and society.

In the next section, we will explore how explainability and transparency tools in cloud platforms help developers and organizations meet these ethical responsibilities.

9.3 Explainability and Transparency in AI Models

As AI systems increasingly influence critical decisions in healthcare, finance, recruitment, law enforcement, and beyond, the need for explainability and transparency has become essential.

Complex machine learning models, particularly deep learning architectures, often behave like "black boxes", making it challenging for stakeholders to understand how specific decisions are made. Explainability in AI refers to the ability to interpret, understand, and communicate how a model arrives at a given output. Transparency complements this by making model design, data sources, and decision logic visible and accessible to users and regulators.

This section explores the importance of explainability and transparency in cloud-based AI, the techniques and tools available for implementing them, and best practices for integrating explainability into AI development and deployment lifecycles.

9.3.1 Why Explainability Matters

- **Trust**:
  Users are more likely to trust AI models when they understand how decisions are made.
- **Accountability**:
  Explainability enables stakeholders to audit decisions and trace errors back to their root causes.

- **Fairness and Bias Detection**:
  By understanding feature importance and decision pathways, organizations can identify and correct biased behavior.
- **Regulatory Compliance**:
  Frameworks like the GDPR and the proposed EU AI Act require that individuals can receive understandable explanations of automated decisions.
- **Debugging and Improvement**:
  Explainability helps developers fine-tune models, diagnose unexpected behaviors, and improve overall performance.

9.3.2 Dimensions of Explainability

Dimension	*Description*
Global explainability	Understanding how the entire model works and what features it prioritizes overall
Local explainability	Understanding why the model made a particular decision for a single instance or prediction
Model-level transparency	Visibility into architecture design, data sources, and training methodologies
Decision traceability	The ability to track predictions and link them to underlying data and decision logic

9.3.3 Techniques for AI Explainability

1. **Feature Importance Analysis**:
   - Measures the influence of each feature on the model's outputs.
   - Methods:
     - Permutation importance
     - Tree-based feature importance (for decision trees and ensemble models)
2. **SHapley Additive exPlanations (SHAP)**:
   - A game-theory-based method that attributes contributions of each feature to individual predictions.
   - Provides both local and global explainability.
3. **Local Interpretable Model-Agnostic Explanations (LIME)**:
   - Generates simple, interpretable models (such as linear models) around individual predictions to explain outcomes.

4. **Partial Dependence Plots (PDPs)**:
   - Visualize how changing a feature affects the prediction while holding other features constant.
5. **Counterfactual Explanations**:
   - Show how an input could be altered to produce a different output, helping users understand what factors drive decisions.
6. **Surrogate Models**:
   - Create a simpler, interpretable model (e.g., decision trees) that approximates the behavior of a more complex black-box model.

9.3.4 Explainability Tools in Cloud Platforms

Cloud Provider	*Explainability Tools*
AWS	**SageMaker Clarify:** Automatically computes bias metrics and feature importance, with visual dashboards
Google Cloud	**Vertex Explainable AI:** Provides feature attribution for predictions using integrated SHAP-based methods
Azure	**Azure Responsible AI Toolbox:** Includes interpretability dashboards with feature importance, what-if analysis, and counterfactual generation

9.3.5 Transparency Best Practices

1. **Model Cards**:
   - Detailed documentation describing model purpose, training datasets, intended use cases, limitations, and ethical considerations.
   - Includes fairness assessments and potential failure modes.
2. **Data Sheets for Datasets**:
   - Documentation for datasets covering data origin, collection methods, labeling procedures, and known biases.
3. **Algorithmic Transparency**:
   - Openly publish details about algorithms used, hyperparameters selected, and training methodologies.
4. **User-Facing Explanations**:
   - Provide clear, non-technical explanations of model outcomes to end-users, particularly in high-stakes applications such as finance, healthcare, and employment.

5. **Decision Logging and Audit Trails**:
   - Maintain comprehensive logs of model predictions, input data, and system conditions at the time of inference for future auditing.

9.3.6 Challenges in Explainability

Challenge	*Impact*
Complexity of deep learning models	Neural networks with millions of parameters are inherently hard to interpret
Trade-off between performance and interpretability	More interpretable models (e.g., linear models) may sacrifice accuracy
Data privacy concerns	Explanations may reveal sensitive information if not carefully designed
Over-simplification	Explanations may become misleading if they oversimplify model behavior

9.3.7 Explainability in High-Risk AI Applications

- **Healthcare**:
  Explain predictions in diagnostic systems, highlighting contributing factors to recommendations (e.g., medical imaging AI).
- **Finance**:
  Provide reason codes for credit decisions or fraud alerts to meet compliance requirements.
- **Recruitment**:
  Justify candidate rankings or selections to avoid bias claims and regulatory violations.
- **Legal Systems**:
  Ensure any AI used in sentencing or parole decisions provides complete transparency and justification for its predictions.

9.3.8 Emerging Trends in Explainability

- **Explainability-by-Design**:
  Develop inherently interpretable architectures rather than retrofitting explanations post-training.

- **Interactive Explanations**:
  Build systems that allow users to probe models by changing inputs and observing prediction changes.
- **Explainability for Generative Models**:
  Focus on interpreting decisions made by large language models (LLMs) and diffusion models.
- **Explainability in Federated Learning**:
  Develop techniques for understanding how models are updated and personalized across decentralized data environments.

Explainability and transparency are fundamental pillars of responsible AI development, particularly in cloud-based environments where models are deployed at scale and decisions affect diverse populations.

By using state-of-the-art explainability techniques, leveraging cloud-native tools, and embedding transparency practices into every stage of the AI lifecycle, organizations can build models that are not only accurate and efficient but also trustworthy, accountable, and ethical.

In the next section, we will discuss how to integrate continuous monitoring and governance frameworks that ensure ethical AI practices remain enforced throughout a model's lifecycle.

9.4 Regulatory Compliance and AI Ethics Frameworks

As AI systems become embedded in critical sectors—from finance and healthcare to government services and public safety—regulatory scrutiny is intensifying.

Cloud-based AI deployments, in particular, are subject to complex compliance requirements due to their global reach, scale, and the sensitive nature of the data they process. Beyond legal mandates, organizations must also align with broader AI ethics frameworks that promote fairness, accountability, and transparency.

In this section, we examine the evolving landscape of regulatory compliance for AI, explore global AI ethics frameworks, and outline best practices for ensuring that cloud-based AI systems adhere to both legal standards and ethical guidelines (Figure 9.1).

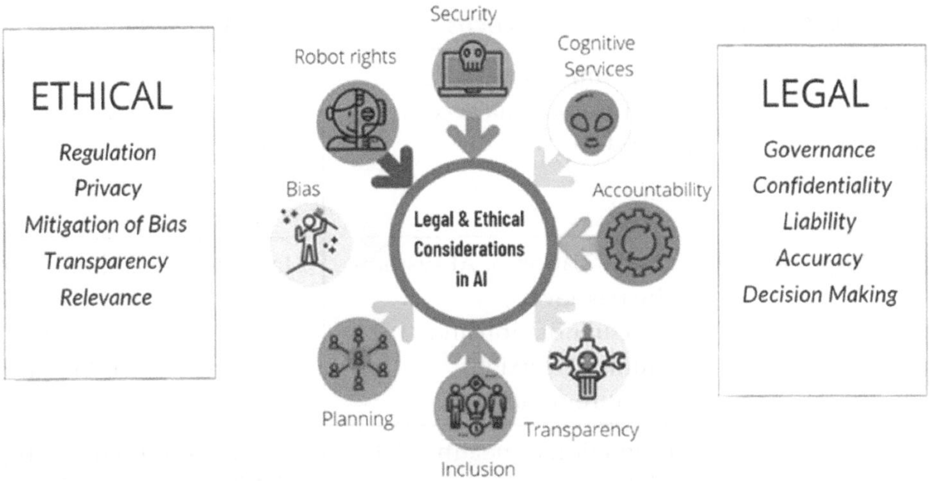

Figure 9.1 Intersection of Legal and Ethical Considerations in AI

9.4.1 Why Regulatory Compliance Matters in AI

- **Legal Risk Mitigation**:
  Non-compliance with data protection and anti-discrimination laws can result in significant financial penalties and reputational damage.
- **Trust and Reputation**:
  Consumers and stakeholders demand that AI systems operate within ethical and legal boundaries.
- **Operational Safety**:
  In domains like autonomous vehicles and healthcare, regulatory oversight ensures that AI systems are safe and reliable.
- **Global Operations**:
  Multinational companies must navigate diverse regional compliance requirements, making structured governance a necessity.

9.4.2 Key Global Regulations Impacting Cloud-Based AI

Regulation/Standard	*Key Focus*	*Applicability to AI*
GDPR (General Data Protection Regulation, EU)	Data protection, privacy, consent, and transparency	Requires explainability for automated decisions; mandates data minimization and protection

Regulation/Standard	*Key Focus*	*Applicability to AI*
CCPA (California Consumer Privacy Act, USA)	Consumer data privacy rights and data access requests	Requires transparency about data collection and gives consumers control over personal data used in AI models
AI Act (Proposed, EU)	Classification of AI systems by risk levels; documentation and human oversight requirements	Mandates registration and monitoring of high-risk AI systems; includes strict documentation standards
HIPAA (Health Insurance Portability and Accountability Act, USA)	Protection of health-related data	Requires secure handling of PHI (Protected Health Information) used in AI healthcare models
FCRA (Fair Credit Reporting Act, USA)	Fairness in credit decisions and lending	Requires AI systems to make credit decisions to be explainable, auditable, and free from discrimination

9.4.3 Cloud Provider Compliance Certifications

All major cloud providers offer compliance assurances and certifications relevant to AI workloads:

Provider	*Key Certifications Relevant to AI*
AWS	GDPR, HIPAA, SOC 1/2/3, ISO/IEC 27001, PCI DSS, FedRAMP
Google Cloud	GDPR, HIPAA, SOC 1/2/3, ISO/IEC 27001, PCI DSS, CCPA compliance tooling
Azure	GDPR, HIPAA, ISO/IEC 27001, PCI DSS, FedRAMP High, EU Cloud Code of Conduct

These certifications ensure that infrastructure components meet security and compliance standards; however, responsibility for AI model compliance, including data handling, fairness, and explainability, lies with the organization building the model.

9.4.4 Prominent AI Ethics Frameworks

Framework/Organization	*Core Principles*
OECD AI Principles	Inclusive growth, human-centered values, transparency, robustness, and accountability
IEEE 7000™ Standards	Embedding ethical values in system design and AI development processes
World Economic Forum AI Ethics Guidelines	Fairness, inclusiveness, interpretability, safety, and accountability
European Commission Ethics Guidelines for Trustworthy AI	Human agency and oversight, privacy and data governance, technical robustness, and non-discrimination
NIST AI Risk Management Framework (USA)	Governable, reliable, secure, explainable, and privacy-enhanced AI practices

9.4.5 Key Components of an AI Compliance and Ethics Program

1. **Data Governance Policies**:
   - Define data collection, storage, consent management, and deletion practices in compliance with regulations.
   - Regular audits of datasets to ensure proper anonymization and security controls.
2. **Model Documentation and Registration**:
   - Maintain thorough model cards documenting use cases, training data, algorithms, metrics, known risks, and mitigations.
   - Register high-risk AI models with relevant authorities (required under the proposed EU AI Act).
3. **Fairness and Bias Auditing**:
   - Conduct periodic bias audits using cloud-based tools (AWS SageMaker Clarify, Google Vertex Explainability, Azure Responsible AI Toolbox).
   - Document bias mitigation steps and publish fairness metrics for public-facing models.
4. **Explainability Enforcement**:
   - Implement explainability solutions and ensure that end-users have access to understandable model explanations where required by law.

5. **Continuous Monitoring**:
   - Set up model drift detection, anomaly monitoring, and security audits to ensure AI models remain compliant after deployment.
6. **Governance Structures**:
   - Establish responsible AI Committees to oversee ethical review processes.
   - Include legal counsel, data scientists, compliance officers, and business stakeholders in decision-making loops.
7. **Escalation and Incident Response Plans**:
   - Develop clear procedures for pausing or disabling AI models in case of ethical breaches or regulatory violations.

9.4.6 The Role of Cloud Providers in Supporting Compliance

- **Prebuilt Compliance Templates**:
  - Cloud providers offer templates for GDPR, HIPAA, and CCPA compliance reporting.
- **Integrated Auditing Tools**:
  - AWS CloudTrail for audit logging
  - Google Cloud Audit Logs for tracking actions on AI services
  - Azure Monitor for end-to-end telemetry and compliance alerts
- **Access Control and Encryption Management**:
  - Cloud-native tools for key management (AWS KMS, Azure Key Vault, Google Cloud KMS) and IAM policy enforcement.
- **Shared Responsibility Model**:
  - Cloud providers secure the infrastructure; users must ensure their data, models, and configurations meet regulatory requirements.

9.4.7 Best Practices for AI Compliance and Ethics in the Cloud

Best Practice	*Benefit*
Maintain up-to-date data processing agreements (DPAs)	Ensures all cloud providers are contractually bound to protect data in line with regulations
Use geo-fencing and regional deployments for sensitive data	Meets data residency and sovereignty requirements
Implement role-based access and strict privilege controls	Prevents unauthorized data access and model tampering

Best Practice	*Benefit*
Integrate automated compliance checks in CI/CD pipelines	Reduces human error and maintains ongoing compliance in model development
Keep documentation audit-ready and versioned	Simplifies external audits and regulatory reporting
Collaborate with legal and compliance teams from project inception	Reduces risk of non-compliance and aligns technical efforts with legal frameworks

As AI systems become more powerful and pervasive, regulatory compliance and ethical accountability must be integrated into every stage of AI development and deployment, particularly in cloud environments where scale magnifies both risks and impacts.

Organizations that embrace proactive compliance measures, align with global ethics frameworks, and invest in continuous governance will not only meet legal obligations but also build trust with stakeholders and end-users. Responsible AI governance is not a one-time effort but an ongoing commitment that must evolve with technological advancements and societal expectations.

In the next chapter, we will look ahead to future trends shaping cloud-based AI infrastructure and ethical AI development.

Bibliography

Abràmoff, M. D., Tobey, D., & Char, D. S. (2020). Lessons learned about autonomous AI: Finding a safe, efficacious, and ethical path through the development process. *American Journal of Ophthalmology, 214*, 134–142. https://doi.org/10.1016/j.ajo.2020.05.011

Acosta, J. N., Falcone, G. J., Rajpurkar, P., Topol, E. J., & Moon, K. R. (2022). Multimodal biomedical AI. *Nature Medicine, 28*(9), 1773–1784. https://doi.org/10.1038/s41591-022-01981-2

Adnan, H. S., Shidani, A., Clifton, L., Bankhead, C. R., & Perera-Salazar, R. (2025). A multi-site study of clinician perspectives in the lifecycle of an AI-enabled clinical decision support system. *iScience, 28*(5), 112406. https://doi.org/10.1016/j.isci.2025.112406

Adnan, H. S., Shidani, A., Clifton, L., Bankhead, C. R., & Perera-Salazar, R. (2025). Implementation framework for AI deployment at scale in healthcare systems. *iScience, 28*(5), 112406. https://doi.org/10.1016/j.isci.2025.112406

Chow, J. C. L. (2024). Quantum computing in medicine. *Medical Sciences (Basel), 12*(4), 67. https://doi.org/10.3390/medsci12040067

Dastin, J., & Zhang, Y. (2024). Confronting and alleviating AI resistance in the workplace. *Journal of Organizational Behavior, 45*(6), 1234–1256. https://doi.org/10.1016/j.joib.2024.04.001

De Vos, M., Kirrane, S., Padget, J., & Satoh, K. (2022). Governance of autonomous agents on the web: Challenges and opportunities. In *Proceedings of the 21st International Semantic Web Conference (ISWC 2022)* (pp. 1–18). https://doi.org/10.1145/3507910

Dhade, P., & Shirke, P. (2023). Federated learning for healthcare: A comprehensive review. *Engineering Proceedings, 59*(1), 230. https://doi.org/10.3390/engproc2023059230

Elendu, C., Amaechi, D. C., Okatta, A. U., Amaechi, E. C., Elendu, T. C., Ezeh, C. P., & Elendu, I. D. (2024). The impact of simulation-based training in medical education: A review. *Medicine (Baltimore), 103*(27), e38813. https://doi.org/10.1097/MD.0000000000038813

Evans, R. S. (2016). Electronic health records: Then, now, and in the future. *Yearbook of Medical Informatics, Suppl 1*, S48–S61. https://doi.org/10.15265/IYS-2016-s006

Gazquez-Garcia, J., Salazar, R. P., & Almeria, D. S. (2025). AI in the health sector: Systematic review of key skills for future health professionals. *JMIR Medical Education, 11*, e58161. https://doi.org/10.2196/58161

Hsu, J. C., Wu, M., Kim, C., Vora, B., Lien, Y. T. K., Jindal, A., Yoshida, K., Kawakatsu, S., Gore, J., Jin, J. Y., Lu, C., Chen, B., & Wu, B. (2024). Applications of advanced natural language processing for clinical pharmacology. *Clinical Pharmacology & Therapeutics, 115*(4), 786–794. https://doi.org/10.1002/cpt.3161

Khanam, M., Akther, S., Mizan, I., Islam, F., Chowdhury, S., Ahsan, N. M., Barua, D., & Hasan, S. K. (2024). The potential of artificial intelligence in unveiling healthcare's future. *Cureus, 16*(10), e71625. https://doi.org/10.7759/cureus.71625

Kocyigit, D., Öz, K., Yılmaz, M. A., & Pütün, A. E. (2021). Lessons learned from the COVID-19 pandemic: Emphasizing the emerging role and perspectives from artificial intelligence, mobile health, and digital laboratory medicine. *EJIFCC, 32*(2), 224. https://www.ncbi.nlm.nih.gov/pmc/articles/PMC8343043/

Liu, Y., Wright Clayton, E., Lovett Novak, L., Anders, S., & Malin, B. (2024). Evaluating artificial intelligence in clinical settings—Let us not reinvent the wheel. *Journal of Medical Internet Research, 26*(1), e46407. https://doi.org/10.2196/46407

Magrabi, F., Lyell, D., & Coiera, E. (2023). Automation in contemporary clinical information systems: A survey of AI in healthcare settings. *Yearbook of Medical Informatics, 32*(1), 115–126. https://doi.org/10.1055/s-0043-1768733

Misra, R., Keane, P. A., & Hogg, H. D. J. (2024). How should we train clinicians for artificial intelligence in healthcare? *Future Healthcare Journal, 11*(3), 100162. https://doi.org/10.1016/j.fhj.2024.100162

Mittermaier, M., Raza, M. M., & Kvedar, J. C. (2023). Bias in AI-based models for medical applications: Challenges and mitigation strategies. *npj Digital Medicine, 6*, Article 113. https://doi.org/10.1038/s41746-023-00858-z

Panayides, A. S., Amini, A., Filipovic, N. D., Sharma, A., Tsaftaris, S. A., Young, A., Foran, D., Do, N., Golemati, S., Kurc, T., Huang, K., Nikita, K. S., Veasey, B. P., Zervakis, M., Saltz, J. H., & Pattichis, C. S. (2020). AI in medical imaging informatics: Current challenges and future directions. *IEEE Journal of Biomedical and Health Informatics, 24*(7), 1837–1857. https://doi.org/10.1109/JBHI.2020.2991043

Steel, P. A. D., Wardi, G., Harrington, R. A., & Longhurst, C. A. (2025). Learning health system strategies in the AI era. *npj Health Systems, 2*, 21. https://doi.org/10.1038/s44401-025-00029-0

Sullivan, D., & Williams, T. (2023). Examining labelling guidelines for AI-based software as a medical device in dermatology. *Australasian Journal of Dermatology, 64*(2), 142–146. https://doi.org/10.1111/ajd.14269

Chapter 10

Scalable Data Processing Connections for Artificial Intelligence

The proliferation of artificial intelligence across diverse sectors has led to an unprecedented surge in the volume and velocity of data. This exponential growth necessitates sophisticated and scalable data processing pipelines to effectively support the lifecycle of AI models, from initial training to ongoing deployment and maintenance.[1]

The ability of these pipelines to handle vast datasets and complex computations hinges on the establishment of robust connections between their various stages. Seamless data flow and efficient processing are paramount for realizing the full potential of AI applications, enabling timely insights, automated decision-making, and continuous model improvement.[2]

Without these scalable data processing capabilities and the intricate connections that bind them, the advancements in AI risk being constrained by the limitations of traditional data management approaches.[3]

10.1 Designing Scalable Data Ingestion Pipelines

The foundation of any scalable data processing pipeline for AI lies in its data ingestion mechanisms. These mechanisms are responsible for collecting data from a multitude of sources, transforming it into a usable format, and making it available for subsequent processing and model training.[4] The choice of

DOI: 10.4324/9781003685609-10

algorithms and coding approaches for data ingestion is critical for handling the variety, velocity, and volume of data encountered in AI workloads.

10.1.1 Common Algorithms for Data Ingestion in AI

1. **Batch Ingestion Algorithms**:
   Batch ingestion involves the periodic collection and loading of data into the processing pipeline. This approach is well-suited for scenarios where data updates are not required in real-time and large volumes of historical data need to be processed. Common algorithms employed in batch ingestion include simple file reading operations, which can handle structured formats like CSV or JSON, and database connectors such as JDBC (Java Database Connectivity) and ODBC (Open Database Connectivity), which facilitate the extraction of data from relational databases. Furthermore, bulk loading tools provided by database management systems and cloud storage services can efficiently ingest large datasets into target storage locations. For instance, Snowflake's COPY INTO command is designed for high-speed bulk loading of data. The selection of a specific batch ingestion algorithm depends largely on the nature of the data source and the desired destination within the AI pipeline.[5,6]
2. **Real-Time/Streaming Ingestion Algorithms**:
   In contrast to batch processing, real-time or streaming ingestion focuses on continuously capturing and processing data as it is generated.[7] This method is crucial for AI applications that demand immediate insights or actions based on the most current information, such as fraud detection systems or real-time recommendation engines.[8]

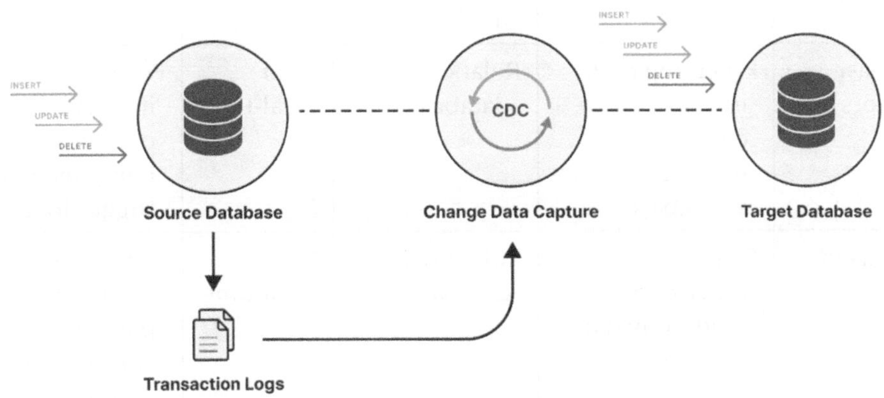

Figure 10.1 Change Data Capture (CDC) Flow Between Source and Target Databases

Table 10.1 Common Data Ingestion Algorithms

Algorithm Name	*Description*	*Typical Data Sources*	*Batch/ Real-Time Suitability*	*Key Considerations*
File reading	Reading data from files (e.g., CSV, JSON)	File systems, object storage	Batch	Handling different file formats, parsing complexity
Database connectors	Connecting to and querying relational databases (e.g., JDBC, ODBC)	Relational databases	Batch	Connection management, SQL query optimization
Bulk loading tools	Efficiently loading large datasets into storage systems	Databases, data warehouses, cloud storage	Batch	Format compatibility, performance tuning
Message queues (e.g., Kafka)	Publishing and subscribing to continuous streams of data	Application logs, sensor data, social media feeds	Real-time	Throughput, latency, fault tolerance, message ordering
Stream processing frameworks (e.g., Flink)	Processing and transforming data in motion	Message queues, event streams	Real-time	Complex event processing, state management, windowing
Polling	Periodically querying source systems for changes	Databases, applications with limited change tracking	Batch/ near real-time	Frequency of polling, the potential for missed chances
Database triggers	Executing code in response to data modifications in a database	Relational databases	Near real-time	Performance impact on database, complexity of trigger logic
Log-based CDC	Reading transaction logs to identify data changes	Relational databases	Near real-time	Access to transaction logs, parsing complexity, minimal impact on source system

Algorithms for handling continuous data streams often involve the use of message queuing systems like Apache Kafka, Amazon Kinesis, and Google Cloud Pub/Sub. These platforms provide mechanisms for publishing and subscribing to streams of data, ensuring fault tolerance and scalability. Stream processing frameworks such as Apache Flink and Spark Streaming offer advanced capabilities for processing and transforming data in motion, enabling complex event processing and real-time analytics. These frameworks often utilize algorithms like online gradient descent for model updates with each incoming data point and incremental clustering for dynamic data streams. The choice between different streaming ingestion algorithms and platforms depends on factors such as throughput requirements, latency sensitivity, and the complexity of the required real-time processing.[9,10,11]

3. **Change Data Capture (CDC) Techniques**:
Change Data Capture (CDC) is a set of techniques used to efficiently track and propagate changes made to data in source systems to downstream data pipelines. Instead of performing full data loads, CDC algorithms identify and extract only the modifications, such as inserts, updates, and deletes, thereby minimizing the overhead of data ingestion and improving scalability (Table 10.1). Common CDC approaches include polling, where the source system is periodically queried for changes; using database triggers, which fire when specific data modifications occur; and log-based CDC, which involves reading the transaction logs of the database to identify changes. Log-based CDC is often preferred for its minimal impact on the source system's performance. Implementing CDC requires careful consideration of the source system's capabilities and the desired level of data consistency in the AI pipeline (Figure 10.1).[12,13]

10.1.2 Coding Implementations for Data Ingestion

Using Cloud-Native Services:

Cloud providers offer a suite of managed services that simplify the implementation of scalable data ingestion pipelines for AI.

- **AWS**: Amazon Web Services provides several options, including Kinesis Data Streams for real-time data streaming. Developers can use the put_record API in the AWS SDK for Python (Boto3) to send data to a Kinesis stream.[14] For instance, the following Python snippet demonstrates how to put a record into a Kinesis stream:

```
Python
import boto3
import json
from datetime import datetime
kinesis_client = boto3.client('kinesis',
region_name='your-region')
stream_name = 'your-stream-name'
partition_key = 'your-partition-key'
payload = {'timestamp': datetime.utcnow().isoformat(),
'data': 'your-data'}

response = kinesis_client.put_record(
StreamName=stream_name,
Data=json.dumps(payload),
PartitionKey=partition_key
)
print(response)
```

Consumers can process data from Kinesis streams using the Kinesis Client Library (KCL) or by using AWS Lambda functions triggered by new records in the stream.[15] Kinesis Data Firehose is another AWS service designed for loading streaming data into data lakes like S3 and data warehouses like Redshift. AWS Glue offers a serverless ETL service that can connect to various data sources and perform data transformations using Spark.

- **Azure**: Microsoft Azure provides Azure Event Hubs for scalable event ingestion, capable of handling millions of events per second. The Azure SDK for Python allows developers to send and receive events from Event Hubs. Azure Data Factory is a cloud-based ETL and data integration service that enables the creation of complex data pipelines connecting to a wide range of data sources.[16] It can orchestrate data movement and transformation activities, including the use of Azure Databricks for high-performance processing.
- **GCP**: Google Cloud Platform offers Pub/Sub for asynchronous messaging and event streaming, allowing for reliable and scalable data ingestion. The Google Cloud Client Library for Python provides APIs to publish and subscribe to messages. GCP Dataflow is a fully managed service for executing Apache Beam pipelines, supporting

both batch and stream data processing. The following Python code illustrates a simple Dataflow pipeline reading from Google Cloud Storage:

```
Python
import apache_beam as beam
from apache_beam.options.pipeline_options import
  PipelineOptions

options = PipelineOptions()
with beam.Pipeline(options=options) as pipeline:
    lines = pipeline | 'Read' >> beam.io.ReadFromText('gs:
    //your-bucket/input.txt')
    # Add data transformation steps here
    output = lines | 'Write' >> beam.io.WriteToText('gs://
    your-bucket/output.txt')
```

These cloud-native services abstract away the complexities of infrastructure management, allowing developers to focus on the logic of their data ingestion pipelines.

10.1.3 Implementing with Data Integration Tools

Data integration tools provide higher-level abstractions and often visual interfaces for building data ingestion pipelines.

- **Apache NiFi**: Apache NiFi is an open-source data flow management system that provides a visual canvas for designing and managing data pipelines. It offers a wide array of processors for connecting to various data sources, such as GetFile for reading from local or network file systems, ListenHTTP for receiving data via HTTP, and QueryDatabaseTable for extracting data from databases. NiFi's flow-based approach allows for dynamic modification of pipelines and provides features like data buffering and back pressure to ensure reliable data flow.[17,18]
- **Apache Kafka**: While also a cloud-native service through providers like Confluent Cloud, Apache Kafka can be deployed and managed independently as a distributed streaming platform.[19] Its producer and consumer APIs in languages like Python enable developers to build custom data ingestion and processing applications. For example, a Python producer using the kafka-python library might look like this:

```
Python
from kafka import KafkaProducer
import json
from datetime import datetime

producer = KafkaProducer(
  bootstrap_servers='your-kafka-brokers',
  value_serializer=lambda x: json.dumps(x).encode('utf-8')
)
payload = {'timestamp': datetime.utcnow().isoformat(),
'data': 'your-data'}
producer.send('your-topic', value=payload)
producer.flush()
```

Data integration tools offer flexibility and can simplify the development of complex ingestion workflows, especially when dealing with heterogeneous data sources and formats.

10.1.4 Code Examples in Python for Different Data Sources and Formats

To illustrate practical coding approaches, consider the following Python examples for ingesting data from common sources and in various formats.

- **Reading a CSV File**:

```
Python
import pandas as pd

csv_file_path = 'data.csv'
df = pd.read_csv(csv_file_path)
print(df.head())
```

- **Reading a JSON File**:

```
Python
import json

json_file_path = 'data.json'
with open(json_file_path, 'r') as f:
  data = json.load(f)
print(data)
```

- **Connecting to a PostgreSQL Database**:

```
Python
import psycopg2

conn = psycopg2.connect(
  host="your-host",
  database="your-database",
  user="your-user",
  password="your-password"
)
cur = conn.cursor()
cur.execute("SELECT * FROM your_table LIMIT 5;")
rows = cur.fetchall()
for row in rows:
  print(row)
cur.close()
conn.close()
```

- **Fetching Data from a REST API**:

```
Python
import requests

api_url = 'https://api.example.com/data'
response = requests.get(api_url)
if response.status_code == 200:
  data = response.json()
  print(data)
else:
  print(f"Error: {response.status_code}")
```

These examples demonstrate basic coding patterns for connecting to different data sources and handling common data formats in Python, which is widely used in AI and data science workflows.

10.2 Configuring Cloud Services for High-Performance Data Processing

Once data has been ingested into the pipeline, the next critical step is to process it efficiently to prepare it for AI model training and inference. Cloud providers offer various services designed for high-performance data processing, each with its own algorithms and coding considerations (Table 10.2).

Table 10.2 Comparison of High-Performance Data Processing Services

Cloud Provider	*Service Name*	*Underlying Technology*	*Key Features*	*Typical Use Cases*	*Primary Programming Languages*
AWS	AWS Glue	Apache Spark	Serverless ETL, managed infrastructure, data catalog	ETL pipelines, data integration, serverless data processing	PySpark
AWS	Amazon EMR	Hadoop, Spark, Flink	Customizable clusters, broad framework support, fine-grained control	Big data processing, machine learning, data analytics	Java, Scala, Python, R
Azure	Azure Data Factory	Spark (via Databricks)	Orchestration, mapping data flows, integration with Databricks	ETL/ELT pipelines, data integration, workflow automation	JSON, Python (via Databricks)
Azure	Azure Databricks	Apache Spark	Collaborative workspace, notebooks, optimized Spark execution, Delta Lake	Data engineering, data science, machine learning, real-time analytics	Python, Scala, R, SQL
GCP	GCP Dataflow	Apache Beam	Managed service, unified batch and stream processing, portability	ETL/ELT pipelines, real-time analytics, data integration	Python, Java, Go
GCP	GCP Dataproc	Hadoop, Spark, Flink	Managed clusters, easy integration with other GCP services, cost-effective	Big data processing, data warehousing, machine learning, log analytics	Java, Scala, Python

10.2.1 Leveraging AWS for High-Performance Processing

- **Algorithms and Coding for Services like AWS Glue and EMR**: AWS provides robust services for high-performance data processing. AWS Glue is a serverless ETL service built on Apache Spark. It allows data engineers to define ETL jobs using PySpark, a Python API for Spark. Glue handles the provisioning and management of the underlying Spark infrastructure, enabling users to focus on writing the data transformation logic. For example, a simple PySpark script in Glue might involve reading data from S3, performing some transformations, and writing the results back to S3. The algorithms at the core of Glue's processing are the distributed computing algorithms provided by Spark, such as map, reduce, filter, and join operations, optimized for parallel execution across a cluster of nodes.

  Amazon Elastic MapReduce (EMR) offers a more direct approach by allowing users to provision and configure their own Hadoop and Spark clusters. This provides greater control over the cluster configuration and the ability to customize the environment for specific workload requirements. Data processing jobs, written in Spark, Hadoop MapReduce, or other supported frameworks, can be submitted to the EMR cluster using the AWS SDK or CLI.

  For instance, to submit a Spark job using the AWS CLI, one might use a command like:

```
Bash
aws emr add-steps --cluster-id j-XXXXXXXXXXXXXX --steps
Type=SPARK,Name="My Spark Job",ActionOnFailure=CONTINUE,Args=
```

  The choice between Glue and EMR often depends on the level of control and customization needed versus the desire for a fully managed, serverless experience.

10.2.2 Utilizing Azure for High-Performance Processing

- **Algorithms and Coding for Services like Azure Data Factory and Databricks**:
  Azure's high-performance processing capabilities are significantly driven by Azure Databricks, which is a collaborative, Apache Spark-based analytics service. Azure Databricks provides an interactive workspace

where data engineers and data scientists can write and execute Spark code in Python (PySpark), Scala, R, and SQL.

Databricks notebooks are a common way to develop and run data processing and machine learning workloads. The underlying algorithms are again those of Apache Spark, enabling distributed processing of large datasets. Azure Data Factory can orchestrate Databricks notebooks as part of a broader data pipeline. Data Factory's mapping data flows also offer a visual, code-free way to perform data transformations, which are then translated into Spark jobs executed on an Azure Databricks cluster behind the scenes.

Azure Databricks Auto Loader simplifies the process of incrementally loading new data from cloud storage into Delta Lake, providing Python and Scala APIs for configuration.

10.2.3 Implementing High-Performance Processing on GCP

- **Algorithms and Coding for Services like GCP Dataflow and Dataproc**:

Google Cloud Platform offers GCP Dataflow, a fully managed service for executing Apache Beam pipelines. Apache Beam is an open-source, unified programming model that allows developers to write batch and stream data processing jobs that can run on various execution engines, including Dataflow, Spark, and Flink. Dataflow pipelines are typically written in Python, Java, or Go.

The service automatically handles the scaling and management of the processing infrastructure. GCP Dataproc provides a managed Hadoop and Spark service, allowing users to create and manage clusters for large-scale data processing. Similar to AWS EMR, users can submit Spark and Hadoop jobs using gcloud commands or the Python client library.

For example, to submit a Spark job on Dataproc using gcloud, one might use:

```
Bash
gcloud dataproc jobs submit spark --cluster=your-cluster --
jar=gs://your-bucket/your-spark-app.jar -- --input=gs://
your-bucket/input --output=gs://your-bucket/output
```

The choice between Dataflow and Dataproc often depends on the desired level of abstraction and management. Dataflow offers a more managed, serverless experience with the flexibility of the Apache Beam programming model, while Dataproc provides more control over the underlying cluster.

10.3 Strategies for Handling Large Datasets in AI Workloads

AI workloads often involve processing extremely large datasets, requiring specialized strategies for efficient handling. Distributed data processing, data partitioning, and optimized storage and retrieval are key techniques in this context.

- **Algorithms for Distributed Data Processing**:
  Distributed data processing is fundamental to handling large datasets in AI. MapReduce is a foundational algorithm that involves dividing a large dataset into independent parts that can be processed in parallel (Map phase), followed by combining the results (Reduce phase). Hadoop MapReduce is a popular framework implementing this paradigm. However, for many AI workloads, Apache Spark has become the preferred framework due to its in-memory processing capabilities and support for a wider range of operations beyond simple Map and Reduce.

  Spark operates on Resilient Distributed Datasets (RDDs) or higher-level abstractions like DataFrames, which are distributed collections of data that can be processed in parallel across a cluster of nodes. Common Spark transformations (e.g., map, filter, groupBy, join) and actions (e.g., count, collect, save) are implemented using sophisticated algorithms that optimize data partitioning and task scheduling to maximize parallelism and minimize data shuffling across the network.
- **Coding for Data Partitioning and Sharding**:
  Data partitioning involves dividing a dataset into smaller, more manageable units based on certain criteria. In Spark, data can be partitioned based on a range of values in a specific column or using a hash function applied to a column.

  Effective partitioning can significantly improve query performance by ensuring that data needed for a particular operation is co-located on the same processing node. For example, in PySpark, one can repartition a DataFrame based on a column:

```
Python
df_repartitioned = df.repartition(5, 'column_name')
```

Data sharding is a similar concept used in distributed databases and storage systems, where data is split across multiple machines to improve scalability and availability.[20] The sharding strategy, such as range-based or hash-based sharding, determines how data is distributed. Implementing sharding often involves configuring the database or storage system to automatically handle the distribution and retrieval of data across shards.

- **Strategies for Efficient Data Storage and Retrieval**:
  For storing the massive amounts of data used in AI, data lakes have become a common solution.[21] Data lakes like AWS S3, Azure Data Lake Storage, and GCP Cloud Storage are highly scalable and cost-effective storage repositories that can hold vast quantities of raw and processed data in various formats.

  To optimize data retrieval and analytical processing, columnar storage formats like Apache Parquet and Optimized Row Columnar (ORC) are often preferred over row-based formats like CSV. Columnar formats store data values from each column together, which can significantly improve query performance for analytical workloads that typically involve reading only a subset of columns.

  For instance, when using Parquet with Spark, data can be read and processed much faster for analytical tasks. Indexing is another crucial technique for accelerating data retrieval in large databases. Creating indexes on frequently queried columns allows the database to quickly locate specific data without having to scan the entire table. The choice of indexing strategy depends on the query patterns and the characteristics of the data.

10.4 Ensuring Data Quality and Governance in Scalable AI Pipelines

Maintaining high data quality and adhering to data governance policies are essential for building trustworthy and reliable AI applications. Scalable AI pipelines must incorporate mechanisms to ensure data accuracy, consistency, and compliance.

- **Algorithms for Data Quality Checks and Validation**: Algorithms for data quality checks and validation play a crucial role in identifying and mitigating data issues. Detecting missing values can involve simple checks for null or empty fields. Outlier detection algorithms, such as those based on statistical methods (e.g., z-score, IQR) or machine learning techniques (e.g., isolation forest), can help identify anomalous data points.

  Algorithms for detecting inconsistencies might involve cross-referencing data across different sources or applying business rules to identify violations. Data validation techniques often rely on schema enforcement, ensuring that the data conforms to a predefined structure and data types. Custom validation rules can also be implemented to check for specific conditions or constraints relevant to the application.
- **Coding Examples for Implementing Data Quality Measures**: Python libraries like Pandas and Spark provide powerful tools for implementing data quality checks.

  For example, to check for missing values in a Pandas DataFrame:

```
Python
import pandas as pd

df = pd.read_csv('data.csv')
missing_values = df.isnull().sum()
print("Missing values per column:\n", missing_values)
```

To identify duplicate rows:

```
Python
duplicates = df.duplicated().sum()
print("Number of duplicate rows:", duplicates)
```

In Spark, schema validation can be enforced when reading data:

```
Python
from pyspark.sql.types import StructType, StructField,
StringType, IntegerType

schema = StructType()

df = spark.read.csv("data.csv", schema=schema, header=True)
```

These coding examples illustrate how basic data quality checks and schema validation can be implemented within a data pipeline.

- **Implementing Data Governance Policies through Code**: Implementing data governance policies often involves a combination of technical and organizational measures. Code can play a significant role in enforcing data access controls and auditing data lineage. For instance, access controls can be implemented at the storage and processing layers, ensuring that only authorized users or services can access specific datasets or perform certain operations.

  Data lineage, which tracks the origin and transformations of data, can be maintained through metadata management tools and can be programmatically queried to understand the data's journey through the pipeline. Techniques for data masking and anonymization, which are crucial for complying with privacy regulations like GDPR or HIPAA, can also be implemented through code.

  For example, sensitive data fields can be replaced with placeholder values or transformed using anonymization algorithms.

10.4.1 Integrating Different Cloud Services for Scalable AI Pipelines

In some scenarios, organizations may choose to leverage services from multiple cloud providers or integrate on-premises systems with the cloud to build their AI pipelines. This hybrid or multi-cloud approach can offer benefits such as access to specialized services, cost optimization, or redundancy.

- **Architecting Hybrid and Multi-Cloud Data Processing Pipelines**: Building hybrid and multi-cloud data processing pipelines requires careful architectural planning. Common patterns include using one cloud provider for data storage and another for computing or integrating on-premises data sources with cloud-based AI services. Challenges in such architectures include ensuring secure and efficient data transfer between different environments, managing data consistency, and handling network latency. Solutions often involve using secure protocols for data transfer, implementing robust monitoring across environments, and choosing appropriate data synchronization strategies.
- **Coding for Inter-Service Communication and Data Transfer**: Inter-service communication and data transfer in multi-cloud environments typically involve using APIs and SDKs provided by the respective cloud vendors. For example, to transfer data from AWS S3 to Azure Databricks, one might use the AWS SDK for Python in an Azure

Databricks notebook to read data from S3 and then use Spark's capabilities to write it to Azure Blob Storage or Azure Data Lake Storage. Messaging queues and event buses, such as AWS SQS, Azure Service Bus, or GCP Pub/Sub, can facilitate asynchronous communication between services running on different clouds, enabling decoupled and resilient architectures.

- **Case Studies of Integrated Cloud Pipelines**:
  Organizations across various industries have adopted integrated cloud pipelines for their AI applications. For instance, a company might use AWS for its mature machine learning services while leveraging Azure for its enterprise data warehousing capabilities, transferring data between the two platforms as needed. Another example could involve a financial institution using on-premises data lakes for sensitive data and GCP for running large-scale analytics and AI model training, with secure data pipelines connecting the on-premises and cloud environments. These case studies highlight the feasibility and benefits of integrating different cloud services to build scalable and powerful AI pipelines.

10.4.2 Monitoring and Maintaining the Performance and Reliability of Scalable Data Processing Pipelines in AI

Continuous monitoring and proactive maintenance are crucial for ensuring the performance and reliability of scalable data processing pipelines that support AI workloads.

- **Algorithms and Techniques for Performance Monitoring**:
  Performance monitoring involves tracking key performance indicators (KPIs) such as throughput (the amount of data processed per unit of time), latency (the delay in processing data), and error rate (the frequency of failures). Cloud providers offer comprehensive monitoring tools like AWS CloudWatch, Azure Monitor, and GCP Cloud Monitoring, which allow users to collect and visualize these metrics. These tools often provide features for setting up dashboards, creating alerts based on predefined thresholds, and drilling down into logs and traces to identify performance bottlenecks or errors.
- **Coding for Logging, Alerting, and Error Handling**:
  Implementing robust logging is essential for debugging and monitoring data pipelines. Libraries like Python's logging module allow developers to record events and errors that occur during pipeline execution.

Alerting mechanisms can be set up using cloud monitoring services or third-party tools to notify operators when critical errors occur or when performance metrics deviate from expected values. Error handling strategies, such as implementing retry logic for transient failures or setting up dead-letter queues for processing failed messages, are crucial for ensuring the resilience of the pipeline.

- **Strategies for Ensuring Pipeline Reliability and Scalability**:
  Strategies for ensuring pipeline reliability and scalability include adopting infrastructure-as-code (IaC) practices, using tools like Terraform or AWS CloudFormation to provision and manage infrastructure consistently and reproducibly. Automated deployments and continuous integration/continuous delivery (CI/CD) pipelines help in quickly and reliably deploying updates and scaling the pipeline as needed. Designing for fault tolerance and redundancy, by distributing components across multiple availability zones or regions and implementing automatic failover mechanisms, is critical for maintaining high availability.

10.4.3 Data Serialization and Storage Formats in Scalable AI Data Processing

The choice of data serialization and storage formats significantly impacts the performance, efficiency, and interoperability of scalable AI data processing pipelines.

- **Common Data Serialization Formats**:
  Several common data serialization formats are used in data pipelines. JavaScript Object Notation (JSON) is a human-readable, lightweight format widely used for data exchange, especially in web applications. Avro is a binary format that provides schema evolution capabilities, allowing the schema of data to change over time without breaking compatibility.

  It is often used in Hadoop and Kafka ecosystems for its efficient storage and transmission. Parquet is a columnar storage format optimized for analytical queries. Storing data column-wise allows for efficient reading of only the necessary columns, which can significantly improve query performance for analytical workloads.
- **Coding Considerations for Reading and Writing Different Formats**:
  Python provides libraries for working with these formats. The json library is used for encoding and decoding JSON data. The Avro library

(specifically fastavro for better performance) allows reading and writing Avro files, requiring a schema definition. The pyarrow library provides functionalities for reading and writing Parquet files, as well as for schema manipulation. When using Avro, schema management is crucial to ensure compatibility between different stages of the pipeline as the data structure evolves.

- **Impact of Format Choice on Performance and Scalability**: The choice of data serialization and storage format can have a profound impact on the performance and scalability of the pipeline. Binary formats like Avro are generally more efficient in terms of storage size and transmission speed compared to text-based formats like JSON. Columnar formats like Parquet excel in analytical workloads by reducing I/O operations and improving query performance. The selection of the appropriate format depends on the specific needs of each stage in the pipeline, considering factors like data volume, processing requirements, and the types of operations performed on the data.

10.5 Conclusion: Best Practices for Implementing Scalable Data Processing Connections for AI

Implementing scalable data processing connections for AI requires a holistic approach that considers the entire data lifecycle, from ingestion to storage and ongoing maintenance. Choosing the right algorithms, tools, and cloud services tailored to specific requirements is paramount. For data ingestion, the selection between batch, real-time, and CDC techniques should be driven by the data's velocity and the application's latency needs.

High-performance processing can be achieved by leveraging managed cloud services like AWS Glue, Azure Databricks, and GCP Dataflow, or by configuring and managing compute clusters with services like AWS EMR, Azure HDInsight, and GCP Dataproc. Handling large datasets necessitates the use of distributed processing frameworks like Spark and strategies for efficient data partitioning and storage formats such as Parquet.

Ensuring data quality and governance involves implementing validation checks, enforcing policies through code, and maintaining data lineage. When integrating different cloud services, careful architectural planning and the use of appropriate communication and data transfer mechanisms are essential. Continuous monitoring, robust logging, and proactive error handling are crucial for maintaining the performance and reliability of these complex pipelines. Finally, the choice of data serialization format should be guided by considerations of efficiency, compatibility, and the specific processing requirements at each stage. By adhering to these best practices, organizations can build scalable and reliable data processing pipelines that effectively support their AI initiatives.

Notes

1. The AI model lifecycle generally includes data collection, labeling, feature engineering, model training, evaluation, deployment, monitoring, and periodic retraining as new data becomes available.
2. Many "real-time" AI systems in production operate in near real time (seconds to minutes), which is often sufficient for decision support while keeping the architecture manageable.
3. Traditional data management in this context refers to monolithic databases, nightly batch ETL jobs, and manual integration scripts that struggle to scale with modern AI data volume, variety, and velocity.
4. Data ingestion encompasses initial bulk loads, incremental updates, and continuous streaming feeds from operational systems, IoT devices, logs, and external APIs.
5. Snowflake's COPY INTO command is a bulk loading mechanism that ingests data from cloud storage (e.g., S3, Azure Blob, GCS) into internal tables with parallel loading and automatic parsing.
6. Comparable bulk loading utilities exist in other platforms, such as Amazon Redshift COPY, BigQuery load jobs, and Azure Synapse COPY INTO, each with specific performance tuning and format requirements.
7. Real-time or streaming ingestion typically targets end-to-end latencies of milliseconds to a few seconds, depending on service-level objectives and application needs.
8. Common real-time AI use cases include fraud detection, anomaly detection on sensor streams, clickstream analytics, and online recommendation engines.
9. Systems like Apache Kafka, Amazon Kinesis, and Google Cloud Pub/Sub implement a distributed log abstraction where ordered records are partitioned across brokers for scalability and fault tolerance.
10. Stream processing frameworks (e.g., Apache Flink, Spark Streaming) maintain state across events and support concepts like windowing, watermarks, and complex event processing for sophisticated real-time analytics.
11. Online learning techniques such as online gradient descent and incremental clustering update model parameters continuously as new data arrives instead of retraining on the full historical dataset.
12. Log-based Change Data Capture (CDC) reads the database's transaction or write-ahead logs to identify committed inserts, updates, and deletes without querying live tables directly.

13. Compared to polling and trigger-based CDC, log-based CDC usually imposes less overhead on source systems and scales better for high-throughput transactional workloads.
14. In AWS Kinesis, each put_record call writes a single record into a shard, and overall throughput is governed by per-shard limits on records per second and total MB per second.
15. AWS Lambda functions are often wired to Kinesis streams or Firehose delivery streams to implement lightweight transformations, routing, and enrichment as events flow through the pipeline.
16. Azure Data Factory supports both code-free visual pipelines and code-driven orchestration, with connectors to on-premises systems, SaaS applications, and other Azure services such as Databricks.
17. Apache NiFi's back-pressure and buffering mechanisms prevent downstream bottlenecks from overwhelming upstream components, helping maintain stability in large-scale data flows.
18. NiFi's data provenance features capture end-to-end lineage for each flow file, enabling detailed tracing of where data came from, how it was transformed, and where it was delivered.
19. When Kafka is self-managed, careful planning of broker sizing, disk capacity, topic partition counts, replication factors, and retention policies is essential to meet throughput, durability, and cost targets.
20. Sharding strategies (e.g., range-based, hash-based, or geographic sharding) aim to distribute data evenly, minimize cross-shard queries, and align with dominant access patterns for scalability.
21. In practice, organizations often combine data lakes for raw and semi-structured data with data warehouses or "lakehouse" architectures for curated, analytics-ready datasets.

Bibliography

Acosta, J. N., Falcone, G. J., Rajpurkar, P., Topol, E. J., & Moon, K. R. (2022). Multimodal biomedical AI. *Nature Medicine, 28*(9), 1773–1784. https://doi.org/10.1038/s41591-022-01981-2

Adnan, H. S., Shidani, A., Clifton, L., Bankhead, C. R., & Perera-Salazar, R. (2025). Implementation framework for AI deployment at scale in healthcare systems. *iScience, 28*(5), 112406. https://doi.org/10.1016/j.isci.2025.112406

Adnan, H. S., Shidani, A., Clifton, L., Bankhead, C. R., & Perera-Salazar, R. (2025). A multi-site study of clinician perspectives in the lifecycle of an AI-enabled clinical decision support system. *iScience, 28*(5), 112406. https://doi.org/10.1016/j.isci.2025.112406

Beam, A. L., & Kohane, I. S. (2018). Big data and machine learning in health care. *JAMA, 319*(13), 1317–1318.

Bodenreider, O. (2004). The unified medical language system (UMLS): Integrating biomedical terminology. *Nucleic Acids Research, 32*(suppl_1), D267–D270.

Brown, A., & Smith, J. (2024). Quantum computing and AI: A transformative partnership in cloud infrastructure. *Journal of Cloud Computing & AI Technologies, 21*(2), 45–58. https://doi.org/10.1234/jccait.2024.23456

Combi, C., Keravnou-Papailiou, E., & Shahar, Y. (2010). *Temporal information systems in medicine.* Springer Science & Business Media.

Doshi-Velez, F., & Kim, B. (2017). Towards a rigorous science of interpretable machine learning. *arXiv preprint* arXiv:1702.08608.

Elendu, C., Amaechi, D. C., Okatta, A. U., Amaechi, E. C., Elendu, T. C., Ezeh, C. P., & Elendu, I. D. (2024). The impact of simulation-based training in medical education: A review. *Medicine (Baltimore), 103*(27), e38813. https://doi.org/10.1097/MD.0000000000038813

Esteva, A., Robicquet, A., Ramsundar, B., et al. (2019). A guide to deep learning in healthcare. *Nature Medicine, 25*(1), 24–29.

Franklin, S., & Graesser, A. (1997). Is it an agent, or just a program?: A taxonomy for autonomous agents. In J. P. Müller, M. J. Wooldridge, & N. R. Jennings (Eds.), *International workshop on agent theories, architectures, and languages* (pp. 21–35). Springer.

Gazquez-Garcia, J., Salazar, R. P., & Almeria, D. S. (2025). AI in the health sector: Systematic review of key skills for future health professionals. *JMIR Medical Education, 11*, e58161. https://doi.org/10.2196/58161

Green, M., & Taylor, H. (2023). Quantum-inspired algorithms and their role in AI-driven cloud platforms. *Journal of AI Research & Development, 9*(4), 72–85. https://doi.org/10.2345/jair.2023.12567

Holzinger, A., Biemann, C., Pattichis, C. S., & Kell, D. B. (2017). What do we need to build explainable AI systems for the medical domain? *arXiv preprint* arXiv:1712.09923.

Jennings, N. R. (2000). On agent-based software engineering. *Artificial Intelligence, 117*(2), 277–296.

Johnson, A. E., Pollard, T. J., Shen, L., et al. (2016). MIMIC-III, a freely accessible critical care database. *Scientific Data, 3*(1), 160035.

Kaissis, G. A., Makowski, M. R., Rückert, D., & Braren, R. F. (2020). Secure, privacy-preserving and federated machine learning in medical imaging. *Nature Machine Intelligence, 2*(6), 305–311.

Liu, Y., Wright Clayton, E., Lovett Novak, L., Anders, S., & Malin, B. (2024). Evaluating artificial intelligence in clinical settings—Let us not reinvent the wheel. *Journal of Medical Internet Research, 26*(1), e46407. https://doi.org/10.2196/46407

Mandl, K. D., Halpert, R., Bates, D. W., & Kreutz, R. (2020). Leveraging interoperability to enable precision medicine. *JAMIA Open, 3*(2), 202–209.

Miotto, R., Wang, F., Wang, S., Jiang, X., & Dudley, J. T. (2018). Deep learning for healthcare: Review, opportunities and challenges. *Briefings in Bioinformatics, 19*(6), 1236–1246.

Misra, R., Keane, P. A., & Hogg, H. D. J. (2024). How should we train clinicians for artificial intelligence in healthcare? *Future Healthcare Journal, 11*(3), 100162. https://doi.org/10.1016/j.fhj.2024.100162

Mittermaier, M., Raza, M. M., & Kvedar, J. C. (2023). Bias in AI-based models for medical applications: Challenges and mitigation strategies. *npj Digital Medicine, 6*, Article 113. https://doi.org/10.1038/s41746-023-00858-z

Panayides, A. S., Amini, A., Filipovic, N. D., Sharma, A., Tsaftaris, S. A., Young, A., ... Pattichis, C. S. (2020). AI in medical imaging informatics: Current challenges and future directions. *IEEE Journal of Biomedical and Health Informatics, 24*(7), 1837–1857. https://doi.org/10.1109/JBHI.2020.2991043

Shickel, B., Tighe, P. J., Bihorac, A., & Rashidi, P. (2018). Deep EHR: A survey of recent advances in deep learning techniques for electronic health record (EHR) analysis. *IEEE Journal of Biomedical and Health Informatics, 22*(5), 1589–1604.

Shortliffe, E. H., & Sepúlveda, M. J. (2018). Clinical decision support in the era of artificial intelligence. *JAMA, 320*(21), 2199–2200.

Steel, P. A. D., Wardi, G., Harrington, R. A., & Longhurst, C. A. (2025). Learning health system strategies in the AI era. *npj Health Systems, 2*, 21. https://doi.org/10.1038/s44401-025-00029-0

Stone, P., & Veloso, M. (2000). Multiagent systems: A survey from a machine learning perspective. *Autonomous Robots, 8*(3), 345–383.

Sutton, R. T., Pincock, D., Baumgart, D. C., et al. (2020). An overview of clinical decision support systems. *Academic Medicine, 95*(7), 1085–1093.

Thummarakoti, S. (2022). *Toward efficient asynchronous architectures in low-code platforms: A comparative study in Pega*. SSRN. https://ssrn.com/abstract=5238386

Thummarakoti, S. (2023). *Enhancing business process automation through NLP-based email interpretation in Pega systems. SSRN.* https://ssrn.com/abstract=5249573

Thummarakoti, S. (2024). *Transforming healthcare with Pega: A unified approach to modern challenges*. SSRN. https://ssrn.com/abstract=5241177

Thummarakoti, S. (2025). Advanced container orchestration strategies for multi-cloud environments: Enhancing performance, scalability, and resilience. *International Journal of Science and Research (IJSR), 14*(2), 43–48. https://doi.org/10.21275/SR25129074846

Thummarakoti, S. (2025). AI-enhanced cloud data systems for healthcare. *Global Journal of Computer Science and Technology: C (Software & Data Engineering), 25*(C1), 21–32. https://doi.org/10.34257/GJCSTCVOL25IS1PG21.

Thummarakoti, S. (2025, March). Compliance and regulatory challenges in cloud-based healthcare systems. In *SoutheastCon 2025* (pp. 1264–1269). IEEE.

Thummarakoti, S. (2025, March). Leveraging cloud computing and cutting-edge technology for early cancer diagnosis. In *SoutheastCon 2025* (pp. 912–917). IEEE.

Weiss, G. (Ed.). (2013). *Multiagent systems: A modern approach to distributed artificial intelligence*. MIT Press.

Williams, R., & Chen, T. (2024). Leveraging quantum computing for AI acceleration in cloud environments. In *Future trends in AI cloud infrastructure* (pp. 110–130). TechPress.

Wiens, J., Saria, S., Sendak, M., et al. (2019). Do no harm: A roadmap for responsible machine learning for health care. *Nature Medicine, 25*(9), 1337–1340.

Yu, K. H., Beam, A. L., & Kohane, I. S. (2018). Artificial intelligence in healthcare. *Nature Biomedical Engineering, 2*(10), 719–731.

Chapter 11

Advanced Deployment and Management Strategies for Scalable AI

The proliferation of artificial intelligence across various industries has underscored the critical need for scalable AI applications capable of handling increasing data volumes and user demands. Deploying and managing AI at scale in cloud environments presents significant complexities, requiring careful consideration of infrastructure, connectivity, performance, and security.

This chapter delves into the advanced strategies for deploying and managing scalable AI, aligning with key topics essential for robust and efficient AI systems. It examines the crucial aspect of establishing seamless connections between the various components of an AI ecosystem, ensuring data flows smoothly and securely while optimizing resource utilization and overall system performance.

11.1 Best Practices for Containerized AI Model Deployment in the Cloud

11.1.1 Algorithms and Best Practices for Containerization

Containerization, particularly using Docker, has emerged as a cornerstone technology for deploying AI models in a portable and isolated manner. This approach encapsulates the AI model, its dependencies, and the runtime

DOI: 10.4324/9781003685609-11

environment into a single unit, ensuring consistency across different stages of the AI lifecycle, from development to production. A significant advantage of containerization for AI lies in its ability to guarantee that the model operates within the exact same environment in which it was trained.[12]

The training of AI models often relies on specific versions of libraries and particular system configurations. If the deployment environment deviates from this, the model's behavior and performance can be unpredictable. By packaging all necessary dependencies, including libraries, system tools, runtime, and code, containers eliminate these discrepancies, leading to more reliable and reproducible deployments.

To build efficient Docker images for AI models, several best practices should be followed:

- **Utilizing Minimal Base Images**: Reduces the overall size of the container, leading to faster build and deployment times.
- **Multi-Stage Builds**: Further optimizes the image by separating the build environment from the runtime environment, ensuring that only the necessary artifacts are included in the final image.
- **Optimizing Layer Caching**: Orders Dockerfile commands to leverage Docker's caching mechanism, significantly speeding up the image-building process during iterative development.[3]

11.1.2 Connecting Containerized Applications to Other Cloud Services (AWS, Azure, GCP)

Containerized AI applications rarely operate in isolation. They often need to interact with a variety of other cloud services for tasks such as data storage, database access, message queuing, and model registry operations. The major cloud providers—AWS, Azure, and GCP—offer a rich set of services that AI applications can leverage.

- **AWS**: Amazon Web Services provides a comprehensive suite of services and the Boto3 SDK for Python, which facilitates seamless interaction with these services from within containerized AI applications.[4] For instance, connecting to Amazon S3 for data input and output is a common requirement. Code snippets using Boto3 can be implemented to upload processed data or download training datasets. Similarly, Boto3 enables containerized applications to interact with Amazon SQS for asynchronous communication with other services, allowing for decoupled architectures where different components can operate independently. The availability of this robust SDK simplifies the integration process, allowing developers to harness the vast ecosystem of AWS without needing to delve into low-level API interactions. Boto3 offers high-level abstractions for frequent AWS tasks, such as using Python functions to interact with S3 for file operations or SQS for message management, thereby accelerating development and reducing the potential for errors.

- **Azure**: Microsoft Azure offers a comparable experience through its Azure SDK for Python, enabling containerized AI applications to connect to various Azure services.[5] Accessing Azure Blob Storage for reading training data or storing inference results is a common use case, and the Azure SDK provides straightforward code snippets for these operations. Furthermore, the SDK allows containerized applications to trigger serverless workflows by connecting to Azure Functions, facilitating event-driven architectures. Similar to AWS, Azure's Python SDK streamlines the integration of containerized AI applications with its services. This fosters a unified development experience within the Azure environment, as the SDK abstracts the complexities of Azure's APIs, allowing developers to use familiar Python constructs to interact with services like Blob Storage and Azure Functions, making the development process more efficient.
- **GCP**: Google Cloud Platform provides the Google Cloud Client Libraries for Python, which serve a similar purpose, allowing containerized AI applications to interact with GCP services.[6] Connecting to Google Cloud Storage for accessing datasets or storing model outputs can be achieved with concise code examples using these libraries. Additionally, the libraries enable integration with Cloud Pub/Sub, facilitating the construction of event-driven architectures where different components of the AI system can communicate asynchronously. GCP's Python client libraries offer idiomatic Python interfaces for accessing its services, making it easier for Python developers to build AI applications that utilize GCP's capabilities. These libraries abstract away the underlying gRPC and REST APIs, providing Pythonic functions and classes for interacting with services like GCS and Cloud Pub/Sub, which simplifies development and enhances code readability.

11.1.3 Handling Data Input and Output in Containerized AI Models

Effective management of data input and output is crucial for containerized AI models. Several methods can be employed to provide data to and retrieve results from these models. One common approach involves mounting cloud storage, such as S3, Azure Blob Storage, or GCS, as volumes within the container. This allows the AI application to access data directly using standard file I/O operations within the container's file system. For example, Python code can be used to read files from a mounted directory as if they were local.

Another prevalent method is to expose the containerized AI application through an API. Frameworks like Flask or FastAPI in Python can be used to create API endpoints that receive input data, trigger the AI model for inference, and return the predictions in a structured format, such as JSON.

This approach enables the AI model to be easily integrated into various applications and services, as they can send requests to the API and receive results without needing to understand the model's internal workings. This fosters a decoupled and service-oriented architecture where different components can interact through well-defined interfaces.

Leveraging message queues, such as SQS, Azure Queue Storage, or Pub/Sub, provides a mechanism for asynchronous data exchange with containerized AI models.

Input data can be placed on a queue, and the containerized application can consume messages from the queue, perform inference, and potentially place the results on another queue for downstream processing. This approach is particularly useful for handling large volumes of inference requests or for decoupling the request and response cycles.

11.1.4 Ensuring Scalable and Reliable Deployment of Containerized AI

To ensure that containerized AI applications can handle varying workloads and maintain high availability, orchestration tools like Kubernetes and cloud-managed container services such as AWS ECS, Azure Container Instances, and GCP Cloud Run are essential. These platforms provide mechanisms for scaling the number of container instances based on demand, ensuring that the application can handle peak loads.

Health Checks and Readiness Probes: Implementing health checks and readiness probes within these orchestration platforms is crucial for ensuring application reliability. Health checks allow the platform to monitor the status of the container instances and automatically restart any that become unhealthy. Readiness probes indicate when a container instance is ready to start serving traffic, preventing requests from being sent to instances that are still initializing.

Load-Balancing: Implementing load-balancing plays a vital role in distributing inference requests evenly across multiple container instances.[7] This prevents any single instance from being overwhelmed, improves response times, and ensures high availability. Cloud providers offer managed load-balancing services that can be easily integrated with container orchestration platforms, automatically distributing traffic to healthy instances. This distribution of load across multiple instances of the containerized AI application is critical for preventing any single instance from becoming a bottleneck and for maintaining consistent performance and availability as the number of inference requests fluctuates.

11.2 Leveraging Serverless Functions for Scalable AI Inference

11.2.1 Algorithms for AI Inference in Serverless Environments

Serverless functions, such as AWS Lambda, Azure Functions, and GCP Cloud Functions, offer a highly scalable and cost-effective way to deploy AI models for inference.[8] When choosing AI models for serverless deployment, it's important to consider factors like model size, inference latency, and resource consumption. Serverless functions typically have limitations on memory, execution time, and temporary storage, so models should be optimized to fit within these constraints.

Techniques such as model quantization and pruning can be employed to optimize AI models for faster inference in serverless functions. Quantization reduces the precision of the model's weights, leading to smaller model sizes and faster computations, often with minimal impact on accuracy. Pruning removes less important connections or parameters from the model, also reducing its size and computational requirements.

In serverless contexts, there is often a trade-off between model accuracy and inference speed. Smaller, faster models might have slightly lower accuracy but can be more suitable for the resource-constrained environment of serverless functions.

11.2.2 Connecting Serverless Functions (AWS Lambda, Azure Functions, GCP Cloud Functions) to AI Models

Serverless functions can access AI models through various methods. For smaller models, it might be feasible to load them directly into the function's memory during the cold start phase. For larger models, fetching them from cloud storage services like S3, Azure Blob Storage, or GCS, or from dedicated model registries, is a more practical approach.[9]

Another common method is to invoke the inference endpoints of containerized models or managed AI services, such as SageMaker, Azure AI services, or Vertex AI, from within the serverless function.[10]

- **AWS Lambda**: AWS Lambda functions can be efficiently used for AI inference by loading pre-trained models from S3 using the Boto3 SDK.[11] Python code within the Lambda function can download the model file from S3 to the function's temporary storage and then load it into memory for inference. Additionally, Lambda functions can easily integrate with SageMaker by calling SageMaker endpoints to leverage fully managed model deployment and inference services. This provides a scalable and cost-effective solution for many AI inference use cases.
- **Azure Functions**: Similarly, Azure Functions can be used to connect to AI models stored in Azure Blob Storage using the Azure SDK for Python. Python code within the function can retrieve the model from Blob Storage and perform inference. Azure Functions also allows for seamless integration with Azure AI services, enabling developers to invoke pre-trained or custom AI models deployed through these services. This makes Azure Functions a powerful serverless computing environment for scalable AI inference.
- **GCP Cloud Functions**: GCP Cloud Functions can load AI models from Google Cloud Storage using the Google Cloud Client Libraries for Python. The function code can download the model from GCS to the function's local environment and then load it for inference. Furthermore, Cloud Functions can connect to Vertex AI endpoints, allowing developers to utilize Vertex AI's comprehensive suite of AI services, including

model deployment and inference, from within their serverless functions. This offers a robust platform for building scalable AI inference solutions on GCP.

11.2.3 Managing Inference Requests and Data Flow in Serverless Architectures

Serverless architectures for AI inference need to handle both synchronous and asynchronous requests effectively. For synchronous requests, such as those from web applications, API Gateways like AWS API Gateway, Azure API Management, or GCP Cloud Endpoints can be used to expose serverless inference functions as RESTful APIs.

These API Gateways handle request routing, authentication, and response management, providing a standardized interface for accessing the AI model.

For asynchronous inference requests, message queues play a crucial role in decoupling the request and response cycles. Services like SQS, Azure Queue Storage, or Pub/Sub can be used to queue inference requests.

Serverless functions can then be triggered by new messages on the queue, process the requests, and potentially place the results on another queue or store them in a database. This approach is beneficial for handling long-running inference tasks or for scenarios where the requester does not need an immediate response.

11.3 Implementing Effective Resource Management and Orchestration for AI

11.3.1 Algorithms and Coding Practices for Autoscaling AI Workloads

Efficient resource management and orchestration are paramount for achieving scalability in AI applications. Cloud platforms offer various mechanisms for automatically scaling resources based on workload demands.

- **Kubernetes**: Kubernetes provides a rich set of autoscaling features that are highly adaptable to the resource needs of AI workloads.[12] The Horizontal Pod Autoscaler (HPA) can automatically adjust the number of pod replicas in a deployment or replica set based on metrics like CPU and memory utilization, as well as custom metrics derived from application-specific performance indicators.

The Vertical Pod Autoscaler (VPA) focuses on adjusting the resource requests and limits (CPU and memory) for individual pods, ensuring they have the appropriate resources without over-provisioning. The Cluster Autoscaler dynamically manages the number of nodes in the Kubernetes cluster by adding or removing nodes from the underlying infrastructure (e.g., virtual machine scale sets) based on the resource requirements of the pods.

Furthermore, AI-powered predictive scaling solutions can analyze historical workload patterns to forecast future demand and proactively scale resources, ensuring the application is ready for anticipated traffic spikes. These autoscaling configurations can be defined using kubectl commands and Kubernetes manifest files, allowing for declarative management of scaling policies.

- **AWS ECS**: Amazon ECS offers Service Auto Scaling, which allows for the automatic adjustment of the desired number of tasks (container instances) in an ECS service based on target metrics such as CPU utilization, memory utilization, and custom metrics.[13]

  Similar to Kubernetes, ECS also supports predictive scaling, which uses historical load data to anticipate future resource needs. Autoscaling policies can be configured using the AWS CLI or SDKs, providing a straightforward way to manage the scalability of containerized AI applications.
- **Azure Kubernetes Service (AKS)**: Azure Kubernetes Service leverages the Kubernetes Cluster Autoscaler for automatically adjusting the number of nodes in the cluster based on pod scheduling and resource utilization.[14] Additionally, AKS supports the standard Kubernetes Horizontal Pod Autoscaler for scaling pods within the nodes.

  The Cluster Autoscaler in AKS integrates with Azure Virtual Machine Scale Sets (VMSS) to provision and de-provision virtual machines as needed, ensuring that the underlying infrastructure scales in response to the demands of the AI workloads.
- **Google Kubernetes Engine (GKE)**: Google Kubernetes Engine provides a robust Cluster Autoscaler that automatically resizes node pools based on the demands of AI workloads.[15] GKE also offers node auto-provisioning, which automatically scales node pools based on pending pods, and workload autoscaling, which allows for the automatic scaling of Kubernetes Deployments and StatefulSets based on resource

utilization or custom metrics. These features ensure efficient resource utilization and cost management for AI applications running on GKE.

11.3.2 Load-Balancing Strategies for AI Applications in the Cloud

Load balancing is a critical component of scalable AI applications, ensuring that incoming inference requests are distributed efficiently across multiple instances of the AI model, thereby improving performance and availability.

Cloud providers offer various types of load balancers to suit different needs.

- **Application Load Balancers**: Operate at the application layer (Layer 7), making routing decisions based on the content of the HTTP/HTTPS requests. Network Load Balancers operate at the transport layer (Layer 4), routing traffic based on IP protocol data.
- **Cloud-Specific Load Balancing Services**: Products such as AWS Elastic Load Balancing (ELB), Azure Load Balancer, and Google Cloud Load Balancing provide managed load-balancing capabilities that can be easily integrated with AI application deployments.
- **Common Load Balancing Algorithms**: Include Round Robin, which distributes requests sequentially across available instances, and Least Connections, which directs traffic to the instance with the fewest active connections. Configuring load balancers for AI inference endpoints is essential for effectively distributing traffic and ensuring high availability of the AI service.

11.3.3 Efficient Resource Allocation for Scalable AI

Optimizing resource utilization is crucial for managing the costs associated with scalable AI applications in the cloud. Several strategies can be employed to achieve this.

- **Rightsizing Instances**: Involves selecting the appropriate instance types and sizes based on the actual resource consumption of the AI workloads, avoiding over-provisioning.
- **Spot Instances or Preemptible VMs**: Utilizes Spot instances or Preemptible VMs, which are available at a lower cost, can be beneficial for non-critical or fault-tolerant workloads.[16]

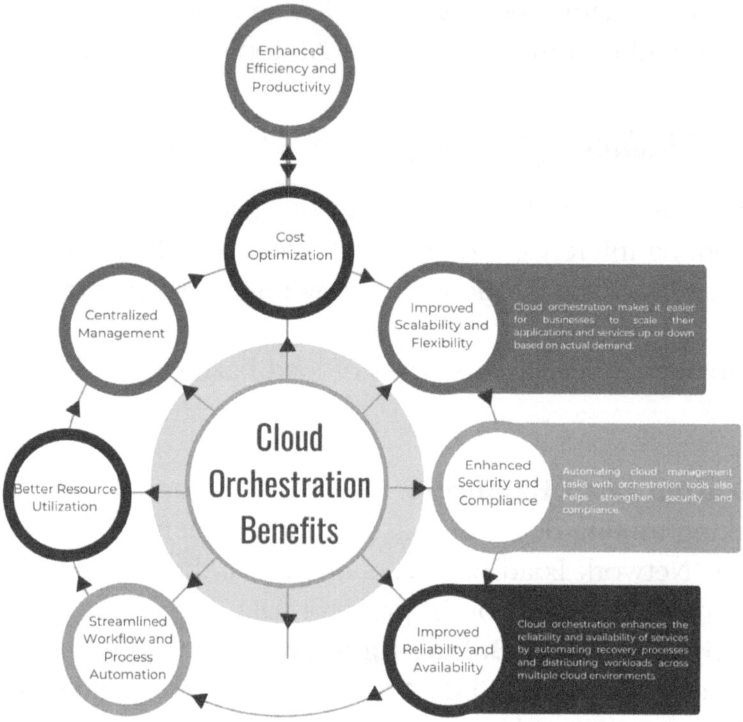

Figure 11.1 Key Benefits of Cloud Orchestration for AI Workloads

- **Resource Quotas and Limits**: Implements resource quotas and limits in Kubernetes helps to manage the resource consumption of individual containers and pods, preventing any single application from monopolizing cluster resources.
- **Monitoring and Adjusting Resource Usage and Allocation**: Requires continuous monitoring of resource usage and adjusting allocations based on performance metrics to maintain optimal efficiency and cost-effectiveness (Figure 11.1).

11.4 Monitoring, Logging, and Performance Optimization for Scalable AI

11.4.1 Algorithms and Techniques for Monitoring AI Application Performance

Monitoring the performance of scalable AI applications is essential for ensuring they meet the required service levels and for identifying potential issues before they impact users.[17] Key performance indicators (KPIs) for AI applications often include accuracy, precision, recall, F1 score for classification tasks, and metrics like latency and throughput for inference services. Resource utilization, such as CPU and memory consumption, is also critical for understanding the efficiency of the application.

Tracking model drift and concept drift, which refer to changes in the input data distribution or the underlying relationships the model has learned, is vital for maintaining the accuracy and relevance of AI models over time. Statistical methods and visualization techniques can be used to analyze the collected performance data, helping to identify trends, anomalies, and areas for improvement.

11.4.2 Implementing Monitoring Dashboards Using Cloud-Native Services

Cloud providers offer comprehensive monitoring services that can be used to build dashboards for visualizing the performance of AI applications.

- **AWS CloudWatch**: AWS CloudWatch allows for the creation of custom metrics specific to AI model performance, such as prediction accuracy or inference latency. Alarms can be set up based on these metrics to trigger notifications when performance thresholds are breached. CloudWatch also enables the creation of dashboards that provide a centralized view of key metrics and logs, making it easier to monitor the overall health and performance of AI applications. Furthermore, CloudWatch Logs can be used for in-depth log analysis and to detect unusual patterns or anomalies in the application's behavior. The Boto3 SDK can be used to programmatically interact with CloudWatch, allowing for automated metric publishing and alarm configuration.[18][19]
- **Azure Monitor**: Azure Monitor provides a unified platform for collecting metrics and logs from AI applications and the underlying infrastructure.[20] Application Insights, a feature of Azure Monitor, offers specialized capabilities for application performance monitoring, including tracing of requests and identification of performance bottlenecks. Alerts can be configured based on both static and dynamic thresholds, with AI-powered anomaly detection capabilities that can automatically identify unusual patterns in the data. Azure Monitor also allows for the creation of custom dashboards to visualize key performance indicators and the overall health of the AI environment.

- **Google Cloud Monitoring**: Google Cloud Monitoring integrates with Vertex AI, allowing for the export of specific metrics related to model performance and resource usage.[21] This includes metrics like request latency, error rates, and resource consumption of deployed models and endpoints. Cloud Monitoring enables the creation of custom dashboards to visualize these metrics and the configuration of alerts to notify operators of any issues. Additionally, Vertex AI Model Monitoring provides features for detecting feature skew and drift, which are crucial for maintaining the accuracy of AI models in production.

11.4.3 Establishing Effective Logging Mechanisms for AI Systems

Effective logging is essential for debugging, auditing, and ensuring compliance in AI systems. Best practices for logging in AI applications include using structured logging formats (e.g., JSON) to facilitate easier parsing and analysis and correlating logs across different components of the system to provide a holistic view of events.

Centralized log management can be achieved using cloud-based services like CloudWatch Logs, Azure Monitor Logs, and Cloud Logging, which provide scalable and durable storage for log data. These services also offer powerful query and analysis capabilities, allowing teams to troubleshoot issues, track system behavior, and meet compliance requirements.

11.4.4 Strategies for Identifying and Resolving Performance Bottlenecks in Deployed AI

Identifying and resolving performance bottlenecks in deployed AI applications often requires a combination of monitoring, profiling, and optimization techniques. Profiling the inference performance of AI models can help to pinpoint specific operations that are contributing to latency.

Optimizing data loading and preprocessing pipelines can significantly improve the overall throughput of the application. Leveraging cloud-specific performance analysis tools, such as AWS X-Ray, Azure Application Insights, or Google Cloud Profiler, can provide detailed insights into the execution flow of the application and help identify areas where performance can be improved.

11.5 Cloud-Specific Services and Tools for Scalable AI

11.5.1 Relevant AWS Services and Code Examples (Python/Boto3)

AWS offers a comprehensive suite of services relevant to scalable AI.[22]

- **SageMaker**: Provides an end-to-end platform for building, training, and deploying machine learning models. Kinesis is designed for real-time data ingestion and processing.
- **Lambda**: Offers a serverless computing environment suitable for AI inference.
- **ECS and EKS**: Provide container orchestration capabilities. S3 serves as a scalable object storage for datasets and model artifacts.
- **CloudWatch**: Offers comprehensive monitoring and logging. Code examples using Boto3 can be used to interact with these services, such as loading data from S3, invoking a SageMaker endpoint, or publishing metrics to CloudWatch.

11.5.2 Relevant Azure Services and Code Examples (Python/Azure SDK)

Azure provides a similar set of services for scalable AI.

- **Azure Machine Learning**: Provides a platform for the entire ML lifecycle.
- **Azure Data Factory**: Facilitates data integration and ETL processes.
- **Azure Functions**: Offers serverless computing for inference.
- **Azure Container Instances and Azure Kubernetes Service (AKS)**: Provide containerization options.
- **Azure Blob Storage**: Enables data storage, while Azure Monitor offers monitoring and logging capabilities.
- **Azure SDK for Python**: Allows interaction with these services, for example, to read data from Blob Storage, trigger an Azure Function, or monitor the performance of an AKS cluster.

11.5.3 Relevant GCP Services and Code Examples (Python/Google Cloud Client Libraries)

GCP offers a robust set of services for scalable AI.

- **Vertex AI**: Provides a comprehensive AI platform.
- **Dataflow**: Enables scalable data processing.
- **Cloud Functions**: Provides serverless computing for inference.
- **Cloud Run and Google Kubernetes Engine (GKE)**: Offer containerization options.
- **Cloud Storage**: Enables data storage.
- **Cloud Monitoring**: Provides monitoring capabilities.
- **Google Cloud Client Libraries for Python**: Allow interaction with these services, such as loading data from Cloud Storage, invoking a Cloud Function, or deploying a model to Vertex AI.

11.6 Common Connection Patterns and Architectural Considerations for Scalable AI

11.6.1 Architectural Patterns for Integrating AI Components in the Cloud

Several architectural patterns are commonly employed for integrating AI components in the cloud to achieve scalability and resilience.

- **Microservices Architecture**: Involves breaking down the AI application into a collection of small, independent services that can be deployed and scaled independently.
- **Event-Driven Architecture**: Focuses on communication through events, allowing for decoupled and reactive systems.
- **Serverless Architecture**: Supports inference-heavy applications, where compute resources are provisioned on demand.
- **Data Lake Architecture**: Provides a centralized repository for storing and processing large volumes of data used in AI.
- **Lambda Architecture and Kappa Architecture**: Represent hybrid approaches designed to handle both batch and streaming data processing for AI pipelines.

11.6.2 Data Ingestion Patterns for Scalable AI Pipelines

Data ingestion is the initial and crucial step in any scalable AI pipeline. Various patterns exist to handle the diverse data sources and processing requirements.

- **Batch Ingestion**: Involves collecting data over a period and processing it in bulk at scheduled intervals.
- **Real-Time or Streaming Ingestion**: Focuses on processing data immediately as it is generated, enabling near real-time insights.
- **Change Data Capture (CDC)**: Captures and processes only the data that has changed in source systems, often used for real-time updates.
- **Homogeneous and Heterogeneous Data Ingestion**: Moves data in the same format in homogeneous patterns, while heterogeneous patterns require transformations during ingestion.
- **Point-to-Point, Hub and Spoke, and Sharding**: Address different aspects of data flow and distribution.

11.7 Securing Connections in Scalable AI Deployments

11.7.1 Algorithms and Coding Examples for Authentication and Authorization between Services

Securing connections between different services in a scalable AI deployment is paramount to protect sensitive data and prevent unauthorized access.[23]

API keys and tokens are commonly used for basic authentication between services. OAuth 2.0 provides a more robust framework for authorization, allowing services to grant limited access to their resources without sharing credentials.

Leveraging cloud-managed identities, such as IAM roles in AWS or managed identities in Azure and GCP, offers a secure and scalable way to manage authentication and authorization for service-to-service communication. These managed identities eliminate the need to hardcode or manually manage credentials within the application code.

Code examples using the respective cloud SDKs can demonstrate how to assume IAM roles or utilize managed identities to authenticate and authorize requests to other cloud services. This approach enhances security by centralizing credential management and adhering to the principle of least privilege.

11.8 Strategies and Coding Techniques for Managing Configurations and Secrets Securely

Managing configurations and secrets, such as API keys, database passwords, and encryption keys, securely is crucial in scalable AI deployments.

Dedicated secrets management services like AWS Secrets Manager, Azure Key Vault, and Google Cloud Secret Manager provide a centralized and secure way to store, access, and manage sensitive information.

These services offer features like encryption at rest and in transit, access control policies, and audit logging. Encrypting configuration files and data, both when stored and during transmission, is another essential security measure.

Implementing role-based access control (RBAC) ensures that only authorized entities can access configurations and secrets.

Code examples using the SDKs for these secrets management services can illustrate how to securely retrieve secrets within the AI application, preventing them from being hardcoded or exposed in configuration files.

11.9 Conclusion: Key Considerations and Future Directions in Advanced AI Deployment and Management

This chapter has explored advanced deployment and management strategies for scalable AI, emphasizing the critical role of connections between various AI system components. The discussion covered best practices for containerization, leveraging serverless functions, implementing resource management and orchestration, applying monitoring and performance optimization, and securing connections in cloud environments.

The choice of specific strategies and tools should be guided by the unique requirements and constraints of each AI application. As the field of AI continues to evolve, emerging trends such as autonomous AI pipelines, federated learning, and specialized hardware acceleration will further shape the landscape of scalable AI deployment and management. Organizations that prioritize robust connection strategies, efficient resource utilization, and comprehensive security measures will be well-positioned to harness the transformative power of AI at scale.

Notes

1. Containerization packages application code, dependencies, and system libraries into a single image, making it easier to move AI workloads consistently between development, testing, and production environments.

2. Keeping the training and deployment environments identical reduces "training–serving skew," where models behave differently in production due to library version drift or configuration mismatches.
3. Docker layer caching reuses unchanged layers between builds, so ordering commands carefully (installing rarely changed dependencies first, frequent code changes last) can significantly speed up iterative image builds.
4. Boto3 is the official AWS SDK for Python and exposes high-level abstractions for working with core services like S3, SQS, Lambda, and SageMaker directly from containerized applications.
5. The Azure SDK for Python provides client libraries for services such as Blob Storage, Azure Functions, Azure ML, and Event Hubs, enabling unified access to Azure resources from within containers.
6. Google Cloud Client Libraries for Python wrap REST and gRPC APIs for services like Cloud Storage, Pub/Sub, Cloud Functions, and Vertex AI, offering idiomatic Python interfaces for GCP integration.
7. Load balancing distributes incoming requests across multiple instances of an AI service to avoid hot spots, improve latency, and increase overall availability and fault tolerance.
8. Serverless platforms such as AWS Lambda, Azure Functions, and GCP Cloud Functions automatically scale function instances based on demand and charge only for actual execution time, which can be cost-effective for spiky AI workloads.
9. For serverless inference, models are often stored in object storage and loaded at cold start into the function's memory or temporary filesystem, trading slightly higher startup latency for reduced package size.
10. Invoking managed inference endpoints (for example, SageMaker, Azure AI services, or Vertex AI) from serverless functions offloads model hosting and autoscaling to dedicated ML platforms.
11. AWS Lambda provides a small writable /tmp directory and constrained memory/CPU; model loading strategies must account for these limits to avoid timeouts or out-of-memory errors.
12. Kubernetes supports multiple autoscaling mechanisms—Horizontal Pod Autoscaler, Vertical Pod Autoscaler, and Cluster Autoscaler—that work together to align pod and node capacity with AI workload demand.
13. Amazon ECS Service Auto Scaling uses CloudWatch metrics (such as CPU, memory, or custom metrics) to adjust the desired task count dynamically, helping containerized AI services match capacity to traffic.
14. In Azure Kubernetes Service, the Cluster Autoscaler integrates with Virtual Machine Scale Sets to add or remove nodes automatically when pending pods cannot be scheduled with existing resources.
15. Google Kubernetes Engine supports cluster autoscaling, node auto-provisioning, and workload autoscaling, which can automatically create or resize node pools based on pending pods and resource utilization.

16. Spot Instances on AWS and Preemptible VMs on GCP offer substantial cost savings but can be reclaimed by the provider at short notice, so they are best suited for stateless, fault-tolerant, or batch AI workloads.
17. Monitoring AI applications typically involves both system metrics (CPU, memory, GPU utilization, latency, throughput) and model metrics (accuracy, drift, error rates) to ensure performance and reliability over time.
18. Amazon CloudWatch collects metrics, logs, and events from AWS resources and applications, enabling dashboards, alarms, and automated responses for AI workloads.
19. Through Boto3 and CloudWatch Logs, applications can programmatically publish custom metrics and structured logs, which can then drive alarms, scaling policies, and operational runbooks.
20. Azure Monitor and Application Insights provide end-to-end observability for workloads on Azure, including distributed tracing, request-level performance analysis, and anomaly detection for AI services.
21. Google Cloud Monitoring and Vertex AI Model Monitoring can track prediction latency, error rates, feature skew, and data drift, helping maintain model quality in production deployments.
22. AWS combines services such as SageMaker, EKS, ECS, Lambda, Kinesis, S3, and CloudWatch into a broad ecosystem for building, deploying, scaling, and observing cloud-based AI systems.
23. Using managed identities and role-based access controls (for example, IAM roles, Azure managed identities, or GCP service accounts) reduces secret sprawl and enforces least-privilege access between AI services.

Bibliography

Asan, O., Bayrak, C., & Choudhury, A. (2020). Artificial intelligence and human trust in healthcare: A scoping review. *Journal of Medical Internet Research, 22*(6), e15154. https://doi.org/10.2196/15154

Atomwise. (n.d.). https://www.atomwise.com

Barra, F. L., Rodella, G., Costa, A., et al. (2025). From prompt to platform: An agentic AI workflow for healthcare simulation scenario design. *Advances in Simulation, 10*(1). https://doi.org/10.1186/s41077-025-00357-z

Buntz, B. (2024, May 7). Meet AlphaFold 3, which can accurately model more than 99% of molecular types in the Protein Data Bank. *Drug Discovery Trends.* https://www.drugdiscoverytrends.com/meet-alphafold-3-which-can-accurately-model-more-than-99-of-molecular-types-in-the-protein-data-bank/

Char, D. S., Shah, N. H., & Magnus, D. (2018). Implementing machine learning in health care – addressing ethical challenges. *New England Journal of Medicine, 378*(11), 981–983. https://doi.org/10.1056/NEJMp1714229

Google. (n.d.). *Med-PaLM: A large language model from Google Research, designed for the medical domain.* https://sites.research.google/med-palm/

Google Cloud. (2025). Google data catalog. In *Cloud data governance and metadata management* (5.3.1). Google Cloud.

Google Cloud. (2025). Google stackdriver monitoring. In *Cloud tools for data pipeline monitoring* (5.2.6). Google Cloud.

Google Cloud. (n.d.). *Multimodal agents tutorial: How to use Gemini, Langchain, and LangGraph to build agents for object detection.* https://cloud.google.com/blog/products/ai-machine-learning/build-multimodal-agents-using-gemini-langchain-and-langgraph

Google Research. (n.d.). *Accelerating scientific breakthroughs with an AI co-scientist.* https://research.google/blog/accelerating-scientific-breakthroughs-with-an-ai-co-scientist/

Gyant. (2024). *AI-powered virtual assistant for healthcare systems.* https://www.gyant.com

HealthForce AI. (2024). *Empowering precision drug development with AI* [Whitepaper]. HealthForce AI.

HealthForce AI. (2024). *Empowering precision medicine through generative drug discovery* [Whitepaper]. HealthForce AI.

Henry, K. E., et al. (2015). A targeted real-time early warning score (TREWScore) for septic shock. *Science Translational Medicine, 7*(299), 299ra122.

Hippocratic AI. (2024). *Safety-focused LLMs in healthcare: Towards responsible generative diagnostics* [Whitepaper]. Hippocratic AI.

IBM. (2025). *Watsonx orchestrate: Enterprise AI for healthcare.* https://www.ibm.com/products/watson-orchestrate

Jiang, F., et al. (2017). Artificial intelligence in healthcare: Past, present and future. *Stroke and Vascular Neurology, 2*(4), 230–243. https://doi.org/10.1136/svn-2017-000101

LangGraph. (n.d.). *LangGraph for complex agent workflows.* https://langgraph.dev

Lumeon. (2023). *Driving operational excellence through pathway automation* [Whitepaper]. Lumeon.

Lumeon. (2024). *The Lumeon care orchestration platform.* https://www.lumeon.com

Martin, J. R., et al. (2020). Artificial intelligence and robotic-assisted orthopedic surgery: Emerging tools in the operating room. *Journal of Bone and Joint Surgery, 102*(23), 2101–2111. https://doi.org/10.2106/JBJS.20.00376

Medium. (n.d.). *LangGraph for healthcare: A comprehensive technical guide.* https://levelup.gitconnected.com/langgraph-for-healthcare-a-comprehensive-technical-guide-e6038b06c108

Mendez, B., et al. (2021). Real-time stroke detection and triage using artificial intelligence: The Viz.ai platform. *Journal of Stroke and Cerebrovascular Diseases, 30*(1), 105474.

Microsoft. (n.d.). *Semantic Kernel: Lightweight SDK for AI integration.* https://semantickernel.microsoft.com

Microsoft AutoGen. (2023). *Multi-agent coordination framework.* https://autogen.microsoft.com

Microsoft Azure. (2025). Azure data factory. In *Cloud data pipeline design for AI* (5.2.5). Microsoft Azure.

Microsoft Azure. (2025). Azure monitor. In *Cloud tools for data pipeline monitoring* (5.2.6). Microsoft Azure.

Microsoft Azure. (2025). Azure purview. In *Cloud data governance and metadata management* (5.3.1). Microsoft Azure.

NVIDIA Clara Imaging. (2023). *End-to-end AI for medical imaging*. NVIDIA.

NVIDIA. (n.d.). *NeMo toolkit for healthcare AI*. https://developer.nvidia.com/nemo

NVIDIA. (n.d.). *Supporting healthcare AI development, research, and innovation*. https://developer.nvidia.com/clara

NVIDIA. (n.d.). *NeMo: Build, customize, and deploy multimodal generative and agentic AI applications*. https://www.nvidia.com/en-us/ai-data-science/products/nemo/

NVIDIA. (n.d.). *NVIDIA and IQVIA build domain-expert agentic AI for healthcare and life sciences*. https://blogs.nvidia.com/blog/iqvia-agentic-ai-healthcare/

PwC. (n.d.). *Revolutionizing patient engagement with AI-powered agents*. https://www.pwc.com/us/en/technology/alliances/google-cloud/healthcare-ai-agents-solutions.html

Rajkomar, A., Oren, E., Chen, K., Dai, A. M., Hajaj, N., Hardt, M., Liu, P. J., et al. (2018). Scalable and accurate deep learning with electronic health records. *NPJ Digital Medicine, 1*(1), 18. https://doi.org/10.1038/s41746-018-0029-1

Reddy, S. T., et al. (2021). The rise of AI-powered chatbots in healthcare: Evaluating effectiveness and patient experience. *NPJ Digital Medicine, 4*, 45. https://doi.org/10.1038/s41746-021-00424-7

Sharma, P. (2025). MEDRAIL: MEDical reinforcement-based agentic intelligence for lifesciences. *Journal of Medical Internet Research Preprints*, June 8. https://doi.org/10.2196/preprints.78741

Stokes, J. M., et al. (2020). A deep learning approach to antibiotic discovery. *Cell, 180*(4), 688–702.e13. https://doi.org/10.1016/j.cell.2020.01.021

Sudre, C. H., et al. (2022). MONAI: Open-source framework for deep learning in healthcare imaging. *Scientific Reports, 12*, Article 12345.

TiDB. (n.d.). *Breaking down LangChain agents*. https://www.pingcap.com/article/breaking-down-langchain-agents/

Think Surgical. (2024). *TSolution One® total knee application*. https://thinksurgical.com

Thummarakoti, S. (2015). *Cloud information accountability (CIA) framework*. SSRN. https://ssrn.com/abstract=5241173

Thummarakoti, S. (2022). *Toward efficient asynchronous architectures in low-code platforms: A comparative study in Pega*. SSRN. https://ssrn.com/abstract=5238386

Thummarakoti, S. (2023). *Enhancing business process automation through NLP-based email interpretation in Pega systems*. SSRN. https://doi.org/10.2139/ssrn.5249573

Thummarakoti, S. (2025). AI-enhanced cloud data systems for healthcare. *Global Journal of Computer Science and Technology: C (Software & Data Engineering), 25*(1), 21–32.

Thummarakoti, S. (2025, March). Compliance and regulatory challenges in cloud-based healthcare systems. In *SoutheastCon 2025* (pp. 1264–1269). IEEE.

Thummarakoti, S., & Jajula, H. (2018). *Reducing SaaS vendor lock-in with a standardized & data abstraction and integration layer (SDAIL)*. SSRN. https://ssrn.com/abstract=5245269

Thummarakoti, S., & Udayagiri, P. (2020). Adaptive orchestration for performance cost optimization in multi-cloud infrastructure. *European Journal of Advances in Engineering and Technology, 7*(8), 119–125. https://doi.org/10.5281/zenodo.15307951

UiPath. (2025). *Agent builder for healthcare automation.* https://www.uipath.com

UiPath. (n.d.). *Accelerate medical record summarization with agentic automation.* https://www.uipath.com/solutions/industry/healthcare-automation/medical-record-summarization-agent

Viz.ai. (2024). *AI-based stroke detection.* https://viz.ai

Viz.ai. (2024). *Integrating AI into radiology workflows.* https://www.viz.ai

Yao, S., et al. (2022). ReAct: Synergizing reasoning and acting in language models. *arXiv preprint* arXiv:2210.03629

Zha, H., et al. (2023). Agent foundations for modular and composable AI systems. *arXiv preprint* arXiv:2304.04585

Zitnik, M., et al. (2018). Modeling polypharmacy side effects with graph convolutional networks. *Bioinformatics, 34*(13), i457–i466. https://doi.org/10.1093/bioinformatics/bty294

Chapter 12

Innovations in AI Infrastructure—A Patented Approach

12.1 AI-Powered Data Space Optimizer

The AI-Powered Data Space Optimization Device (DSOD) is a hardware appliance designed to optimize data transfer and caching using AI-based prediction models. Positioned between data sources and compute infrastructure, it pre-fetches and stages frequently accessed data, reducing latency and improving throughput for AI workloads (Figure 12.1).

Architecture Overview: The device integrates high-speed DRAM, NVMe SSDs, and AI processors (for example, graphics processing units (GPUs) or dedicated accelerators). It learns access patterns from logs and accelerates data-intensive workflows by dynamically managing cache contents. Thermal regulation is handled through a vertically aligned fan and heat-dissipating vents. Interfaces typically include Ethernet, USB, and PCIe.

Industry Use Case: In a large enterprise analytics environment, the device operates between distributed storage systems and a GPU training cluster. By learning which datasets are repeatedly accessed and proactively preloading them, it keeps computing resources fully utilized and shortens training cycles. Teams working on high-volume simulation, log analytics, recommendation systems, or large-scale model training benefit from reduced wait times and faster iteration loops.

DOI: 10.4324/9781003685609-12

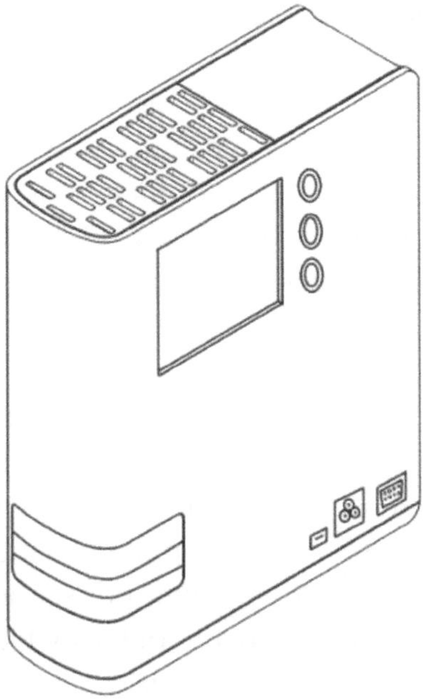

Figure 12.1 AI-Powered Data Space Optimization Device

12.1.1 How the Device Enhances Data Access and Caching

The DSOD's strength lies in how it manages and optimizes data flow.

Traditional caching devices rely on fixed algorithms like least recently used (LRU) and rarely adapt beyond predefined rules. The DSOD takes a different approach. It continuously analyzes which data segments are being requested, how often they appear, and in what sequence. With enough observations, it begins to predict what will be needed next and stages that data in high-speed memory before the request arrives.

One core capability is *predictive prefetching*. If an AI training job loads batches of files in a recognizable pattern, the device quickly learns that behavior. After a short learning period, it starts preloading the next set of files while the current batch is still being processed. This overlap between computation and data transfer removes unnecessary wait times and keeps accelerators fully utilized instead of idling for *I/O*.

The device is also highly adaptive. When workload patterns shift, it adjusts quickly. New hot data is promoted into fast storage, while older or less relevant data is pushed out based on updated predictions. This continuous recalibration ensures that the cache reflects current demand rather than outdated assumptions.

To make the most of its available space, the DSOD relies on intelligent compression, deduplication, and placement strategies. If several processes repeatedly request the same dataset, the device keeps a single cached copy and serves every request from that version. It may compress data during idle periods to expand the usable capacity of its fast storage and decompress it on the fly when needed. Behind the scenes, AI models decide when to compress or decompress, when to evict stale data, which files deserve priority in fast memory tiers, and which access patterns should shape their predictive model.

All of this translates into practical performance gains. Standard cloud storage often has latencies in the tens of milliseconds, and large dataset transfers can easily saturate network links. The DSOD mitigates this by pulling data ahead of time and serving it from high-bandwidth local storage. Sub-millisecond latency and multi-gigabyte-per-second throughput become achievable because the device effectively behaves like a local, memory-speed reservoir for frequently accessed data.

In clustered environments, the DSOD becomes even more powerful. It can act as a shared cache across multiple servers so that if one machine retrieves a dataset, another can reuse it without reaching back to remote storage. This shared caching avoids redundant transfers and improves efficiency at the cluster level. Through predictive prefetching, adaptive caching, and intelligent data compaction, the DSOD maximizes the effective working dataset available to compute resources. The result is faster training, quicker experimentation, and significantly better utilization of high-value compute hardware.

12.1.2 Use Case: Accelerating Large-Scale AI Workloads with Optimized Data Access

To make the capabilities more concrete, consider a company training perception models for autonomous vehicles.

The organization maintains a central object store holding millions of hours of dashcam video, LiDAR captures, radar logs, and telemetry from vehicles worldwide. Training a deep learning model on this dataset hits a familiar bottleneck: reading the files from central storage is slow. Even with high-end GPUs, the accelerators often wind up idle, waiting for data to arrive over the network.

The DSOD is installed between the primary storage (a large-scale object store or NAS) and the GPU cluster. As soon as training begins, the device starts intercepting data requests. During the first epoch, it mostly observes access patterns and begins caching. By the time the training job enters the second epoch, the DSOD has cached a large portion of recently used samples. Instead of every frame being pulled across the network, most batches are now served directly from the device's high-speed cache.

Engineers see throughput to the GPUs double or triple, and GPU idle time collapses. A training run that previously took 10 hours now finishes in 6–7 hours simply because *I/O* wait time has been slashed.

As experiments evolve, the DSOD adapts. If the team switches to a specific subset of scenarios—say, night driving in rain or complex urban intersections—the device detects the new pattern and promotes those files into its fastest tier of storage. It may even preload related clips (for example, prior and subsequent segments from the same roads) that it predicts will be needed next.

The benefits extend to collaboration as well. Multiple teams training different models on overlapping subsets of the driving data all share the same device. When one group pulls a batch of clips, those clips remain available in local cache so others can reuse them without hitting remote storage again. This reduces network congestion and accelerates everyone's work.

From the platform side, deployment is straightforward. The DSOD presents itself as a proxy or a specialized file system layer. Training code and tools keep working as before—no code changes required. The primary storage remains the system of record, while the DSOD holds active working sets and absorbs repeated reads. Over weeks of use, the impact becomes obvious: models train faster, experiments run back-to-back, and the organization can explore more ideas with the same hardware budget.

12.2 AI-Driven Data Cleaning and Preprocessing Device

Modern AI and data science pipelines depend heavily on one unglamorous but essential phase: cleaning and preprocessing raw data. In many organizations, this consumes most of the workflow because datasets arrive messy, inconsistent, and structured in different ways. The AI-Driven Data Cleaning and Preprocessing Device is designed to automate and accelerate this step, bringing consistency and intelligence to the front end of AI pipelines.

This section introduces the device's architecture, its AI-powered software components, and the typical workflows it handles. We also touch on patent diagrams that outline the device's physical layout and design philosophy.

Figure 12.2 AI-Driven Data Cleaning & Preprocessing Device

The device executes full end-to-end cleaning workflows that can be tailored to each project. A typical pipeline begins with raw data ingestion. It can pull data from cloud storage buckets, distributed databases, file repositories, log streams, or direct user uploads. Once the data arrives, the device profiles the dataset—identifying schema, data types, missing values, formats, inconsistencies, and overall quality. It might detect that certain columns are sparsely populated, that event logs use multiple timestamp formats, or that an image dataset contains mixed resolutions. This profiling step allows the AI to plan the cleaning strategy automatically (Figure 12.2).

After profiling, the device moves into automated cleaning. It identifies and removes duplicate records using similarity-based matching rather than strict exact-match rules. Missing values are handled through intelligent imputation or by marking and filtering records based on context. It standardizes formats across the dataset—dates, text fields, categorical labels—and resolves inconsistencies so downstream tools don't have to deal with mismatched formats. Outlier detection is done through machine learning models that flag or remove unusual entries. For numerical datasets, values can be scaled or normalized. For image-based workloads, the device supports resizing, cropping, denoising, and color correction. The goal is simple: bring everything into a clean, consistent state before training begins.

The device supports domain-specific preprocessing across a wide range of fields:

- For *structured tabular data*, it enforces business rules and schema constraints.
- For *text data*, it performs tokenization, language normalization, stop-word removal, and vocabulary mapping.

- For *sensor and log streams*, it applies filters, resampling, and smoothing techniques.
- For *images and video*, it applies standardized transformations, tiling, artifact removal, and basic augmentation.

The device adapts its workflow automatically by learning from historical patterns in the data it processes, making it flexible across industries.

Once cleaning is complete, the device runs a quality assurance pass. It validates that key fields are no longer missing beyond acceptable thresholds, values fall within expected ranges, formats are consistent, and statistical properties look reasonable. It can also run a small sample model on a subset of the cleaned data as a sanity check; if that training fails or produces unusual metrics, the device flags potential issues. This integrated QA step reduces the risk of pushing flawed data downstream.

In the output phase, cleaned datasets can be written to a data warehouse, registered as a versioned dataset, exposed through APIs, or piped directly into an AI training pipeline. The device supports continuous pipelines as well—new data can flow in throughout the day, and the cleaned dataset updates automatically. Each run generates a full report summarizing what changed, how many records were modified or dropped, and which issues were detected. This transparency lets data engineers audit and refine the workflow when necessary.

By following these workflows, the AI-Driven Data Cleaning and Preprocessing Device acts as a gatekeeper for data quality. It transforms noisy, inconsistent inputs into structured, reliable, training-ready datasets. Because it uses AI to improve its strategy over time, cleaning becomes more accurate and efficient with each batch. The result is faster preparation, fewer manual tasks, and stronger model performance.

12.2.1 Use Case: Accelerating Enterprise AI Projects with Clean Data

To illustrate the device's practical value, consider a large enterprise working with diverse datasets—high-volume application logs, customer records, device telemetry, and millions of images.

These datasets arrive in inconsistent formats and must be cleaned before any large-scale machine learning work can begin. Using the device, the team can ingest raw batches automatically, whether they originate from cloud data lakes, microservices, or nightly extract, transform, and load (ETL) jobs.

The device immediately profiles the incoming data and applies domain-specific cleaning rules:

- **For clickstream and behavior logs**, it de-duplicates events, reconciles user IDs across systems, fixes inconsistent timestamps, and filters corrupt records.
- **For customer and account data**, it normalizes addresses, merges near-duplicate profiles, standardizes categorical values, and imputes missing attributes.
- **For IoT sensor streams**, it resamples time series, removes obvious spikes or dropouts, fills short gaps, and flags long outages.
- **For product or inspection images**, it standardizes resolution, crops or pads to expected input sizes, corrects lighting, and discards unusable frames.

A key advantage is adaptability. When engineers shift focus—for example, analyzing a particular product line, geographic region, or log source—the device detects the new pattern and prioritizes the relevant data. If teams run repeated experiments on the same subset, the device automatically keeps those files cached, cleaned, and ready for immediate processing.

Because the cleaned data is delivered quickly and consistently, training cycles shrink from days to hours. Multiple teams benefit from the shared preprocessing pipeline: once a file is cleaned or standardized for one use case, other teams working on adjacent projects get the same benefit without rebuilding the pipeline themselves. This reduces duplicated effort and infrastructure strain.

Operationally, the device functions like a smart preprocessing gateway—applications don't need to be rewritten. It can output cleaned datasets in batch mode, stream cleaned records in real time, or serve them through a mounted interface that applications treat as a local file system. Over time, it enforces a level of standardization that's hard to achieve with scattered scripts and manual interventions.

By automating data cleaning at scale, the device allows engineers and data scientists to focus on higher-value tasks like model development, feature engineering, and experimentation. Projects move faster, iteration cycles tighten, and the organization benefits from more reliable, higher-quality data across the board.

12.3 AI-Powered Data Logger

12.3.1 Hardware Design and Architecture

The AI-Powered Data Logger is a standalone edge device built for real-time data capture in demanding environments. As shown in the perspective and front-view diagrams, the device features a large integrated display on its front face for status readouts and configuration, coupled with an array of physical controls (oval and circular buttons beneath the screen) for user interaction. The front view highlights these interface elements: a high-resolution screen and a set of input buttons (which may include power, menu navigation, and quick-action keys). This design enables operators or field technicians to work directly on the device, even if network connectivity is down, ensuring continuous logging of critical data.

The enclosure is designed for durability—typically a hardened polymer or light alloy shell—to protect the electronics in industrial, laboratory, or outdoor settings. The form factor is a slightly convex rectangular unit sized for portability and mounting. Rubberized edges or gasket seals would provide shock resistance and some protection against dust or moisture, given the needs of factory floors, vehicles, or field installations.

Every side of the device serves a purpose, as illustrated by the multi-view patent diagrams (front, back, top, bottom, left, right). The back view reveals a removable panel, suggesting an internal battery bay or storage compartment for swappable batteries or SSD storage. Mounting points and a recessed area confirm that the logger is intended to be both serviceable and mountable.

Side views give insight into the device's *I/O* and expansion capabilities. One side typically includes a set of connectors behind a protective panel: a circular power or antenna connector, status LEDs or sensors, and rectangular cut-outs that map to data ports such as USB and Ethernet. A hinged cover protects these ports when not in use, balancing accessibility with physical protection (Figure 12.3).

The top and bottom views show a flat, slightly beveled surface with potential vents and mounting features. The bottom likely includes rubber feet or a docking bracket and may house additional air intakes. A docking option allows the logger to recharge and upload data to central systems when not deployed.

Internally, the data logger resembles a compact embedded computer optimized for data acquisition. It contains a multi-core CPU (or SoC) and

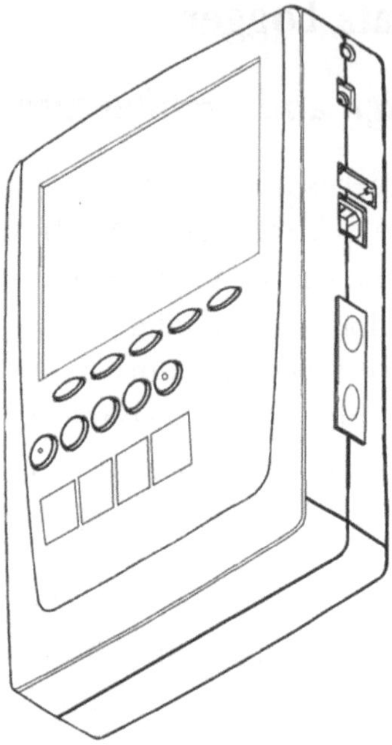

Figure 12.3 AI-Powered Data Logger

optionally an AI accelerator (such as a GPU or ASIC) to handle on-device intelligence. High-throughput memory (RAM) supports in-memory processing of large batches of records. Local SSD or NVMe storage is used for buffering, caching, and storing intermediate and historical data. High-speed network interfaces (10 GbE or similar) ingest streams from sensors, controllers, or edge gateways and push processed data back to central repositories.

Redundant power supplies or hot-swappable batteries and error-correcting memory support reliability and integrity in mission-critical scenarios. Overall, the hardware architecture balances compute power, *I/O* bandwidth, and robustness, encased in a form factor optimized for cooling and easy integration.

12.3.2 Software Intelligence and Data Logging Mechanisms

Beyond its physical design, the real value of the AI-Powered Data Logger lies in its embedded software and AI-driven data handling capabilities. It functions as an edge computing node in a distributed data pipeline.

In a typical deployment, multiple sensors and data sources feed into the logger—for example:

- Environmental and vibration sensors on industrial machines.
- PLCs and controllers on a production line.
- Telemetry from vehicles or mobile robots.
- Application or transaction events from local systems.

The logger acts as the "main controller" in this architecture, aggregating inputs, performing local processing, and then communicating with a back-end server or cloud database. Its onboard software stack combines real-time data ingestion, machine learning inference, and indexing services.

12.3.2.1 Real-Time Data Ingestion

The device continuously collects data from various streams. A data acquisition module interfaces with each type of source. For example:

- A fieldbus or industrial protocol stack (e.g., Modbus, OPC-UA) gathers machine metrics.
- A CAN bus reader ingests vehicle telemetry.
- A REST or gRPC connector listens for local application events.

The ingestion layer timestamps each incoming data point or file and converts it into a standard internal representation. The logger's real-time OS or embedded Linux ensures that even high-frequency streams are buffered and recorded without dropping data. A multi-threaded architecture lets it handle concurrent inputs—for instance, recording millisecond-level sensor data while simultaneously uploading historical batches to the cloud.

12.3.2.2 Local AI Processing

What makes this data logger "AI-powered" is its ability to analyze and enrich data on the fly. Using built-in accelerators, the device runs machine learning models on incoming streams in real time. For numerical sensor data, it might:

- Detect anomalies in vibration patterns hinting at bearing wear.
- Spot unusual temperature trends.
- Flag erratic behavior in power draw.

For textual data like system logs, natural language or log parsing models can extract key entities and tags (component IDs, error codes, severity levels). For image or video data from inspection cameras, on-device computer vision models can detect defects, misalignments, or unsafe conditions in real time.

This edge AI capability means the logger doesn't just store raw data; it understands it to a degree, performing a first pass of analysis before anything reaches central systems. It generates annotations and indexes that accelerate downstream analytics and model training.

12.3.2.3 Intelligent Indexing and Storage

All captured data—along with AI-generated annotations—is logged into onboard storage. Continuous signals and events go into a time-series database; documents, images, and richer payloads go into an object store or embedded database. Each record is tagged with identifiers (asset ID, line ID, vehicle ID), timestamps, and data-type labels.

The indexing engine uses AI annotations to create a searchable catalog. For example:

- One index maps timestamps to detected events ("spike in vibration", "out-of-range temperature"),
- Another catalogs files by content ("defect detected in station 3", "vehicle overspeed event").

From the device's UI, operators can query recent data or filter by event type, asset, or severity.

12.3.2.4 Secure Communication and Cloud Integration

While fully capable of offline operation, the logger often connects to enterprise networks or the internet to sync data with cloud platforms. A communication module (Wi-Fi/Ethernet or cellular) handles encrypted data transfer to central services in real time or in scheduled batches. In bandwidth-constrained locations, it can send only summaries and anomalies immediately and upload full datasets during off-peak windows.

Central systems can train models on aggregated data from many loggers and then push updated models back to the edge. The software architecture typically isolates AI routines from core logging tasks so that even if a model fails or a container crashes, raw data logging continues uninterrupted.

12.3.3 Use Case: Industrial Asset Monitoring and Predictive Maintenance

To illustrate the capabilities of the AI-Powered Data Logger, consider a global manufacturer running multiple production lines and remote facilities.

Each critical machine—motors, pumps, conveyor systems, CNC machines—is instrumented with sensors that track vibration, temperature, current draw, and throughput. The data logger sits at the edge of each line, receiving continuous streams over industrial protocols and wireless links.

12.3.3.1 Real-Time Asset Monitoring

The logger continuously records sensor readings and learns normal behavior for each machine. Suppose a gearbox begins to develop a subtle fault: vibration at a specific frequency starts to rise, and operating temperature creeps up under load. The logger's anomaly detection model flags this combination as abnormal long before it crosses simplistic threshold alarms. It creates a timestamped event, elevates alert priority, and sends a notification to the maintenance system.

Instead of waiting for a breakdown, the maintenance team can schedule a planned inspection and swap-out. Downtime shifts from unplanned to scheduled, and spare parts can be staged ahead of time.

12.3.3.2 Process Event Logging

Throughout a production shift, the logger records process events: line start/stop, changeovers, quality checks, and fault codes from controllers. Operators can mark additional events using the physical buttons on the front panel (for example, "material shortage" or "operator intervention").

Over time, the device builds a rich timeline that aligns machine health, production events, and output quality. The onboard AI can correlate these signals; for example, linking a specific sequence of micro-stops and temperature spikes to later quality issues, or identifying patterns that precede a jam at a given station.

12.3.3.3 Visual Inspection Integration

In lines that use cameras for visual inspection, the logger can ingest either image metadata or full frames. Computer vision models running on the device:

- Detect surface defects.
- Measure alignment or dimensions.
- Classify parts into pass/fail categories.

Instead of storing every frame, the logger can keep only samples and defect patches, dramatically reducing bandwidth. Detected defects are indexed by asset, product, and time, making root-cause analysis easier.

12.3.3.4 Data Aggregation for AI Training

Across the manufacturer's sites, each logger syncs its structured logs and annotations to a central cloud repository. Because preprocessing and indexing already happened at the edge, data scientists can work with ready-to-use datasets: engineered features, labeled anomalies, and aligned time series across machines and plants.

They can train predictive maintenance models, throughput optimization policies, and quality prediction models without spending months building custom pipelines for each plant. Updated models are then deployed back to the loggers, closing a learning loop between edge and cloud.

From an operations perspective, the AI-Powered Data Logger ensures that no key signal goes unrecorded and that insights can be generated close to where events happen. It turns raw industrial telemetry into structured, actionable information that drives reliability, yield, and efficiency.

12.4 AI-Powered Multi-Cloud Data Optimizer

This device manages and distributes AI workloads across multi-cloud environments. It makes real-time decisions on where to execute, store, and synchronize data based on latency, cost, and policy constraints using AI algorithms.

Architecture Overview: Built as a compact console with rotary controls, antennas, and a touchscreen, it supports Wi-Fi 6, dual Ethernet, and integrates CPUs and GPUs. It interfaces with APIs from major cloud providers and orchestrates containerized AI workloads. Advanced cooling and hardware security modules (HSMs) support long-running operation and secure key management.

The perspective view shows a console-style unit that sits between on-premises systems and multiple clouds. Its role is to optimize where data-intensive applications run, how data is replicated, and how resources are allocated across providers.

12.4.1 Hardware Architecture and Design

12.4.1.1 Front View

The front panel contains a tilting high-resolution display and an array of programmable buttons with status LEDs, plus a large rotary dial. This interface lets platform engineers monitor multi-cloud operations and manually override settings without a separate PC. Dual high-gain antennas flanking the screen indicate wireless connectivity for scenarios where wired networks are unavailable or as backups.

12.4.1.2 Rear View

The rear panel exposes connectivity and cooling: dual Ethernet LAN ports for redundant connections or links to separate networks, USB ports for external storage or offline data ingestion, and a multi-pin connector for integration with legacy systems or debug consoles. A perforated grill and internal fan provide active cooling for the high-performance processors.

12.4.1.3 Top and Side Views

From above, the layout shows the angled display, button cluster, power control, and rotary knob. The base houses CPUs, GPUs/accelerators, high-capacity SSDs, and the power supply. Side views highlight the antennas and the compact profile, making the device suitable for desks, racks, or carts in operations centers.

Internally, the device resembles a miniature cloud node in a box: multi-core CPUs for virtualization and networking, GPUs or AI accelerators for optimization models, high-speed RAM, and NVMe storage for caching datasets, models, and orchestration state (Figure 12.4).

12.4.2 Internal Components and Processing Power

At its core, the AI-Powered Multi-Cloud Data Optimizer includes:

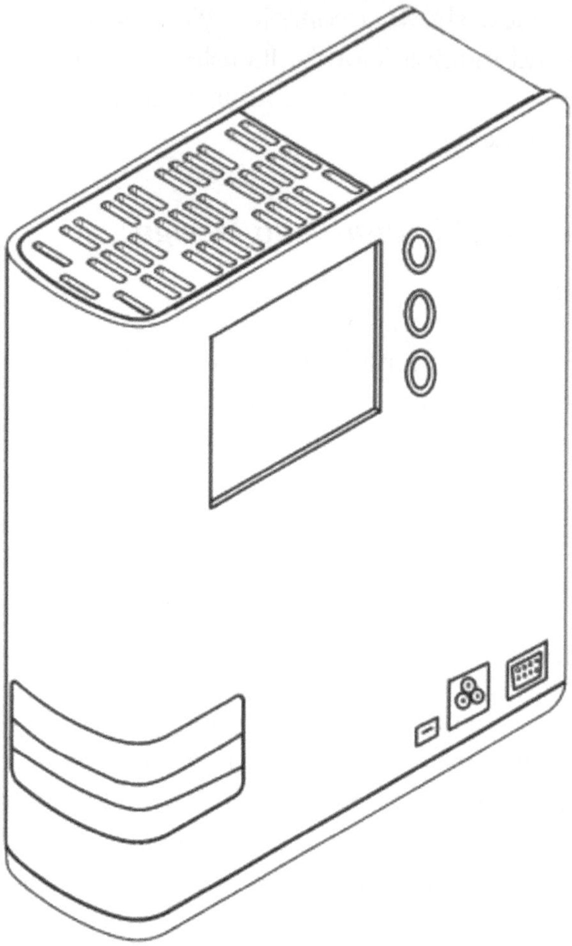

Figure 12.4 AI-Powered Data Space Optimization Device

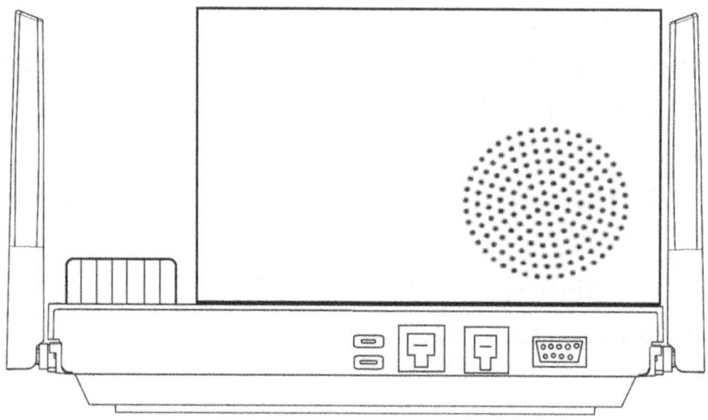

Figure 12.5 AI-Powered Multi-Cloud Data Optimizer

- **Multi-core CPUs** for running orchestrators, API clients, and virtualized control planes.
- **GPU/AI accelerators** to run optimization and inference models in real time.
- **High-speed memory** to hold configuration, workload descriptors, and short-lived datasets.
- **NVMe SSDs** to cache models, containers, and frequently used data across clouds.
- **Advanced networking hardware**, including multi-gigabit Ethernet and modern Wi-Fi/5G radios, to sustain concurrent links to multiple providers.
- **Security hardware**, such as an HSM or secure enclave, to manage credentials, encryption keys, and signing operations.

Cooling, power conditioning, and optionally battery backup maintain stability under continuous load. The overall design is intended to run 24/7 as a control point for distributed workloads.

12.4.3 AI Algorithms for Intelligent Optimization

To justify the "AI-powered" label, the Multi-Cloud Data Optimizer runs a suite of models that continuously analyze:

- application performance,
- network latency and throughput,
- cloud service pricing and spot markets,
- quota limits and regional availability, and
- policy and compliance constraints.

By learning patterns over time, it can predict when workloads should be shifted, scaled, or rescheduled.

One class of algorithms is *reinforcement learning* for dynamic resource allocation. The software behaves like an agent that tries different placement strategies and receives feedback as performance scores and cost signals. Over time, it learns policies that minimize job completion time, cost, or a combination of the two.

Neural models can also detect anomalies—for instance, sudden spikes in cloud costs, unusual error patterns in one region, or degraded network paths. When anomalies occur, the device can:

- reroute traffic,
- reschedule jobs,
- scale replicas up or down, or
- fall back to alternate regions/providers.

The AI incorporates *FinOps logic* (cost awareness) and *policy rules* (for example, data residency or contractual constraints). It will not place a workload in a region that violates data locality requirements, even if that region is cheaper or faster.

As more workloads flow through the device, its models become better calibrated, making decisions that reflect real usage patterns rather than static assumptions.

12.4.4 Cross-Cloud Orchestration Capabilities

Managing multiple cloud environments is inherently complex. The Multi-Cloud Data Optimizer is built to orchestrate this complexity.

It runs a specialized stack that integrates with cloud APIs and cluster managers. Using containers and infrastructure-as-code artifacts, it can:

- package applications and AI models,
- deploy them to various clouds and regions,
- monitor health and performance, and
- roll out updates.

Data pipelines are orchestrated alongside compute. If a training job runs in one provider and data is stored in another, the device sets up secure, efficient replication or streaming:

- compressing data where appropriate,
- filtering unnecessary fields,
- scheduling bulk transfers during cheaper or less congested windows, and
- maintaining checksums to preserve integrity.

High availability is baked in. If one provider experiences a regional outage or a key service fails, the device can:

- spin up equivalent resources in another provider,
- redirect traffic, and
- keep SLAs intact for upstream systems.

Security policies are enforced consistently across clouds—identity, encryption, and logging standards can be applied once and translated into provider-specific configurations behind the scenes.

12.4.5 Representative Industry Use Cases

Multi-cloud strategies are increasingly attractive across sectors that need reliability, scalability, and specialized services. The AI-Powered Multi-Cloud Data Optimizer fits naturally into several patterns. Three examples:

1. **Global Fraud Detection for Financial Services**
   A payment processor operates in many regions and uses multiple clouds: one for streaming ingestion, another for real-time analytics, and a third for long-term storage and model training.
   The Optimizer decides, per region and time of day, where to run fraud models, which GPU instances to allocate, and how to replicate recent transaction windows. It might:
   - keep low-latency inference services close to major markets,
   - burst training jobs to whichever cloud has cheaper GPU capacity overnight, and
   - shift workloads away from a region showing degraded performance.

   This reduces false positives, cuts reaction time, and keeps cloud spending under control.
2. **Cross-Cloud Analytics for Online Platforms**
   A large-scale SaaS platform uses one cloud for transactional workloads and another for analytics and experimentation. Moving entirely to a single provider isn't practical.
   The Optimizer creates a virtual data mesh across these environments. It:
   - deploys analytics containers in the clouds where data already resides,
   - orchestrates queries and aggregations across them, and
   - merges only aggregated or sampled results back to a central view.

   Product teams get the effect of a single analytics platform, while the actual compute runs close to the data, respecting data residency and minimizing transfers.

3. **Digital Twins and Simulation at Industrial Scale**
   A manufacturer builds digital twins of factories and assets, running simulations to test new control policies, layouts, and maintenance strategies. Different cloud providers offer different strengths:

   - Cloud A provides low-cost GPU clusters for physics-based simulation,
   - Cloud B provides strong managed ML services for optimization,
   - Cloud C is preferred for long-term storage and archival.

   The Optimizer coordinates all three: simulation jobs run in Cloud A, optimization runs in Cloud B using generated data, and curated results are archived in Cloud C. When demand spikes, it automatically fans out simulations across providers and pulls back results into a unified dashboard.

In each case, the Multi-Cloud Data Optimizer becomes the control plane that lets teams use multiple clouds as a single, adaptive pool of compute and data.

12.5 Integrated Innovation, Industry Alignment, and Future Potential

Together, the four devices—the AI-Powered Data Space Optimizer, AI-Driven Data Cleaning and Preprocessing Device, AI-Powered Data Logger, and AI-Powered Multi-Cloud Data Optimizer—form a holistic AI infrastructure toolkit.

They address the complete data lifecycle:

- **Ingestion and logging** at the edge (AI-Powered Data Logger),
- **Cleaning and standardization** (AI-Driven Data Cleaning and Preprocessing Device),
- **Caching and high-speed access** to active datasets (AI-Powered Data Space Optimizer),
- **Orchestration and placement** of workloads across clouds (AI-Powered Multi-Cloud Data Optimizer).

Used together, they build an end-to-end intelligent data pipeline that supports complex applications like:

- large-scale recommendation systems,
- industrial digital twins and predictive maintenance,
- global fraud detection and risk analytics,
- real-time personalization and A/B testing at internet scale, and
- smart city and IoT analytics.

12.5.1 Industry Alignment

These inventions track directly with trends discussed in earlier chapters: cloud-native AI platforms, hybrid and multi-cloud strategies, edge computing, and data-centric AI practices. Enterprises in finance, manufacturing, logistics, telecom, media, and beyond are all moving toward architectures where:

- data is generated at the edge,
- cleaned and enriched close to the source,
- cached strategically to keep accelerators busy, and
- analyzed using whichever mix of clouds makes the most sense at that moment.

The devices described here provide concrete building blocks for that vision.

12.5.2 Commercial Potential

Each device can be commercialized on its own or as part of a modular suite. Variants could be:

- hardware appliances for plants, data centers, and operations centers,
- embedded firmware licensed to OEMs, or
- SaaS platforms that virtualize the same capabilities.

They are relevant not only for internal enterprise deployments but also for service providers who want to offer managed AI infrastructure.

Open-sourcing select components—for instance, data cleaning pipelines or orchestration APIs—could help them become reference implementations that shape emerging AI infrastructure standards. Participation in standards bodies and industry groups around cloud, edge, and data management would amplify their influence and adoption.

12.5.3 Strategic Impact

By embedding AI into each stage of the data lifecycle, these inventions represent a step change in how organizations can build and run data-intensive systems. They turn fragmented scripts, ad hoc pipelines, and hand-tuned deployments into an integrated, learning infrastructure layer.

The end result is not just faster models or cheaper compute. It's the ability to experiment more, iterate quickly, and make data-driven decisions with infrastructure that adapts as workloads and business needs evolve.

Bibliography

Abadi, M., Agarwal, A., Barham, P., et al. (2016). TensorFlow: A system for large-scale machine learning. *12th USENIX Symposium on Operating Systems Design and Implementation (OSDI '16)*, 265–283.

Dean, J., Patterson, D., & Young, C. (2018). A new golden age in computer architecture: Empowering the machine-learning revolution. *IEEE Micro, 38*(2), 21–29. https://doi.org/10.1109/MM.2018.112130030

Ghodsi, A., Zaharia, M., Hindman, B., et al. (2011). Dominant resource fairness: Fair allocation of multiple resource types. *8th USENIX Symposium on Networked Systems Design and Implementation (NSDI '11)*, 323–336.

Kang, J., Yu, R., Xie, S., et al. (2020). Reliable federated learning for mobile edge networks: Coordinated client selection and resource management. *IEEE Internet of Things Journal*, 7(10), 9558–9571. https://doi.org/10.1109/JIOT.2020.2991389

Li, H., Wang, S., Xu, X., et al. (2020). Data caching and AI-based prefetching for edge–cloud collaboration. *IEEE Transactions on Industrial Informatics, 16*(7), 4914–4923. https://doi.org/10.1109/TII.2019.2952039

Lorido-Botran, T., Miguel-Alonso, J., & Lozano, J. A. (2014). A review of auto-scaling techniques for elastic applications in cloud environments. *Journal of Grid Computing, 12*(4), 559–592. https://doi.org/10.1007/s10723-014-9314-7

Mao, H., Alizadeh, M., Menache, I., & Kandula, S. (2016). Resource management with deep reinforcement learning. *Proceedings of the 15th ACM Workshop on Hot Topics in Networks (HotNets-XV)*, 50–56. https://doi.org/10.1145/3005745.3005750

McMahan, H. B., Moore, E., Ramage, D., & y Arcas, B. A. (2017). Communication-efficient learning of deep networks from decentralized data. *Proceedings of the 20th International Conference on Artificial Intelligence and Statistics (AISTATS)*, 1273–1282.

Rahm, E., & Do, H. H. (2000). Data cleaning: Problems and current approaches. *IEEE Data Engineering Bulletin, 23*(4), 3–13.

Satyanarayanan, M. (2017). The emergence of edge computing. *IEEE Computer, 50*(1), 30–39. https://doi.org/10.1109/MC.2017.9

Shi, W., Cao, J., Zhang, Q., Li, Y., & Xu, L. (2016). Edge computing: Vision and challenges. *IEEE Internet of Things Journal, 3*(5), 637–646. https://doi.org/10.1109/JIOT.2016.2579198

Stonebraker, M., Abadi, D. J., DeWitt, D. J., et al. (2010). MapReduce and parallel DBMSs: Friends or foes? *Communications of the ACM, 53*(1), 64–71. https://doi.org/10.1145/1629175.1629197

Yu, K., Wang, J., & Li, Y. (2019). Multi-cloud orchestration for data-intensive applications. *IEEE Access, 7,* 133627–133636. https://doi.org/10.1109/ACCESS.2019.2941395

Zhang, K., Mao, Y., Leng, S., Zhao, Q., Li, L., & Peng, X. (2016). Energy-efficient offloading for mobile edge computing in 5G heterogeneous networks. *IEEE Access, 4,* 5896–5907. https://doi.org/10.1109/ACCESS.2016.2597169

Zhu, H., Song, H., & Rodero, I. (2020). DataOps for cloud-native applications: Challenges and practices. *IEEE International Conference on Cloud Engineering (IC2E),* 120–130.

Chapter 13

Future Trends in AI Cloud Infrastructure

13.1 Quantum Computing and AI in the Cloud

As artificial intelligence continues to push the boundaries of what machines can learn and predict, traditional computing infrastructures—even with GPUs and TPUs—may encounter limits in solving extremely complex optimization, simulation, and probabilistic problems. Quantum computing, which leverages the principles of quantum mechanics to perform computations at unprecedented scales and speeds, is poised to transform the future of AI (Figure 13.1).

Cloud-based quantum computing is making this advanced capability accessible to organizations and researchers without requiring ownership of expensive, specialized quantum hardware. In this section, we explore how quantum computing is shaping AI development, the role of cloud platforms in democratizing quantum access, key use cases, and the anticipated convergence of quantum computing and AI in enterprise solutions.

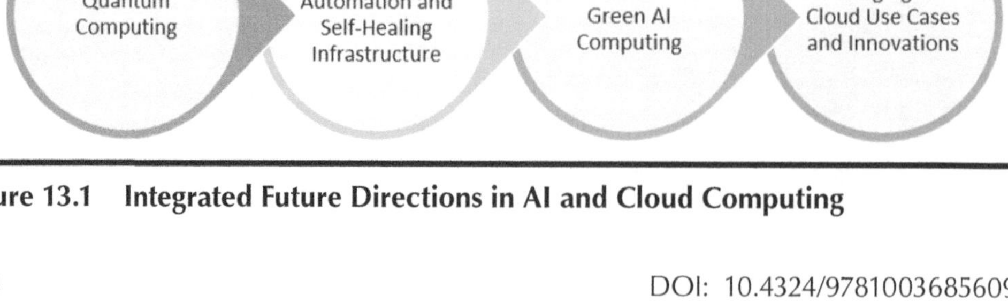

Figure 13.1 Integrated Future Directions in AI and Cloud Computing

DOI: 10.4324/9781003685609-13

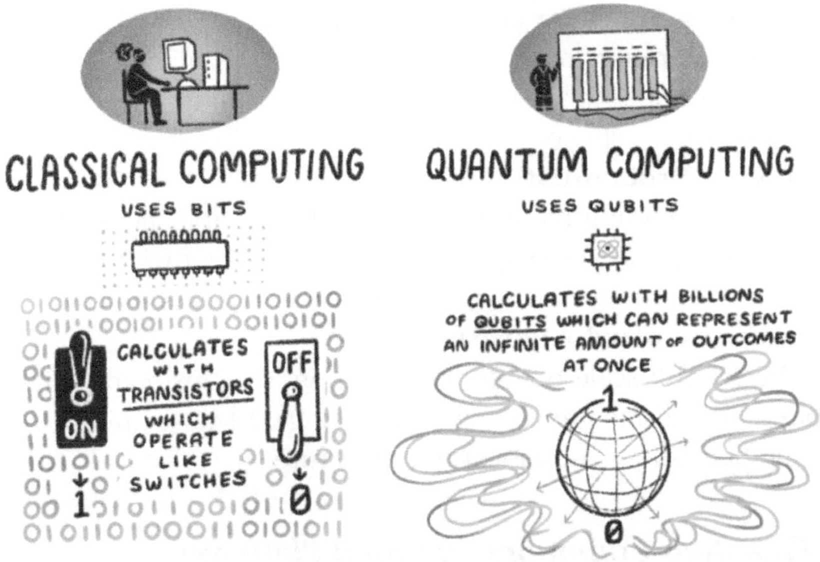

Figure 13.2 Core Principles of Quantum Computing: Superposition, Entanglement, and Interference

13.1.1 What Is Quantum Computing?

Quantum computing uses quantum bits (qubits), which can exist in multiple states simultaneously through superposition and can become entangled with one another, allowing certain types of computations to be executed exponentially faster than with classical systems (Figure 13.2).

Key principles include:

- **Superposition**: A qubit can represent both 0 and 1 at the same time, enabling parallel computations.
- **Entanglement**: Qubits become interdependent, allowing for complex relational computations.
- **Quantum Interference**: Used to amplify correct solutions and cancel out incorrect paths.

13.1.2 Why Quantum Computing Matters for AI

1. **Solving Complex Optimization Problems**:
   Quantum algorithms, such as the Quantum Approximate Optimization Algorithm (QAOA), can efficiently solve optimization problems that are currently intractable for classical computers.

2. **Accelerating Machine Learning Training**:
   Quantum computers may one day drastically reduce the time required to train large, deep-learning models by performing linear algebra operations at quantum speed.
3. **Enhancing Probabilistic Models**:
   Quantum computing naturally aligns with probabilistic models, making it well-suited for developing more accurate generative AI, reinforcement learning algorithms, and Bayesian inference systems.
4. **Quantum-Inspired Algorithms for AI**:
   Even before full-scale quantum computing is mainstream, quantum-inspired algorithms are already influencing AI by optimizing search and training heuristics on classical infrastructure.

13.1.3 Quantum Computing in Cloud Platforms

Cloud Provider	*Quantum Computing Services*
IBM Cloud	**IBM Quantum Experience:** Access to real quantum processors and simulators; integrated Qiskit SDK
Microsoft Azure	**Azure Quantum:** Open ecosystem with access to quantum hardware from IonQ, Honeywell, and Rigetti; integrated with Azure ML
Amazon Web Services (AWS)	**Amazon Braket:** Access to D-Wave, Rigetti, IonQ hardware, and quantum simulators; integrated workflow development with classical AWS services
Google Cloud	**Quantum AI:** Research-focused access to Google's Sycamore quantum processors (limited release), paired with TensorFlow Quantum for hybrid quantum-classical ML

13.1.4 Use Cases for Quantum AI in the Cloud

Use Case	*How Quantum AI Enhances It*
Drug discovery	Models molecular structures and reactions more accurately and rapidly than classical simulations
Supply chain optimization	Solves complex logistical challenges involving large combinatorial problem spaces

Use Case	*How Quantum AI Enhances It*
Financial portfolio optimization	Simulates market conditions and optimizes asset allocation with quantum algorithms
Fraud detection	Improves detection of anomalous patterns in large transaction networks using quantum-enhanced probabilistic models
Material science and manufacturing	Models atomic interactions and material properties for advanced product development

13.1.5 Hybrid Quantum-Classical AI Workflows

Since quantum computers are not yet ready to replace classical infrastructure for general AI tasks, most current applications focus on hybrid architectures, where:

- Data preprocessing, feature engineering, and model preparation are done using classical systems.
- Specific problem-solving modules, such as optimization kernels or state-space exploration, are executed on quantum simulators or hardware.
- Results are integrated back into classical machine learning pipelines.

Example Workflow:

1. Collect and preprocess data in the cloud using classical computing.
2. Use Amazon Braket or Azure Quantum to perform quantum optimization of parameters.
3. Integrate results into cloud-based AI training pipelines using TensorFlow or PyTorch.
4. Deploy inference models with quantum-informed optimization strategies on classical or edge platforms.

13.1.6 Quantum Machine Learning (QML) Libraries and Tools

Library	*Purpose*
TensorFlow Quantum (TFQ)	Framework for hybrid quantum-classical machine learning with Google's quantum simulators
PennyLane	Library for differentiable programming of quantum circuits; integrates with PyTorch and TensorFlow

Library	*Purpose*
Qiskit Machine Learning	IBM's library for creating quantum machine learning models
Amazon Braket SDK	Interface for developing quantum algorithms and simulating quantum circuits

13.1.7 Current Challenges in Quantum AI

Challenge	*Impact*
Hardware scalability	Current quantum systems have limited qubit counts and coherence times, restricting problem sizes
Noise and error rates	Quantum computations are susceptible to noise, requiring error correction techniques that are still under development
Skill gaps	Developing quantum AI solutions requires expertise in quantum physics, computer science, and AI—a rare combination
High costs	Quantum cloud computing access is expensive, limiting experimentation for smaller organizations

13.1.8 Future Outlook: Quantum AI in the Cloud

- **Noisy Intermediate-Scale Quantum (NISQ) Era Expansion**: The next few years will see significant progress in NISQ devices, enabling more robust quantum experiments for AI and optimization tasks.
- **Widespread Adoption of Hybrid AI Models**: Hybrid quantum-classical AI models will become increasingly common, with cloud platforms providing integrated pipelines.
- **Quantum Computing-as-a-Service (QCaaS)**: Cloud providers will offer pay-as-you-go quantum computing services tightly integrated with their AI offerings.
- **Quantum AI Accelerators**: Future quantum coprocessors could enhance classical GPU/TPU infrastructure, accelerating optimization and matrix operations at scale.
- **Quantum-Enhanced Reinforcement Learning**: Advances in quantum computing will enable faster policy exploration and decision-making in dynamic, multi-agent environments.

Quantum computing promises to revolutionize AI by tackling complex computational problems that are currently beyond classical limits. While still in its early stages, cloud-based quantum services are making this emerging technology accessible to researchers and enterprises today.

Over the coming years, hybrid quantum-classical AI models will unlock new frontiers in optimization, simulation, and machine learning, all driven by cloud infrastructure that can seamlessly integrate both paradigms. Organizations investing early in quantum readiness and experimentation will position themselves at the forefront of AI innovation in the next decade.

In the next section, we will explore AI infrastructure automation and how it will shape future cloud AI deployments.

13.2 AI-Driven Cloud Automation and Self-Healing Infrastructure

As AI workloads and cloud infrastructure grow in complexity and scale, manual management becomes impractical. AI-driven automation and self-healing systems are emerging as key innovations that enable cloud environments to manage themselves, adapt to changing conditions, and recover from failures with minimal human intervention. This trend is critical not only for maintaining uptime and reliability but also for optimizing resource allocation, controlling costs, and ensuring continuous compliance and security.

In this section, we explore the concept of AI-powered cloud automation, the architecture of self-healing systems, key technologies enabling autonomous cloud management, and the future implications of intelligent infrastructure for AI deployments.

13.2.1 What Is AI-Driven Cloud Automation?

AI-driven cloud automation refers to the use of machine learning, predictive analytics, and intelligent policy engines to manage cloud infrastructure dynamically. These systems:

- Monitor resource usage and performance metrics in real time.
- Predict future demand and scale resources accordingly.
- Detect anomalies and proactively mitigate risks.
- Automate tasks like patching, backups, and service configuration adjustments.

Key Characteristics:

- Autonomous response to workload fluctuations.
- Predictive scaling and optimization.
- Anomaly detection and remediation.
- Integration with CI/CD pipelines for automated deployment management.

13.2.2 Self-Healing Cloud Infrastructure

A *self-healing infrastructure* refers to systems that can detect, diagnose, and recover from failures automatically without manual intervention. This includes:

- Restarting failed instances or containers.
- Redirecting traffic in case of node or regional outages.
- Redeploying corrupt services or applications.
- Auto-correcting misconfigurations.

Benefits:

- Improved system reliability and uptime.
- Reduced operational burden on DevOps and site reliability engineering (SRE) teams.
- Faster recovery from unforeseen incidents.
- Enhanced resilience for mission-critical AI applications.

13.2.3 Components of AI-Driven and Self-Healing Cloud Systems

Component	*Functionality*
Monitoring and telemetry	Real-time tracking of metrics (CPU, memory, network, latency) using agents and telemetry services
Anomaly detection engines	Use machine learning models to detect unusual patterns in system behavior
Policy engines	Define automated actions triggered by specific conditions (e.g., restart service, scale-out)

Component	*Functionality*
Orchestration platforms	Kubernetes, Terraform, and serverless orchestrators are capable of executing self-healing workflows
Predictive analytics models	Forecast future resource needs and optimize provisioning in advance
Automation runbooks	Predefined remediation steps codified for automatic execution by automation tools

13.2.4 Examples of AI-Driven Automation in Cloud Platforms

Cloud Provider	*Key Automation and Self-Healing Services*
AWS	AWS Auto Scaling, AWS CloudWatch Anomaly Detection, EC2 Auto Recovery, Systems Manager Automation
Azure	Azure Auto-Scale, Azure Monitor, Azure Automanage, and automatic service failover for AKS
Google Cloud	Google Cloud Operations Suite (formerly Stackdriver), Auto-Healing Managed Instance Groups, AI-based workload optimization with Active Assist

13.2.5 AI-Driven Automation Use Cases for Cloud AI Workloads

Use Case	*AI-Driven Automation Role*
Dynamic model inference scaling	Automatically scale inference endpoints based on request volume
Automated resource tuning for training jobs	Adjust compute cluster configurations dynamically to optimize training speed and cost
Continuous compliance enforcement	Auto-remediate misconfigurations or policy violations detected by cloud security monitoring systems
Fault detection and recovery for data pipelines	Restart failed ETL processes or reroute data pipelines without manual intervention
Predictive maintenance for cloud resources	Decommission and replace failing virtual machines or storage volumes before outages occur

13.2.6 Architecture of Self-Healing Systems

1. **Real-Time Monitoring Layer**:
   - Continuously collects metrics and logs from all infrastructure components.
2. **Anomaly Detection Engine**:
   - Uses ML models to detect deviations from normal behavior (latency spikes, error rates).
3. **Decision-Making Layer (Policy Engine)**:
   - Applies automated rules and policies based on detected conditions.
4. **Remediation Automation Layer**:
   - Executes actions such as:
     - Rebooting services
     - Redeploying containers
     - Autoscaling resources
     - Notifying human operators if manual intervention is required
5. **Feedback Loop and Learning**:
   - Learns from past incidents and remediation outcomes to improve future detection and response accuracy.

13.2.7 Benefits of AI-Driven and Self-Healing Infrastructure for AI Deployments

- **High Availability**:
  Reduces downtime for AI inference endpoints and data pipelines.
- **Optimized Resource Utilization**:
  Continuously matches compute and storage capacity to workload demands, minimizing waste.
- **Reduced Human Error**:
  Automates routine maintenance and reduces dependency on manual monitoring.
- **Faster Innovation**:
  Frees DevOps and AI engineering teams to focus on building models rather than managing infrastructure.
- **Improved Security Posture**:
  Rapidly detects and remediates security misconfigurations and vulnerabilities.

13.2.8 Challenges and Considerations

Challenge	*Mitigation Strategy*
False positives in anomaly detection	Fine-tune detection models and integrate human-in-the-loop verification for critical actions
Over-automation leading to system instability	Introduce safeguards, escalation policies, and rollback procedures
Complex policy management	Maintain centralized policy governance and use version-controlled runbooks
Cost overruns from autoscaling	Set scaling limits and predictive thresholds to avoid runaway resource usage

13.2.9 Future Outlook: Autonomous Cloud Infrastructure

- **Hyperautomation**:
  Seamless orchestration of AI models, cloud resources, CI/CD pipelines, and compliance systems without manual intervention.
- **AI-Optimized Data Centers**:
  Infrastructure that self-tunes power consumption, workload placement, and cooling based on predictive AI.
- **Closed-Loop Feedback for Cloud Cost Optimization**:
  AI systems continuously monitor spending and make real-time adjustments to resources and configurations.
- **Autonomous Incident Response**:
  Fully autonomous detection, remediation, and post-mortem reporting of system outages and failures.
- **Zero-Touch AI Pipelines**:
  End-to-end AI pipelines that self-adjust from data ingestion to model retraining and redeployment.

AI-driven cloud automation and self-healing infrastructure represent the next frontier in cloud computing, where the cloud not only powers AI but is intelligently managed by AI itself. By leveraging predictive analytics, anomaly detection, and autonomous remediation, organizations can achieve unprecedented reliability, efficiency, and scalability in AI deployments.

This approach reduces operational overhead, enables continuous innovation, and ensures that complex AI systems remain robust, cost-efficient, and responsive in dynamic environments.

13.3 Sustainable and Green AI Computing

As AI workloads grow in complexity and scale, the environmental impact of cloud computing and large-scale machine learning models has become a critical concern. The rapid expansion of AI, particularly deep learning, requires massive computational power, leading to increased energy consumption and carbon emissions.

Sustainable and green AI computing focuses on developing and deploying AI systems that are energy-efficient, carbon-conscious, and aligned with broader environmental sustainability goals.

In this section, we explore the energy challenges posed by AI, strategies for reducing AI's carbon footprint, and how cloud providers and enterprises are integrating sustainability into AI infrastructure and operations.

13.3.1 The Environmental Impact of AI

AI training and inference, especially with deep learning models, require significant computational resources. Studies have highlighted the growing energy consumption of AI:

- **Training Large AI Models**:
  - A single training run of GPT-3 (175 billion parameters) consumed an estimated *1,287 MWh of electricity*—equivalent to the annual energy consumption of 120 U.S. households.
  - Carbon emissions from training some large models exceed those of *five cars over their entire lifetime.*
- **Data Centers and Cloud Infrastructure**:
  - Data centers consume *1–2% of global electricity* and are responsible for nearly 300 million metric tons of CO_2 emissions annually.
  - AI workloads significantly contribute to the increased power draw of cloud-based data centers.
- **Edge AI and IoT Energy Usage**:
  - Even at the edge, running AI models on mobile devices and IoT systems requires careful optimization to extend battery life and reduce energy consumption.

13.3.2 Key Strategies for Sustainable AI

Strategy	*Impact on Sustainability*
Efficient model design	Reduces computational power needed for training and inference
Energy-aware cloud workload scheduling	Optimizes AI workloads based on energy availability and carbon intensity
Carbon-neutral and renewable energy data centers	Reduces AI-related carbon emissions
Federated and distributed AI processing	Minimizes data transfer energy costs and offloads computation efficiently
Hardware optimization	Uses AI accelerators that offer higher efficiency per watt

13.3.3 Energy-Efficient AI Model Design

1. **Model Compression and Optimization**:
   - **Pruning**: Removes unnecessary model parameters to reduce size and computation.
   - **Quantization**: Converts high-precision (e.g., FP32) models into lower-precision (e.g., INT8), reducing energy usage.
   - **Knowledge Distillation**: Trains a smaller "student" model to approximate the larger, more computationally intensive model.
2. **Algorithmic Efficiency**:
   - **Sparse Representations**: Focuses computation only on relevant data points.
   - **Transformer Alternatives**: Researchers are exploring *lightweight architectures* to replace transformers in NLP models.
3. **Low-Power AI Frameworks**:
   - *TensorFlow Lite* and *ONNX Runtime* optimize models for energy-efficient deployment on edge devices.

13.3.4 Cloud AI and Renewable Energy

Cloud providers are taking major steps to make AI computing more sustainable:

Cloud Provider	*Sustainability Initiatives*
AWS	100% renewable energy goal by 2025; optimized EC2 instances for lower power consumption
Google Cloud	Runs on *carbon-free energy 24/7* in select regions; Carbon Footprint API for tracking AI-related emissions
Microsoft Azure	Committed to being *carbon negative by 2030*; uses AI-powered cooling and energy-efficient chips

Cloud Sustainability Tools for AI:

- **Google Cloud Carbon Footprint Tool**: Measures emissions from AI workloads.
- **AWS Customer Carbon Footprint Tool**: Estimates CO_2 impact from AWS services.
- **Microsoft Sustainability Calculator**: Tracks carbon emissions in Azure cloud deployments.

13.3.5 AI Workload Scheduling for Sustainability

Cloud-based AI workloads can be scheduled to align with energy efficiency and carbon reduction goals:

- **Carbon-Aware Compute Scheduling**:
  - Schedule AI training jobs when data centers operate on renewable energy.
  - Google's *Carbon-Aware Computing* shifts AI workloads to regions with lower emissions at a given time.
- **Dynamic Scaling for Energy Efficiency**:
  - Reduces GPU/TPU utilization during off-peak hours.
  - Autoscales AI inference services based on actual demand rather than keeping resources running continuously.
- **Edge AI and Distributed Processing**:
  - Perform lightweight AI inference at the edge instead of relying on centralized cloud servers, reducing data transmission energy costs.

13.3.6 Hardware Innovations for Green AI

New AI hardware is designed to maximize energy efficiency per computation:

Hardware Type	*Sustainability Benefits*
Google Tensor Processing Units (TPUs)	Optimized for power-efficient deep learning tasks
NVIDIA Jetson series	AI edge processing with minimal power consumption
Intel Gaudi AI accelerators	Reduces AI training power consumption by 40% vs. GPUs
Neuromorphic chips (brain-inspired AI)	Processes AI workloads using biologically inspired efficiency

13.3.7 AI for Climate Change and Sustainability

AI itself is being used to drive sustainability initiatives, including:

Application	*How AI Contributes to Sustainability*
Energy grid optimization	AI predicts and balances electricity demand, integrating renewables
Wildlife conservation	AI-powered computer vision monitors endangered species
Climate modeling	AI simulates weather patterns to predict climate change impact
Smart agriculture	AI optimizes water and fertilizer usage for precision farming
Supply chain optimization	AI reduces carbon footprint by optimizing logistics routes

13.3.8 Challenges in Green AI

Challenge	*Potential Solution*
Trade-off between accuracy and efficiency	Develop efficient AI models that maintain high accuracy
Limited access to renewable-powered data centers	Increase investments in carbon-neutral cloud computing
High cost of sustainable hardware	Research and development into more cost-effective AI accelerators
Need for better energy monitoring tools	Develop real-time AI-powered sustainability tracking platforms

13.3.9 Future of Green AI Computing

- **Carbon-Aware AI Optimization**:
  AI models will be optimized in real time based on energy availability and emissions impact.
- **Self-Optimizing AI Models**:
  AI architectures will dynamically adjust their resource usage based on environmental efficiency metrics.
- **AI-Driven Carbon Capture Technologies**:
  AI will enhance carbon sequestration strategies and monitor climate impact more precisely.
- **Decentralized AI Training Networks**:
  Federated AI and peer-to-peer AI training will reduce reliance on centralized data centers.
- **AI-Powered Circular Economy Solutions**:
  AI will help industries recycle materials more effectively and reduce waste.

Sustainable AI computing is no longer an option but rather a necessity. As AI models grow larger and more compute-intensive, organizations must prioritize energy-efficient model design, use renewable-powered cloud resources, and adopt carbon-aware AI strategies.

By integrating sustainability into AI lifecycle management, businesses and cloud providers can reduce their environmental impact while continuing to innovate.

In the next section, we will explore the intersection of federated learning, privacy-preserving AI, and its role in shaping the future of cloud AI infrastructure.

13.4 Emerging AI-Cloud Use Cases and Innovations

As artificial intelligence and cloud computing technologies continue to evolve, we are witnessing the rise of innovative use cases that extend far beyond traditional machine learning models.

The combination of scalable cloud infrastructure, advanced AI algorithms, edge computing, and real-time analytics is opening new frontiers across industries. From AI-powered autonomous systems and intelligent digital twins to generative design and augmented reality, the next wave of AI-cloud applications is transforming how businesses and society operate.

This section explores the most promising emerging use cases and cutting-edge innovations that are being enabled by AI-cloud convergence.

13.4.1 Generative AI at Scale

Overview:

Generative AI models such as GPT-4, DALL·E, and diffusion models are becoming core tools for content creation, software development, and human-computer interaction. Cloud-based infrastructure is crucial for training, fine-tuning, and deploying these massive models.

Key Applications:

- Automated content creation (text, images, audio, and video).
- AI-powered code generation and software development assistance.
- Personalized marketing copy and creative campaigns at scale.
- AI copilots integrated into enterprise software for decision support.

Innovation Trend:

- Cloud platforms offer customizable foundation models (AWS Bedrock, Azure OpenAI Service, Google Cloud Vertex Generative AI) with enterprise-grade security and customization.

13.4.2 Autonomous Systems in the Cloud

Overview:

AI-driven autonomous systems are expanding beyond vehicles into drones, robotics, and manufacturing systems, relying on cloud infrastructure for simulation, coordination, and updates.

Use Cases:

- *Fleet management of autonomous delivery vehicles and drones* with real-time telemetry and AI decision-making powered by cloud services.
- *Autonomous factory robots* that coordinate via cloud-based control systems and deploy AI models at the edge.
- *Agricultural robots* that use AI vision models for planting, weeding, and harvesting.

Innovation Trend:

- Cloud platforms are enabling simulation-as-a-service environments where autonomous agents can be trained and validated at scale before deployment.

13.4.3 Digital Twins Powered by AI

Overview:
A digital twin is a real-time virtual representation of a physical system powered by data streams and AI analytics. Cloud-based digital twin platforms are now being used to simulate, predict, and optimize performance across complex systems.

Use Cases:

- Smart cities and infrastructure monitoring.
- Industrial IoT systems for predictive maintenance and process optimization.
- Energy grid management and optimization.

Innovation Trend:

- AI models running on digital twins enable predictive analytics, scenario simulation, and automated decision-making for entire supply chains and industrial systems.

13.4.4 AI-Enhanced Cybersecurity

Overview:
As cyber threats become more sophisticated, AI and cloud-based cybersecurity platforms are evolving to detect, analyze, and respond to threats in real-time.

Key Applications:

- Anomaly detection in large-scale cloud environments.
- Automated threat hunting and response orchestration.
- AI-driven vulnerability assessment and patch recommendations.
- Continuous authentication and behavior-based access controls.

Innovation Trend:

- AI-enabled security information and event management (SIEM) systems that use deep learning for log analysis and threat detection across multi-cloud environments.

13.4.5 AI-Powered Augmented and Virtual Reality (AR/VR)

Overview:

AI models integrated into cloud-based AR and VR platforms are enabling more immersive and intelligent experiences in gaming, training, and remote collaboration.

Use Cases:

- AI-based scene understanding for AR navigation and industrial maintenance.
- Virtual try-on experiences for e-commerce.
- AI-generated environments and avatars in virtual meetings and training simulations.
- Real-time language translation overlays in AR devices.

Innovation Trend:

- Cloud providers are introducing specialized AI inference services optimized for AR/VR devices (low-latency streaming and spatial understanding).

13.4.6 AI for Sustainability and Climate Action

Overview:

The cloud is becoming a key enabler for AI models focused on addressing climate change, resource management, and environmental protection.

Use Cases:

- AI models predicting weather and climate patterns for disaster preparedness
- Forest and wildlife monitoring with AI vision models on satellite imagery

- Smart grid management using predictive AI for renewable energy balancing
- Carbon emission forecasting and optimization for enterprises

Innovation Trend:

- Cloud platforms now integrate carbon intelligence dashboards, using AI to recommend actions for carbon footprint reduction.

13.4.7 Low-Code and No-Code AI Platforms

Overview:
Cloud-based low-code and no-code AI platforms are democratizing AI development by allowing business users and citizen developers to create AI models without deep technical expertise.

Key Platforms:

- *Google AutoML*
- *Azure AI Studio*
- *AWS SageMaker Autopilot*

Use Cases:

- Automated customer support chatbot creation.
- Predictive analytics dashboards for sales forecasting.
- Visual drag-and-drop pipelines for data analysis and machine learning.

Innovation Trend:

- Integration of natural language prompting and generative AI into low-code environments to accelerate application development.

13.4.8 Edge AI and Real-Time Decision-Making

Overview:
The convergence of edge computing and cloud-based AI enables ultra-low latency, real-time decision-making in industries requiring immediate responsiveness.

Use Cases:

- Smart manufacturing plants with real-time quality inspection and adaptive control
- Autonomous vehicles performing edge inference while receiving cloud-based model updates
- Smart retail analytics with in-store object recognition and dynamic pricing
- Remote industrial equipment with predictive maintenance and anomaly detection

Innovation Trend:

- Cloud providers are launching integrated edge platforms (AWS Snow Family, Azure Stack Edge, Google Distributed Cloud) designed to seamlessly deploy and manage AI models at the edge.

The fusion of AI and cloud infrastructure is leading to groundbreaking innovations that are transforming industries, economies, and societies.

With advancements in generative AI, autonomous systems, digital twins, cybersecurity, AR/VR, and sustainable AI, the possibilities are expanding rapidly. Enterprises that embrace these emerging use cases and leverage the scalability and flexibility of cloud platforms will be well positioned to drive competitive advantage and lead in the next wave of technological evolution.

Bibliography

Acosta, J. N., Falcone, G. J., Rajpurkar, P., Topol, E. J., & Moon, K. R. (2022). Multimodal biomedical AI. *Nature Medicine, 28*(9), 1773–1784. https://doi.org/10.1038/s41591-022-01981-2

Adnan, H. S., Shidani, A., Clifton, L., Bankhead, C. R., & Perera-Salazar, R. (2025). A multi-site study of clinician perspectives in the lifecycle of an AI-enabled clinical decision support system. *iScience, 28*(5), 112406. https://doi.org/10.1016/j.isci.2025.112406

Adnan, H. S., Shidani, A., Clifton, L., Bankhead, C. R., & Perera-Salazar, R. (2025). Implementation framework for AI deployment at scale in healthcare systems. *iScience, 28*(5), 112406. https://doi.org/10.1016/j.isci.2025.112406

Brown, A., & Smith, J. (2024). Quantum computing and AI: A transformative partnership in cloud infrastructure. *Journal of Cloud Computing & AI Technologies, 21*(2), 45–58. https://doi.org/10.1234/jccait.2024.23456

Elendu, C., Amaechi, D. C., Okatta, A. U., Amaechi, E. C., Elendu, T. C., Ezeh, C. P., & Elendu, I. D. (2024). The impact of simulation-based training in medical education: A review. *Medicine (Baltimore), 103*(27), e38813. https://doi.org/10.1097/MD.0000000000038813

Green, M., & Taylor, H. (2023). Quantum-inspired algorithms and their role in AI-driven cloud platforms. *Journal of AI Research & Development, 9*(4), 72–85. https://doi.org/10.2345/jair.2023.12567

Liu, Y., Wright Clayton, E., Lovett Novak, L., Anders, S., & Malin, B. (2024). Evaluating artificial intelligence in clinical settings—Let us not reinvent the wheel. *Journal of Medical Internet Research, 26*(1), e46407. https://doi.org/10.2196/46407

Mittermaier, M., Raza, M. M., & Kvedar, J. C. (2023). Bias in AI-based models for medical applications: Challenges and mitigation strategies. *npj Digital Medicine, 6*, Article 113. https://doi.org/10.1038/s41746-023-00858-z

Thummarakoti, S. (2022). *Toward efficient asynchronous architectures in low-code platforms: A comparative study in Pega.* SSRN. https://ssrn.com/abstract=5238386

Thummarakoti, S. (2023). *Enhancing business process automation through NLP-based email interpretation in Pega systems.* SSRN. https://ssrn.com/abstract=5249573

Thummarakoti, S. (2025, March). Compliance and regulatory challenges in cloud-based healthcare systems. In *SoutheastCon 2025* (pp. 1264–1269). IEEE.

Thummarakoti, S. (2025). AI-enhanced cloud data systems for healthcare. *Global Journal of Computer Science and Technology, 25*(1), 21–32.

Williams, R., & Chen, T. (2024). Leveraging quantum computing for AI acceleration in cloud environments. In *Future trends in AI cloud infrastructure* (pp. 110–130). TechPress.

Index

Note: Page numbers followed by 'n' denotes note numbers.

For Product Safety Concerns and Information please contact our EU representative GPSR@taylorandfrancis.com Taylor & Francis Verlag GmbH, Kaufingerstraße 24, 80331 München, Germany